GETTING TO
HOWARD

To Jake,
Ho, Ho, Howard !
Tim Wager

Josh
"Size Doesn't
matter"..
Snelly
Paula

GETTING TO
HOWARD

The Odyssey
of an
Obsessed
HOWARD
STERN
Fan

DAN WAGNER

ILICIUM

BOOKS

ILICIUM BOOKS

Ilicium Books, an imprint of Ilicium Publishing, Inc.

LINOPHRYNE ARBORIFER

Lure (Ilicium)

SUBORDER CERATIODEI,
known as SEA DEVILS or deep-sea anglerfishes

An ilicium — from the Latin for allurement, or lure — is a tubular light organ containing luminescent bacteria found on the heads of deep-sea anglerfishes. The ilicium is used to attract prey.

All photographs in this book were taken by the author, Dan Wagner, except for those taken by Michael Vincent Colette on pages 2, 19, 164, 171 bottom, 173, 174 top, 176 bottom, 178, 179 top, 180, 182, and 226. Please visit Dan's website: http://www.danwagner.com

Editor: Amy Goodfellow
Book Design: Barry Simon

Publisher's Cataloging-in-Publication
(Provided by Quality Books, Inc.)

Wagner, Dan, 1957-
    Getting To Howard : the odyssey of an obsessed Howard
Stern fan / Dan Wagner. -- 1st ed.
    p. cm.
    Preassigned LCCN: 98-96297
    ISBN: 0-9665378-7-4

    1. Stern, Howard, 1954- 2. Howard Stern Show.
3. Radio broadcasters--United States--Biography.
4. Wagner, Dan, 1957- 5. Fans (Persons)--United States--
Biography.   I. Title.

PN1991.4.S82W34 1998   791.44'028'092 [B]
                   QBI98-823

10 9 8 7 6 5 4 3 2 1   First Edition

Printed in the United States of America

WARNING & DISCLAIMER

T his book is meant to provide information. Although every effort has been made to make this book as accurate as possible, this text should be used only for entertainment purposes and not as the ultimate authority or source of information.

This book is extremely subjective and reflects the author's thoughts at the time of writing. In some cases the author may have since modified his thoughts and opinions on various aspects of this book. In many instances, the author is clearly pulling the reader's leg and/or acting silly. Therefore, please try to keep an open mind, and take everything in this book in the tongue-in-cheek manner in which it is offered.

This book is not intended to be a "How To" book. Those choosing to use this book as a guide to interacting with Howard Stern, or anyone else for that matter, do so at their own risk.

In conclusion, the author of this book is an obsessed Howard Stern fan. He's not Albert Einstein — to put it mildly. If Dan Wagner jumped off the Empire State Building, would you follow him? Definitely not. Therefore, if you do not wish to be bound by the above, don't read this book. Hey, you can't claim you weren't warned. Good luck.

I dedicate this book to Howard Stern.

I never set out to write a book about him.

It just happened.

ACKNOWLEDGMENTS

First and foremost I thank my family — Amy, Jane and Peter — for their patience with my obsession. Without their love and support this book would not have been possible.

Second, I thank my good friend Barry Simon for the wonderful job he did designing this book. In addition to being a phenomenal designer, Barry is also a loyal Stern fan.

Third, I thank all those who have served as inspirational figures, sounding boards, and contributors to the success of the story told in these pages: Stanley Wagner, Loretta Bolen, Frank Bowden, Don Bowers, Robert Boyd, Rebecca Brantley, Patrick Brown, Joshua Bucklan, Thomas Cipriano, Ralph Cirella, Eugene Clerkin, Clicks Photo Labs, Michael Vincent Colette, Carlo Dano, Gary Dell'Abate, Exact Photo, Frank X. Fallon, Colt .40 Feinberg, Jeff Felmus, Bud Fleisher, Jack Freedman, Ben Friedman, William Glennon, Samuel Goodfellow, Laurence Victor Greenblatt, Julie Griffin, Steve Grillo, James Hanrahan, Denise Harvey, George Harvey, Joel Hecker, Allison Hollett, Ilicium Publishing, Elliot Jaeger, Kenneth Keith Kallenbach, Eric Kampmann, David Katz, Robert Kratzke, Gail Kump, Alison Laird, William Landin, Glenn Laxman, Martin Leeds, Tom Lieber, Rick Maro, Jackie Martling, John Melendez, Jeffrey and Laurie Meltzer, Hal Michaels, Hank Nassiff, Fred-Eric Norris, Ralph Palmieri, Robin Quivers, Kevin Renzulli, Marc Roffman, Beth Schiffer, Fred Schreiber, Brad Searles, Guy Serling, Marvin Shanken, John Shelton, Jean Shepherd, Joanne Sockle, Leonard Sorcher, Denise Souter, Jan-Michael Souter, Howard Stern, Mark Tefft, Andrew Thompson, Uzo, Chris van Zutphen, Paul Viola, Steven Walker, Marc Wasserman.

And finally, I thank all my fellow Howard Stern fans who share my obsession. You, too, can get to Howard if you dare.

"I'm like flypaper for the walking wounded."

— Howard Stern

CONTENTS

FOREWORD

Dear Diary,

Why does history always repeat itself? Lately I have come to believe that I am destined to make the same mistakes endlessly. In early 1995 I made a diary entry about the embarrassment I suffered from interacting with a radio program. I was station surfing on AM radio and eventually decided upon a talk show, which was in the middle of quizzing its listeners on American history. I never win contests, and am in fact so pessimistic regarding my chances of winning, that I seldom bother entering them.

This time, however, the temptation to show off my superior intellect was irresistible. So, I grabbed the phone, and called the talk show. It was surprisingly easy to get through. The talk show host asked me to name President Lincoln's assassin. I proudly gave him the correct answer — John Wilkes Booth. The host excitedly told me that I had won two tickets to the circus for my correct answer. Wow! I had finally won a contest.

Stern fans at the Premiere of "Private Parts"

I was feeling quite proud of myself. The talk show host put me on hold so his producer could find out where to send my prize — and my age. I told him that I was in my late thirties. At this point, the producer's tone changed. He sounded annoyed. I couldn't understand his behavior. After I hung up, I kept listening to the talk show. It turned out that the show was for children. I was totally mortified to discover that I had cheated some poor child out of tickets to the circus.

This kind of mix-up is all too familiar. I vowed never to call a radio station again. At last, I would learn from my mistakes. I dedicated myself to this goal.

My resolve lasted less than twenty-four hours. The following day I called in with my brilliant answer: "Yes, the Vice President's name is Al Gore!" This time the producer was livid. He said that he would put call-blocking on my phone number, so that I would no longer be able to call into the show. He asked, "What sort of pathetic human being calls into children's talk shows and cheats kids out of prizes?" I said, "Does this mean I'm not getting the Power Rangers doll?" Hey, I have kids. It's not as if I were trying to benefit personally from the prizes. The producer hung up on me. I wish I could say that I never tried to call the talk show again. But, true to his word, the producer had blocked my calls. Secretly, I was grateful to him.

For more than eight months I stayed clean. No talk show calls. No contest entries. No radio interaction whatsoever. Perhaps I was finally cured. Right! On November 6, 1995 I suffered a terrible setback. I blame it all on Howard Stern. I was in my photo studio working on a few product shots for a well-known magazine. Howard's show played in the background. On a whim, I faxed Howard a comment about the show.

Within a few minutes Howard read my fax on the air. I was hooked. The flood gates to my obsession had been thrown wide open.

Consider this book a ship's log. It describes the amazing journey that I embarked upon as a direct result of hearing Howard Stern read my fax on-air. My journey led me to hitherto unknown regions of my psyche. I felt like a swimmer stuck in a strong, unbeatable current, with no choice but to go with the flow. At each twisting turn, I discovered more about myself. I found out that I like to write and make people laugh, enjoy playing practical jokes on people, and hearing my own voice on the radio. I became better acquainted with my sense of irony and satire.

Ultimately, I learned that you can't build a dam to stem an obsession. Sometimes, the obsession must simply run its course and play itself out. As to whether my own obsession has run its course, only time will tell.

I also learned much more about Howard Stern. I discovered just what appeals to his sense of humor. I got to know his fans and their idiosyncrasies. From the vast pool of Stern fans, I made numerous friends and acquaintances. I went to Howard's

Miss America book signings, and explored the many ways that his audience acts out its hunger for his unique brand of humor and social satire. I used this newfound knowledge to "get to" Howard, in other words con my way onto his show, a once-in-a-lifetime experience.

During my journey I constantly reminded myself to remain ever vigilant and open-eyed. I didn't want my fascination with Howard Stern to blind me to my own actions. I tried to stay objective, daily checking my pulse for signs of insanity — although these measurements were not always accurate or unbiased. Sometimes I would reread one of my postings on the Prodigy Howard Stern Fan Club Bulletin Board and be absolutely flabbergasted that I could say the things I said, and in public, too!

Who is the real Howard Stern? Does he really believe all that he espouses on-air? Is it all just an act? These questions have been debated time and again by the media. Howard is quite often deliberately vague on this issue. It's been said that there's no such thing as bad publicity, as long as they spell your name right. This seems to be Howard's creed. Over the last fifteen or so years, Howard has become an expert (in Howard-speak, "the king") at manipulating the media. He has taken this skill to the bank time and again.

Howard knows what people want, and he gives it to them. If people want tits and ass, Howard is only too happy to oblige. If the audience enjoys locker room humor, then Howard stands ready to belch and fart to their delight. When people need an outlet to voice their jealousy over celebrities, Howard is there. Taking celebrities down a peg or two is one of Howard's favorite pastimes. Just ask Kathie Lee Gifford. If he can't do it personally, then Howard will send a minion like Stuttering John to ask celebrities embarrassing and annoying questions. Even Howard's detractors admit that he is entertaining and funny.

But is there a flip side to Howard's humor? Is his audience capable of judicious discrimination? Can they separate the wheat from the chaff? Many critics argue that Howard's audience is too low-brow and immature to think for itself. In the wake of Howard's words, these critics foresee the creation of a culture of depravity and insincerity. A world in which women are demeaned by vulgar comments about their bodies. A world in which racial and religious differences are fair game for satire. A world in which serious discussions can't take place. In short, Howard's detractors are worried that his listeners will develop a myopic tunnel vision that will blind them to the complexities of modern life and consequently usher in a return to the dark ages.

Personally, I think the critics are all wrong. My Howard Stern experiences have led me to conclude that while most fans are extremely dedicated to Howard, they still are willing to listen to opposing viewpoints. As with any outspoken public figure there are heated debates regarding the validity of Howard's opinions. Sometimes the debates sink to the level of crude name calling and finger-pointing. Other times the debates rise to transcendent heights and invoke literature, art, and religion. Even Talmudic scholars have occasionally joined the fray to pitch in their two cents. Perhaps Howard Stern's popularity lies in his ability to tap into his public's frustrations.

So, does Howard have any shortcomings? Maybe. I think one of Howard's drawbacks is that he is too insulated from the world around him by virtue of his celebrity status. Howard seems to be trying to distance himself from some of his immature antics. He seems to have mellowed somewhat. Perhaps the F.C.C. (Federal Communications Commission) fines are at the heart of this change. I prefer it when Howard bares his fangs. Sometimes the hypocrisies in the world require a sharp tongue to cut through them.

But enough profundity. Like Howard, this book should be entertaining and fun. For some unknown reason, Howard Stern became my muse. Thanks to Howard, I have journeyed into the twin regions of obsession and inspiration. Millions of people have heard Howard and Robin "perform" my faxes on the air. Listeners have also heard my on-air appearances with Howard. And quite a few people in cyber-land have read my postings to the Howard Stern Fan Club Bulletin Board. Here then, without further ado, is my odyssey of *Getting to Howard.*

Stern fans at the Premiere of "Private Parts"

GETTING TO
HOWARD

CHAPTER 1

OBSESSIVE COMPULSIVE FAXING DISORDER

O ne perfect November morning in 1995, I was at work (as a photographer) minding my own business. The Howard Stern Show played on my radio, as I photographed some products for a magazine. Howard was giving his co-worker, Fred Norris, a hard time. Fred's wife was in the play *Tony And Tina's Wedding*. Her role entailed kissing and grinding against a male cast member. Howard and his minions were cruelly and unmercifully exploiting Fred's situation. Fred was clearly suffering. It was great radio and immensely funny. I wished I could be at Howard's side, participating in the fun. Then I realized I could make my wish come true.

Fred & Allison

On a whim I scribbled this comment about Fred's situation, and faxed it to Howard.

```
*******************************************************************
*                                                            P.01  *
*                     TRANSACTION REPORT                           *
*                     ──────────────────                           *
```

Hi Howard,   11/6/95

    Regarding *Tony And Tina's Wedding*. Do they have an actor playing the part of a janitor with a mop to wipe up the puddles under Fred's wife? — or does she just wear a pad?

Sincerely,
Claus Von Bulow

Just five minutes later Howard read my faxed comments on-air. I couldn't believe it. I was transfaxed — I mean transfixed. Imagine, millions of people had just heard, and perhaps even laughed at, my impulsive fax. This was an unexpected thrill.

That night, while falling asleep, my mind replayed my successful faxing episode. It had been so easy to get my fax read on the air. Was it possible to repeat my success? I soon discovered that I could.

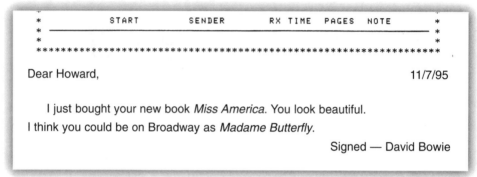

Dear Howard,   11/7/95

   I just bought your new book *Miss America*. You look beautiful. I think you could be on Broadway as *Madame Butterfly*.

Signed — David Bowie

Wow, I was two for two. Like sex, the rush from hearing my fax read on the air, was even greater the second time around. I bragged to my friends and my wife. Did Howard believe he was getting faxes from Claus Von Bulow and David Bowie? I doubt it. I only dropped names in the hope of being noticed. The next day I hit three for three with this item:

Dear Howie: 11/8/95

   These are truly exciting times we live in! I just got your book. I feel as privileged as if this were Czarist Russia, and I was able to buy the first Dostoyevsky, Gogol, or Ivan Turgenev masterpiece hot off the press. Your book is a twentieth-century masterpiece. It is both literature, and multi-media, thanks to the cartoons, photos, and wacky typefaces. You are truly a Renaissance man!

Your literary compatriot, Alexander Solzhenitsyn

I came on heavy with the Classic Russian authors to improve the chances of being read, since I knew this kind of cultural allusion would appeal to Robin

Quivers, Howard's newswoman and sidekick. (Robin attends the opera and takes riding lessons.) I was quickly rewarded. Robin and Howard both squealed in self-congratulatory delight over my shameless compliments.

Robin Quivers

I felt like a shark after its first taste of flesh — ravenous! I needed a larger meal. Satisfaction hinged upon getting a more outrageous fax read.

I began to listen more closely to Howard's show, searching for ways to improve my faxes. To be more successful, I would have to answer these questions: 1) What subject matter appeals to Howard? — Anything that hyped Howard's projects (such as his new book *Miss America*). 2) What approach would captivate Howard? — An easy one! — Anything with blatant sexual overtones. 3) What criteria would catch Robin's eye (Robin pre-screens the faxes.) — Answer, credibility and sensationalism, all wrapped up in a tidy package.

I incorporated my new insights into this fax:

Dear Howard: 11/9/95

Your book caused me great embarrassment yesterday. I was on the L.I.R.R. (Long Island Rail Road) reading the chapter on cybersex. It was so engrossing that I forgot where I was. I had my hand in my pocket, engaged in a good game of pocket billiards. Around Hicksville I felt as though I was being watched, so I looked up. Sitting across from me was a beautiful blonde wearing gray sweatpants. Our eyes met. She was smiling one of those stupid smirking kind of smiles. Then she glanced towards my lap. I looked down. It was tent-pole city. I must have turned beet red. I quickly got off at the next stop, which wasn't my own. It cost me twenty dollars (the same price as your book) for a taxi to get to my car, which was parked in the garage at my own station. Your book is truly dangerous.

Sincerely,
King of All Lubricants

Howard read my fax on-air. My studiously developed criteria had worked. I hyped *Miss America* with a prurient, yet believable, story. *King of All Lubricants* was my first double entendre nom de plume. And Robin howled with laughter when she heard it.

Not only did Howard read my fax, he also engaged in a lengthy discussion with Robin and the rest of the crew about it. I had become a regular, though anonymous, contributor to the show. Howard has to fill up five hours of air time every day, five days a week. Five of those fifteen hundred minutes now belonged to me.

Over dinner that evening, I trumpeted my triumph to my wife, in a fit of hyperbolic hubris. In other words, I acted like an obnoxious horse's ass. I was high as a kite over my successful streak.

My wife diagnosed me as being obsessed. I disagreed. I told her in the words of a true addict, "I can quit anytime I choose. I only enjoy faxing Howard for its value as a creative writing exercise." Yeah, I was hooked. I had O.C.F.D. (Obsessive Compulsive Faxing Disorder).

The next day, I got to work two hours early. I needed the time to compose my next opus. I decided to write a sequel to the *King of All Lubricants* saga.

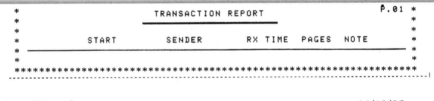

Dear Howard,   11/10/95

My ass is grass! Yesterday you read my fax on the air. As you may recall, I wrote to you regarding my embarrassing experience on the L.I.R.R.. I was the person caught getting his jollies while reading your book's chapter on cybersex. In a nutshell — a beautiful blonde in grey sweat pants caught me sporting a woody. Consequently I ran off the train before my stop and had to take a taxi to complete my trip. This caused me to arrive home over an hour late.

Although my wife is usually a good fellow, on this occasion she acted like a Femi-Nazi. Angry at having ruined dinner, due to my late arrival, she demanded an explanation. I lied and told her that my train had mechanical trouble.

To make a long story short, my wife heard you reading my fax on the air and put two and two together. I was busted. She was returning from driving my daughter to school and almost crashed into a tree. As soon as she got home she called me at work. She told my secretary it was an emergency and was put right through.

Unfortunately my secretary accidentally put her through on conference call. I was in the middle of closing a big deal (I sell oil and other lubricants to gas stations). All of a sudden I hear my wife's voice booming through my office. She is screaming at the top of her lungs. She called me a low-life masturbating exhibitionist scumbag! My clients heard it all! I was devastated. My assistant said I turned the color of a 30 weight motor oil.

Finally, I managed to disconnect her, but the damage had been done. My clients beat a hasty retreat. That night I had to sleep at my brother's apartment.

I am now too afraid to go home, ride the LIRR, or resume reading your book. I said it before: Your book is truly dangerous. It has ruined my life!

Sincerely,

King of All Lubricants

This fax also made it on-air. But Robin paraphrased the contents to Howard. Even though it still got some laughs, as an "artist", I hated to see my work mutilated.

What a wonderful learning experience. After being out of school for fifteen years, I was a student again, at the internationally acclaimed "School of Stern". I was improving my grasp of Howard and Robin's likes and dislikes. Call me Danny the Disciple. What better way to learn than at the feet of the Master. If Howard got tongue-tied while reading my faxes, then I was being too verbose. If Howard changed or omitted part of my fax, then I could learn from that, too. Talk about a correspondence course!

For my next "lesson" I decided to shift gears, as well as my gender. Here is the resulting fax:

```
*                                                                        *
*           START        SENDER        RX TIME   PAGES   NOTE            *
*       ----------------------------------------------------------       *
*                                                                        *
**********************************************************************
--------------------------------------------------------------------------
```

Dear Howard Hot Buns: 11/11/95

I can hardly walk anymore, and it's all your fault! I bought your book two days ago at the Barnes and Noble on 48th street. I was so eager to read your book, that I went to a diner near the theater district for a cup of coffee and a chance to crack open *Miss America*.

Before I go any further let me give you my vital statistics. I am a twenty-six year old bi white actress, 5'8" tall, 119 pounds, 35-24-34 measurements, long auburn hair, green eyes, and an awesomely toned body. (I look like the redhead on *Melrose Place*.)

Anyway, I was in the diner with your book, reading the cybersex chapter, when I noticed a real cute Alec Baldwin look-alike who was also reading your book. I asked him to pass the cream for my coffee. In the process of giving me the cream, he noticed my copy of your book. It turned out that he was an actor, too. He was reading for a play later in the week and asked me back to his apartment to help him with his lines. I said okay, but only if we could read the lines from your cybersex chapter first. He quickly agreed.

I stayed at his apartment till 7AM this morning. We ordered in and never left the bed. All I can say is thank God he buys rubbers by the dozen. I am now a three-input, very satisfied woman with a new boyfriend who drives a red Porsche. I owe it all to you and your book. I feel that I owe you one, if you [wink, wink] know what I mean!

Love and kisses,
Sheila, Queen of All Thespians

(Howard dethroned me by changing my handle to Sheila, a Thespian. How sexist. I wanted to file suit. Is royalty a "dick" thing?)

Howard read my fax word for word. I seemed to have reached the fax "A-List". I was so happy!

Being a repeat faxer led to complications. I doubted Howard would read so many faxes from one individual so I needed to disguise my many identities.

I used a word processor which gave me numerous stylistic options.
• Different typefaces
• Larger or smaller type size
• Varying page setups (margins, line-spacing etc.)

And since the sender's fax number is printed on the recipient's fax, it was important to reprogram my fax machine to display:
• assorted phone numbers

- different area codes from locations appropriate to the supposed senders (e.g. Los Angeles is 310 or 213).

I don't think my actions were dishonest or unethical. I was only emulating Howard Stern himself. Howard always sends his crew out to perpetrate pranks for the greater glory of the show and his own amusement. How could Howard possibly be offended by someone pulling one over on him?

I wrote another fax after watching the television show *20/20*. They had just aired a story about Howard. The story was predictably handled. The people from *20/20* acted very smug and superior and treated Howard with contempt. Howard was presented as a "Shock Jock" pandering to the worst aspects of human nature. Howard was used and abused for his popularity in order to enhance *20/20's* ratings. As far as I'm concerned, Barbara Walters and Hugh Downs are the real phonies.

Unfortunately my fax blasting Baba was never read. Perhaps it was due to my sending it on the thirteenth of the month. Still, I should have been ecstatic. I'd had an unbroken streak of six faxes read in a row. But, no. When one fax didn't make the air, I pouted. Danny the Disciple, indeed. It was back-to-school time.

By this time, my whole circle of friends and acquaintances was aware of my penchant for faxing Howard's show. Some suggested that I come out of the woodwork and reveal myself. "Hello, I am the mysterious faxing maniac." I'm sure Howard and Robin would have been thrilled. But I believed that blowing my cover would spoil my fun. What could "coming out" accomplish? Would Howard invite me to be a guest on his show? Would I be offered a job as a writer? I didn't think so.

But I wondered how much longer I could maintain my breakneck pace. I was in withdrawal from doing without my fix of public acknowledgement. It had been a week since I had struck gold. Had Howard caught on to my chicanery?

I decided the radio station's fax machine was broken and in a desperate maneuver, I re-faxed my unread material. Self-doubt loomed large. I'd been able to get my faxes read before. Had it only been beginner's luck?

New York is a huge radio market. Howard has the lion's share of the weekly 6AM to 11AM drive-time audience. Note: Howard's fax line is always busy. It usually takes ten to thirty minutes to get through so be prepared to set redial and monopolize the fax machine. Some days it seems like the whole world is faxing Howard since getting a fax read on-air is a truly competitive sport, I'm proud to have had even one fax read.

My next fax violated one of my own rules and perhaps that was its downfall. It was too good to be true.

```
  *  ────────────────────────────                    *
  *                                                   *
  *      START      SENDER     RX TIME  PAGES  NOTE   *
  *  ─────────────────────────────────────────────    *
```

Dear Howard: 11/28/95

I am a page on the David Letterman show. I have been with the show since it was
bought by C.B.S. and moved to the old Ed Sullivan Theater.

Lately, things have been very tense. Ratings are down. Dave is under enormous strain,
and it shows. Dave has us pages positioned in the halls with walkie talkies. Our job is to
make sure that the halls are clear anytime he walks through. It's all so 007. Dave has also
been pre-occupied with light switches. If a switch is off, he puts it on, and vice versa. Some
of the pages mess with his head, and change the switches before, or after, he gets to them.
Maybe Dave has O.C.D. (Obsessive Compulsive Disorder). Dave's penis might be bigger
than yours, but you're twice the man because you conquered your O.C.D..

Many of the pages are worried about their jobs. I am no exception. If this gig blows up,
I would like to land on my feet. Perhaps there are some openings in your organization. How
difficult can it be to cook a germ-free potato? Hey, who knows, maybe if I stay here you will
come to us. It would be cost effective and good for the network. Renaming the theater could
be done in a day. We have an excellent telephone system.

The whole facility is first-rate. Your general manager, Tom Chiusano would have a brain
hemorrhage if he knew what this place costs!

When Dave first moved here the ratings were so much better. One day, prior to a really
successful show, I brought Dave his coffee. It was in a red cup. At the time, I was recovering
from a case of poison ivy. I was scratching my left arm.

Ever since that day Dave has demanded that I bring his coffee in the same cup and scratch
my arm. This is driving me crazy. I can't take personal days, lest I miss my appointed round with
destiny and Dave's coffee cup.

As a gay man, I am used to strange requests. I have yet to meet a man who I can't con-
nect with in some way, much less fail to please. Dave may prove to be the exception.

My name is Nigel. I am from England, and in possession of all the required working
papers. I dress tastefully, and I'm very perky and easy to have around. I will be sending your
office my resumé. Although I find Gay Rich very attractive, I can assure you that my behavior while at work will always be professional and above board.

Respectfully yours,

Nigel Llewelyn

I later refined my Nigel personality into Chaz, and perpetrated a successful prank on one of the show's interns. The following fanciful fax and the one before it were never read. However, this next fax attracted a lot of attention behind-the-scenes. Steve Grillo (one of Howard's interns) phoned me in the hopes of securing a place to live. I couldn't believe he was so gullible. I managed to tape part of the call, during which I spoke in my most affected "fey" voice. As you might imagine, Steve beat a very hasty retreat. I guess he was afraid to share a bunk-bed with *Chaz*.

Steve Grillo

```
* * * * * * * * * * * * * * * * * * * * * * * * * * * * * * * * * * * * * * * * * * * * * * * * * * *
*                        TRANSACTION REPORT                              P.01   *
*                        _____                                    *
*                                                                               *
*        START          SENDER        RX TIME    PAGES    NOTE          *
*        _____ *
```

Dear Howard,   11/30/95

I understand from yesterday's show that two of your interns (Steve Grillo and Mike Gange) will soon be homeless. I would hate to see them pan-handling on Madison Avenue and living in the subways of New York City. I know Steve Grillo has aspirations of being on Broadway someday; but I'm sure those hopes do not include sleeping on Broadway. Perhaps I can be of some assistance to your assistants.

I have a studio apartment in Soho. It would be an easy commute for the boys to get to work at your show. They would have no excuses for tardiness. That's for sure. As luck would have it, my former roommates just moved to San Francisco to open a hair salon. So there's now a bunk-bed and some slightly worn leather clothing available.

I'm a very easy-going landlord. My only rules are as follows: A) My make-up and cross-dressing outfits are off-limits. So stay out of the closet. Steve that means you! Sorry. The only exception is during the Halloween Parade in Greenwich Village. B) No using my Lady Gillette on your legs. C) If you look at my *Blue Boy* magazines, please put them back in chronological order and don't remove the Post-it notes. D) Don't mess with my Barbie Collection. E) Never stop my Judy Garland albums in the middle of a song. F) Buy your own K-Y. That's it. Loud, frisky parties are okay. Grillo's theater friends are always <u>very</u> welcome! Richard Simmons, Mark Harris, Berry Boy Ralph, and Gay Rich can sleep over anytime.

Wow, I am so excited. This will be like *Three's Company* or *Friends*. The boys are welcome to use my Thigh Master and Butt Buster. The rent will be on a "sliding" scale, or can be taken out in trade for services rendered. I will show the boys a side of New York that they never even knew existed. We will be so happy together! It will be like the Robin Williams movie, *Dead Poets Society*. Carpe Interniem! Seize the intern!

Sincerely — Chaz

P.S. I have never been convicted of a sex crime. I work in the cosmetics department at Macy's, and my last HIV test was negative.

Oh happy day! The drought ended. The old magic was nearly back. This next fax was not read word-for-word on-air. Instead, I got the next best thing. Robin paraphrased my story to Howard, for about three minutes of hilarity. I used a favorite Howard target, Indians.

∗∗∗

Dear Mr. Stern, 12/10/95

A most unusual thing happened to me recently. I was on a flight out of New Delhi bound for The United States. At the New Delhi duty free shopping area I purchased your new book *Miss America*. I was seated next to a very fetching Hindu woman. I am Moslem, but I can pass for Hindu. As I read your book I could tell that the woman was, as you Americans say, reading over my shoulder. Everyone on the plane had their shoes and socks off as is the Indian custom. The air in the plane was charged with a primal odor. These earthy scents combined to make my reading of your cybersex chapter truly dynamic. I felt as randy as a goat during the feast of Ramadan. I had visions of joining the Mile High Club with the Hindu woman seated next to me. I longed to rub chutney all over her womanhood and then slowly lick it off. My fondest desire at the time was to caress her from the red dot on her forehead all the way down to her five-inch toenails.

When I reached the picture titled "Ba Ba Buddha Stern", my blood boiled like the Ganges in the month of Sha'ban. In my country you could get arrested for such sacrilege. I know that you are a man of the humor, and were just making with the jokes. Unfortunately, the Hindu woman next to me was not so enlightened. She summoned the stewardess. The stewardess came and then brought the captain. The captain confiscated my copy of *Miss America*. I was ordered to leave my first class seat. They made me sit with the Untouchables in coach. It was so humiliating! Even Vishnu could not rescue me from my terrible fate.

After we landed at Kennedy Airport, the captain returned my book. The page of you as "Ba Ba Buddha Stern" had been removed. I am no longer allowed to fly on Air India. Please advise your Indian listeners to cover the controversial parts of your book (especially Jackie's hind-quarters!) when they are in public places. Your most humble servant,

Punjab — The Raj of All Tantric Sex

This next fax is my favorite. I view it as my crowning achievement. Danny the Disciple, a.k.a. The Graduate, was finishing the "School of Stern" Summa Cum Laude. In fact, when Robin Quivers asked, "Is that the greatest letter ever?", Howard exclaimed, "Yes it is!" Jackie Martling was howling with laughter in the background. Fred Norris played pig squealing noises at appropriate points during the reading. It occupied almost four minutes of air time. I made my weekly time quota with this fax alone. I also managed to tape 95% of the reading. The rush I got from this experience lasted through the holidays and well into the New Year. Whenever I'm feeling blue, I pop this cassette into my tape player and feel rejuvenated.

```
*******************************************************************
  *                                                       P.01  *
  *                  TRANSACTION REPORT                          *
  *                                                              *
  *        START        SENDER        RX TIME  PAGES  NOTE       *
```

Dear Mr. Stern,   12/18/95

I am an inmate at Ossining State Prison. For the last seven years I have run the prison library. Your new book has created a real stir in Stir! I am unable to keep your book in stock. All fifteen copies are in constant circulation. You are the most widely read prison author ever! Even inmates who cannot read demand their time with *Miss America*. They must really enjoy the pictures. Inmates have offered as much as a carton of cigs for a chance to get a peek at your book. The warden says he has never seen anything like this before!

I personally know of one inmate who is very grateful to you. He is a fair-haired, tender, young white boy. A real "CHICKEN"! He bought his way out of a "BLAN-

KET PARTY" which was to be held in his honor with a copy of *Miss America* that had been in a care package to him.

I just ordered twenty more copies of your book. *Private Parts* and Robin's book have received renewed interest. In fact these three books hold the top three slots on the prison's most-wanted list by an enormous margin. The copy of Colin Powell's book is in solitary confinement — literally. The inmates say that Powell's book is worse than being denied parole! We all wonder what's up at *The N.Y. Times.* How could they lie and say your book was no longer number one on the *Best Seller List?* Some of the inmates would love to stick a shiv in the people at the *Times* responsible for disrespecting you.

Howard, you the man! I owe you a debt of gratitude. Being the gate-keeper for your book has made me a big man in stir! I now enjoy the top bunk in my cell, as well as first crack at the new fish. Please send me a signed copy of your book. (Would you mind placing a file and some money or dope inside the binding?)

Stir Crazy After All These Years,
King of All Prison Librarians

P.S. The picture of Jackie's butt is a hit. I had to put plastic lamination over his page! If Jackie ever finds himself behind bars, it will give new meaning to the popular anthem "F. JACKIE"!!!

Howard guffawed at my request for "placing a file, and some money or dope inside the binding". To make the fax more convincing, I programmed my fax machine with Ossining Prison's real fax phone number. I also did my research. I found out that the prison really has an inmate-run library.

After this fax aired, I noticed that Howard was getting more wacky faxes than usual. I felt like Lewis and Clark — Trailblazer Danny! One married male listener even claimed to be shanghaied for his sperm by a pair of baby lusting lesbians. I wish I had tried that angle. What could be next? Abduction by aliens? Martian invasions?

Jackie Martling

John Hinkley had a fatal fixation for Jody Foster. I was developing a similar, though hopefully less harmful, fascination for Robin Quivers. I felt like Robert De

Niro in *Taxi Driver.* When Robin commented on my faxes, I would look at my radio and say out loud, "Hey, are you talking to me?" From my vantage point, Robin sounded breathless and eager (like my wife does when there is a sale at Barneys), whenever she introduced one of my faxes. She had every word and nuance of my faxes memorized. If Howard left anything out while reading one of my faxes, Robin would pipe in. I savored her appreciation for my efforts. She also has a bodacious bosom!

So far I had faxed Howard descriptions of *Miss America* as a catalyst for numerous adventures such as: getting laid, saving a prison inmate from a "blanket party", being kicked out of first class on an Air India flight, etc. Now, I would top myself. I scoured the newspapers daily for inspiration. In my next fax *Miss America* saved a soldier's life.

	START	SENDER	RX TIME	PAGES	NOTE	

Dear Mr. Stern,   1/5/96

Mere words cannot express my sincere heartfelt gratitude to you. Your new book *Miss America* is responsible for saving my son's life.

My son in an Army Sergeant. I sent him a signed copy of your book as an early Christmas present. He was stationed in Germany at the time. My son was thrilled with the gift. He is a big fan of yours. All his Army buddies loved your book, too. In fact, they loved it so much that they convinced my son to disobey regulations and bring *Miss America* with him to Bosnia.

My son's unit landed in Bosnia on Christmas Day. Once there, they were ferried by chopper to a remote security checkpoint. My son was opening his unit's new orders, when a gust of wind from the chopper's blades blew the orders out of his hands. He chased after the papers. The noise from the chopper prevented him from hearing his buddie's shouted warnings. My son was running into a mine field! A moment later he stepped on a "Bouncing Betty" mine. The mine exploded—sending my son ten feet into the air. He landed in a water-filled ditch. Your book was in my son's backpack. It saved his life! Five long pieces of razor-sharp shrapnel were embedded in *Miss America*. My son only suffered a mild concussion. He is due to receive a Purple Heart Medal. (He wants to give it to you for saving his life). .

(At this point, Robin piped in with, "Wow, is that true?". Howard came back with, "I made the book very thick — remember Letterman said, 'It's a thick book.'")

In an amazing coincidence, my son's pregnant wife broke her water the same day. She gave birth to a beautiful seven-pound baby boy. They are naming him Howard, in your honor. Would you be so kind as to send a signed copy of your book for my son? The one he has now was ruined. God Bless you!

Sincerely,
A Grateful Mom

P.S. Jay Leno was a real flop with the troops. The boys all wish you and the gang could come to Bosnia and entertain them.

Imagine, Howard refused to send this poor "lady" a copy of his book. He said, "No, I will not send a signed copy, I am not signing any more copies!" The weird thing about this fax is that a month later a soldier in Bosnia, was actually blown up by a mine — score extra points for believability. At the end of this fax, Boy-Gary commented that he thought it strange for a soldier to get a Purple Heart just for being

Gary Dell'Abate

blown up. Howard said, "You ever been blown up? You deserve a medal."

Howard and Robin were very suspicious of the authenticity of this fax, and yet they played along — God, I love these guys!

I decided to bring my family into the act. I even bribed my daughter with a dollar bill to write this next letter to Howard. The words and spelling are her own. As far as I'm concerned, my daughter has the show down cold. I bet her letter seeking an internship is of a higher caliber than Howard's show usually receives. Although Howard didn't read this fax on-air, I'm sure it must have amused him.

Dear Howerd, 1/25/96

I am a eight year old second grader I am a girl. I love your show. My bus driver listens to your show all the kids love it. Jackie is a big jackais! I want to work on your show durring easter vacation. I will anser your mail. I know how to use a coputer. I know how to cook on the mickerwave. I can cook potatos meat sandwichis and vegatabels. I take a bath three times a week. My favorite person on the show is Roben. I know a lot of bad words and what they mean. I dont say them my self. My dad farts a lot like you. When I grow up I want to write books. I want to read your book. You look better in a drees!!!!!!!!! I asked my dad to facs you this letter.

From, Jane

This next fax was read on 2/20/96 at around 7AM. I heard it over my tiny portable radio while commuting to work by train. I was so excited my fellow commuters probably thought I was having a heart attack. I wanted to tell the whole train. However, I usually sit in the same car, with the same people each morning, and thought I'd better not make a fool of myself.

```
*************************************************************
*                                                         *
*                  TRANSACTION REPORT          P.01       *
*                                                         *
*                                                         *
*     START        SENDER       RX TIME  PAGES   NOTE     *
*                                                         *
*                                                         *
*************************************************************
```

Dear Howard, 2/20/96

I just got back from Los Angeles, where I was working as a waitress at a trendy restaurant in Malibu. The place was always filled with Hollywood types. Producers, directors, writers, and actors. The talk at all the tables was about you and the upcoming movie adaptation of your book "Private Parts". The "buzz" is that everyone wishes they were "on board" your project. Hollywood is such an incestuous and jealous place. Some people would say nasty things to their fellow diners about your work. Moments later these phonies would get on their cell phones and beg their agents to get them in your movie. I wish you could have heard them. It was so pathetic! Personally, I am honest enough to admit that I would do ANYTHING to be in your movie!

Speaking of "Private Parts" I can play a kazoo with mine! This has always amused

my boyfriends. The songs I play on the kazoo with my private parts are even recogniz-
able. My best song is "How Dry I Am". Of course I'm really wet — but that's besides the
point. After all you have to be more than just slightly moist for it to work anyway. If you
like, I could send you a tape. (*Howard said, "Ma'am, if you're out there listening, please
send me the tape!"*) I can also make pussy-farts and coughing noises. You should see the
impression I do in my bathtub of "Old Faithful", the geyser at Yellowstone National Park.

I think my ability must be hereditary, because my mother is Thai. My father met my
mom while on R and R during the Vietnam War. She was working as an "entertainer and
comfort-girl" at a Bangkok Bistro. My mother used her private parts to steal my father's
heart. Mom is far more skilled with her privates than I am. In fact she can blow smoke
rings, make icing decorations for a cake, and shoot objects such as darts and Milk Duds
across the room through a tube. After we finish a roll of paper towels, there is always a
fight over who gets to play with the cardboard tube. I'm the only one in the family, however, who can play two Kazoos at once (one with my upper mouth and one with my
lower one).

I can also sing and accompany myself on kazoo at the same time. This makes me feel
like Bob Dylan. I would be willing to perform for you, if you felt it might interest your
audience. All I need to perform is a mini-skirt, a picture of Brad Pitt, and a microphone
clamped to the front of my chair seat. Howard, you are the greatest! I would love to sere-
nade you. Take care, and best of luck with your movie.

Sincerely,

Mai-Ling Postino

P. S. I am Eurasian, 23 years old, 5'6" tall, 117lbs., 36-24-36, and have long, shiny, jet
black hair down to my bottom. I look just like the woman who stars as an exotic dancer
in the new George Clooney movie *Dusk Till Dawn*. By the way, to improve my instru-
ment, I have shaved my private parts. My twin sister Mai-Lynn can use her privates to
play the slide flute, and crack open walnuts. My father calls us his Vaginal Vaudeville
Virtuosos!

(Postino means mailman in Italian — was I being obvious or what? Anyway,
Howard and the gang bought it hook, line, and sinker. Maybe they were just playing along.)

My moonlighting for the Howard Stern show was having an impact on my
career as a photographer and thus my finances. Howard consumed ever increasing
amounts of my time. Instead of thinking of new ways to improve my photography, I was concentrating on my Howard Stern activities. I found myself cutting
corners and rushing my assignments to completion. For every picture I took, I
wrote a thousand words about Howard.

I insisted on listening to Howard, every morning, without fail, even during photo shoots. I couldn't risk missing one of my faxes being read. Howard is not everyone's cup of tea. My clients were sometimes uncomfortable. Usually this discomfort broke along gender lines. Most guys could tolerate Howard, while women had less patience for him.

Perhaps I was coming across like a street corner fanatic. It took every ounce of self-control that I possessed to avoid going too far. Preaching to the confirmed is one thing. But, preaching to non-believers is another matter. Fortunately, I somehow managed to walk this tightrope without winding up in bankruptcy court.

My Howard fixation, also ate away at my personality like a flesh-eating disease. I was neglecting my family, especially on weekends. My sleeping and eating patterns had all changed to accommodate my Howard Stern chores. At social gatherings, I quickly became a one-topic conversationalist. That topic was of course Howard. My wife's friends were concerned. When I referred to Howard Stern, I would just say Howard. I acted as though there was only one person named Howard in the whole world. Yet, until my wife pointed out this fact, I was completely unaware of it. Too bad there isn't a 12-step program for Howard Stern sufferers!

My disease had spread far beyond faxing. I was also heavily engaged in surfing the Net for Howard Stern pages and spending three hours a day on the Prodigy Howard Stern Bulletin Boards. I used some of my rejected faxes as material for board postings. My on-line charges went

Howard Stern

through the roof. How could I justify my excessive spending to my family? These feelings of guilt caused me to become secretive. Never in my wildest fantasizing could I have imagined myself capable of such behavior. If you had suggested to me the year before that I could act this way I would have thought *you* crazy.

Lately, I have been pondering this question: Why is it so rewarding to hear my faxes on the radio? It took some time to figure out. A big part of the reason is vanity. But the other part is that having Howard read your fax is like having Pavarotti sing your song, or Rembrandt paint your portrait. The ultimate result is masterful. Howard brings my faxes to life. Besides, advertisers pay thousands of dollars per minute for Howard to read their material. I get it for free!

Well, there you have it. From a one-line fax, an empire grew.

CHAPTER 2

THE BOOK SIGNING FROM HELL

T he armed services have boot camp. Mountain climbers have Mount Everest. Runners have the Boston Marathon. Fraternities have hazing. For a Howard Stern fan, it's a book signing.

Getting one's book signed by the King of All Media is an occasion that truly separates the men from the boys. Fellow fans regard anyone claiming to be a fan with utter contempt if their copies of *Private Parts* or *Miss America* lack Howard Stern's John Hancock.

It takes Howard approximately four seconds to sign each book. This comes to nine hundred books per hour. Most books signings are attended by more than seven thousand people. Howard always stays until the last fan gets his or her book signed. This means that the person at the end of the line must wait more than seven hours. Allow an extra hour for Howard to take a break or two and the basic wait exceeds eight hours. And that doesn't even include the time spent waiting for the book signing to begin, or travel time to and from the signing. The faint of heart should stay home as this is survival training of the highest order — only the fittest will survive.

1 minute = 60 seconds
60 minutes = 1 hour = 3,600 seconds

3,600 seconds ÷ 4 seconds per book = 900 books per hour
7,000 fans ÷ 900 books per hour = 7.8 hours

Ironically, the person at the end of the line may have a shorter wait overall than the person at the beginning of the line. The leader of the pack has to camp out for days to secure the prime real estate. As always it's location, location, location — the benefits of which include media attention and a live on-air interview with Howard. The early bird catches the worm, while the rest are left to scratch and peck in the dirt.

Book signings resemble a circus, Woodstock, and a Roman orgy all rolled into one. At least that's the impression gained from the media coverage devoted to each signing. Following each event, the faxes fly in to Howard's show at a fast and furious pace. Some listeners claim abduction by sex crazed aliens, while others meet their future spouses, or discover that they're gay. The only conclusion to be drawn from all this is that every copy of *Miss America* should come with a free box of rubbers.

Perhaps Howard's next book should be titled *Caligula*. It would make for a great bookcover. Howard could wear a toga with a crown, carry a book, and hold a dildo over his head. Or he could go Greek. Plato meets Hugh Hefner. An erudite man with an erection! Maybe he could dress up as President Theodore Roosevelt, with a Panama hat, white suit, glasses, and a cigar. A man, a plan, a vaginal canal. Sounds like a winner to me.

My experiences with radio personality book signings date back to the early nineteen seventies. As a teenager I listened to my childhood idol Jean Shepherd, on WOR radio. My stepmother was meaner than Cinderella's. I had a very early bedtime. She hated my guts and wanted me out of her sight. I was always too wide awake to sleep. So I hid a radio under my pillow and secretly listened to Jean. It was great. I don't know what percentage of my personality I owe to him. I only wish I were one tenth the storyteller he is.

When I was fifteen I got Jean Shepherd's books *In God We Trust, All Others Pay Cash*, and *Wanda Hickey's Night Of Golden Memories and Other Disasters*. They are great books, well within the reading abilities of the average teenager. They remind me of comedic *Nancy Drew* or *Hardy Boys* mysteries. To promote his books, Jean held book signings. For some unfathomably stupid reason Jean chose the A&S department store in downtown Brooklyn as the location for one of his signings. I cut school early and took a train to A&S. The store was really seedy, with less charm than the average K-Mart.

I had never seen Jean before. His voice sounded deep, gravelly, and very virile so I imagined him to be a tall, broad-shouldered, ruggedly handsome man — the kind of outdoors man a young teenaged boy could look up to. When I rounded a corner I came upon a small crowd of approximately twenty people gathered around a pudgy, balding old man. I thought that the man was a sales clerk or a publicist. When I discovered that it was Jean Shepherd, my boyhood idol, I almost passed out.

Eventually, I composed myself. I decided to make the best of the occasion. I remembered that my reason for coming was to show support for a man who had made my unreasonable bedtime bearable. I decided to mingle with my fellow fans who were all much older than I. Many of the fans were old ladies with droopy stockings. What the hell was going on? My nightmare grew worse when I discovered that many of my supposed fellow fans were actually bored shoppers. Some of them even thought it was a cooking demonstration. The only reason they had stayed was for the free samples. I was crestfallen. Life had added another humiliation to my already full plate. I was a nerdy teenager who never fit in. And now, to make matters worse, I was surrounded by losers in a department store waiting to have a book signed by a pudgy old baldy. A smarter person would have cut their losses and split. True to form — I stayed.

Before the signing began, Jean talked to the crowd. Then he asked for comments and questions. Jean was just killing time. The actual signing could only take two or three minutes at most, even with breaks and chit-chat. He was doing his best to act important. He even stood on a step-stool so he could look down on everyone.

Jean often played the Jew's Harp, while humming, and doing glockenspiel (resonant head-thumping) on his radio program. It was usually pretty amusing, but I enjoyed his stories more. Anyway, I raised my hand and waited for Jean to recognize me. When called upon for my comment or question, I asked Jean to do a little glockenspiel. To this day, my head still has a sore spot from my own pubescent attempts at emulating my hero. Jean looked at me and said in a curt and nasty voice that he was not there to perform. Bam! That was it. What a creep! I was the youngest person in the whole store, with a simple request, and expensive hardcover editions of his books, and this was the way he chose to treat me. I told him to go shove it, and threw my book in the nearest trash can while he watched in wide-eyed disbelief.

Considering my history with book signings, attending another one required all the faith, hope, and courage that I could muster. I had no intention of waiting in line with another bunch of "losers" to get my copy of *Miss America* signed. (I hadn't gone to the first book signing for *Private Parts*.) But in the two months before *Miss America* was published I'd upgraded my fan status from passive to active. I had evolved into the species more formally known as Faxis Fantasticus — dangerous, predatory, compulsive, rabid, meat-eating, devil-worshipping, and crazed.

Yet, like Dr. Jekyll, I tried to deny my true nature. While running a work-related errand near the Brentano's Bookstore in New York City on the day of Howard's first *Miss America* book signing, I decided to see what all the fuss was about. The line of people waiting to have their books signed was enormous. It began at 48th Street and Fifth Avenue and stretched all the way past 54th Street and Madison Avenue. The line was at least four people wide. I was amazed. There was a carnival atmosphere in the air. Television crews roamed around interviewing fans. A group of scraggly, long-haired hippies dressed from head-to-toe in black and carrying guitars entertained the masses with a spirited rendition of a song appropriately titled "Miss America". The upbeat, expectant, and excited behavior of the crowd was infectious. I wished I could join them. However, my copy of *Miss America* was at home, and I had too much work that day.

I followed the crowd like a river to its source — the front of Brentano's Bookstore. The entrance was blocked with blue police barricades. I staked out a perfect spot to view Howard's arrival. This spot was located beneath a traffic light directly across the street from Brentano's. I planned on climbing to the base of the light to gain a three-foot height advantage. Onlookers, were covering the ground like a thick, tightly woven rug. We were jammed so closely together that a penny thrown into our midst would never hit the ground.

Suddenly, a huge, spontaneous, roaring wall of sound tumbled closer and closer. It was the sound of the crowd voicing its approval and excitement at the appearance of Howard's limousine. I clung to the safety of my perch to avoid being crushed and to get a clearer view of the spectacle. Howard emerged from his limo dressed in full drag, wearing a lovely gown, high heels, a feathered boa, and sporting a huge bouffant hairdo. Hair to toe, he must have been at least eight feet tall. Clearing a path before him was a rose-petal-throwing midget in top hat and tails.

Howard is undeniably a great showman. The late Princess Di would have been hard-pressed to make such an exciting entrance. Even P.T. Barnum would have been impressed. Everyone was going crazy. It was well-behaved, semi-out-of-control chaos. I loved it. Howard waved to everyone before entering the bookstore. The King of All Media really knows how to act regally! I reluctantly tore myself away and headed back to my studio. On the way, I passed several late arrivals running full tilt in the hopes of beating the cut-off time for getting in line for the signing. I had always thought myself immune to mass hysteria over a media figure, but now I wasn't so sure. I was really disappointed at not being in line with my fellow fans to get my copy of *Miss America* signed. I thought I'd missed my chance.

Fortunately, Lady Luck intervened on my behalf with a second chance. Howard announced that he was going to have a book signing at the Barnes and Noble book-store in Carle Place, Long Island (a twenty-minute drive from my house) on Saturday November 18, 1995. The timing was perfect. My wife and kids were planning to visit relatives in Maryland. I would be home alone with *Miss America* and an empty dance card. I decided to take *Miss America* out for a day on the town so I could get her properly accessorized! Then I planned to bring her home and celebrate. *Miss America* was about to loose her cherry. I would finally be promoted to the rank of die-hard fan.

As I backed my Subaru out of my driveway the words of John Babsone Lane Soule rang out true and clear in my head: "Go west, young man." Good advice. I needed an appropriate sign to display on the way to my first Howard Stern book signing. On a sheet of orange oak-tag I wrote "Howard Stern or Bust!", figuring that Howard would appreciate the "Bust" part.

It seemed as though the whole seven million plus populace of Long Island had decided to join me. The traffic slowed to a crawl by the time I came within sight of Barnes and Noble. I regretted not having left earlier. Perhaps I should have driven there the previous night and slept in my car. I was almost tempted to turn back, but my curiosity got the best of me. Eventually I managed to find a parking spot in "Siberia," — a good twenty-minute walk from the bookstore. I considered myself lucky to get a space at all. I wasn't very comfortable with parking my new Subaru in such a desolate area. But destiny doesn't like to be kept waiting.

I fell in with my fellow fans, and journeyed with them to the promised land. We were in high spirits. Little did we realize how difficult our pilgrimage to Mecca would be. It was a damp, overcast, and bone-chilling day. I was fighting a bad cold and my nose was running. My pockets were stuffed with tons of tissues — enough to last the length of my maiden voyage or so I hoped. The day was starting to feel apocalyptic. I considered changing my sign from "Howard Stern or Bust!" to "This Is The End!" I was heading towards the end of the line anyway. I took out my black marker and made the necessary changes on the back of my "Howard Stern or Bust!" sign.

The first leg of my trip took me and my fellow late arriving fans past, and parallel to, the front of the winding serpentine line of eager fans. We were prevented from cutting ahead in line, and thus joining our early bird brethren, by a chain-link fence topped with barbed wire. The perimeter was patrolled by the storm troopers of the Nassau County Police Department mounted on horseback. These measures wound up protecting and benefitting those of us at the back more than those fans at the head of the line.

In fact, I was very grateful to have a secure barrier separating myself from this ungodly rabble. I would have bet all my money that a low-rent tour bus from Brooklyn had unloaded its foul cargo of mafia guidos at the head of the line. They were truly obnoxious and disgusting. They looked like a bunch of night-club bouncers in a uniform of loud, multi-colored baggy clothing. I'm no Beau Brummel myself, but I reserve my workout duds for the gym.

These idiots were primed and loaded for bear — or at least primed and loaded with beer. They had to be drunk or stoned — the only explanation I can produce for their behavior. They shouted various dimwitted obscenities at us as we passed. Women fans endured the lion's share of their abuse.

Needless to say, I was very relieved when we were out of earshot, and they had a whole new crop of fans behind us to jeer at. My only lingering concern was whether Howard would turn tail and head for the hills when he saw the dregs of society inhabiting the front of the line.

Luckily, only the front one-percent of the line was poisonous. The line was like a deadly rattle snake: only the head was dangerous. Howard was due to arrive at noon — in an hour and a half. Could the guidos last that long? I had my doubts.

Penny Crone from *Fox 5 News* was interviewing some fans. I asked her if the rumors that she and Howard were having an affair were accurate. She gave me an ear-to-ear smile and laughed. She said the rumors were true. I couldn't believe that she was such a good sport. I had once heard her cry when a man pointed his finger at her during a Howard Stern press conference. She became very irrational. I guess she hates to be pointed at. Go figure.

I bought a cup of tea to soothe my cold, and trekked back nearly 3/4 of a mile to the end of the line. I later learned that about six and a half thousand fans were in line that day. We lined up in a winding configuration on the parking lot tarmac surrounding the stores next to and across from Barnes and Noble. I purchased a Howard Stern Rules sweat shirt from an enterprising soul to help keep me warm. It was a wise purchase. The length of the line was very intimidating. While Howard had promised to stay until everyone had their book signed, I doubted my own fortitude.

Since there were no Portapotties available, many fans were urinating behind a beat-up van. Others tried to use the restroom at Ben's Deli, which had agreed to donate free hot dogs to the fans as a publicity stunt and goodwill gesture. Personally, I think the owners of Ben's should receive a humanitarian award. One can only guess how many lives they saved.

A woman employee from Barnes and Noble came by and handed everyone a copy of the official Howard Stern book signing rules. This is what she gave me:

ATTENTION HOWARD STERN FANS!

**Welcome to the Howard Stern signing for <u>Miss America</u>
at Barnes & Noble!**

Following are some tips to make the signing easier:

• YOU DO NOT HAVE TO ENTER THE STORE TO PURCHASE YOUR COPY OF *MISS AMERICA* FOR THE SIGNING! The line for the signing will be in the south end of our parking lot on the other side of Ben's Deli. Upon arrival go immediately to this line. If you are bringing a pre-purchased copy of *Miss America*, please alert our bookseller at the end of the outside line who will mark your book with a sticker.

• Once on line, you will eventually come to a register where you will purchase your book(s). You will be given a receipt. IT IS VERY IMPORTANT THAT YOU DO NOT LOSE THIS RECEIPT AS IT WILL BE CHECKED TWICE BEFORE YOU LEAVE THE STORE. You will not be given your actual books until you have been at the signing table and your books have been signed.

• Once in the store, you will enter the signing area, a Barnes & Noble employee will give your book(s) to Howard to be signed and then they will be given to you as you exit.

• You will not be able to enter the rest of the store following the signing to insure that all fans can get their books signed. A clear exit aisle will be marked and you will exit the store at the front door where you will be asked for your receipt and your book will be bagged.

• Do not bring shopping bags, purses or backpacks with you. They will not be allowed into the store.

• No photographs are allowed! Do not bring cameras or video cameras into the store.

• Howard is only signing *Miss America* —- NO EXCEPTIONS! Please do not bring any photographs, memorabilia, baseballs, etc. There will also be no personalization!

A chorus of groans and epithets followed this foolishly brave woman as she worked her way through the line disseminating her fascist flyers. Everyone in line had backpacks, cameras, and copies of *Private Parts* and/or *Miss America* in need of signing. I was no exception, being loaded down like a pack mule. In fact, after only a half hour, my own copy of *Private Parts* felt like a two-ton albatross around my neck. My shoulders were killing me from the effort of lugging so much stuff. Many fans had packed food, water, and other survival gear. It was quite clear that the fans were on their own. Barnes and Noble had made the paltriest of efforts to provide for our physical or emotional well-being. We tried to help each other. The strongest and most well-equipped fans helped the weakest. We took inventory of our supplies and rationed them out equitably. The more we were oppressed by outside forces, the more we banded together. The solidarity was heartfelt. I was touched and proud to count myself among their number.

A flock of entrepreneurs descended upon us like vultures to hawk their wares. First came a gaggle of local merchants. They held reams of flyers to their breasts with claw-like grasps. Then came the food-vendor-for-a day militia armed with beer, pizza, and other highly nutritional and insanely overpriced foodstuffs. Not to be outdone were the souvenir sovereigns. Every time they made the rounds, their desperation driven prices would drop at least ten percent. They had tee shirts, sweat shirts, Howard Stern for President buttons, collectible Howard Stern videos, posters, and counterfeit *Miss America* promotional car mirror danglers.

One of the strangest profiteers was an emaciated quadriplegic in a wheel chair pushed by his sleazy partner. This dynamic duo worked the crowd for spare change. Howard Stern fans are generally not known for their sympathy or generosity. Whenever there is a disaster in the world, Howard Stern and company are the first to exploit the situation for its humor value. However, against all reasonable expectations, the dynamic duo did quite well. I guess behind the stern exteriors of Howard's fans, beat hearts of gold.

Eventually the truly vile characters descended upon the tired and unsuspecting fans like an evil plague of locusts. We were punished by Howard Stern's mangy stray cats. These obscene felines, the people whose "fame" was entirely due to Howard, had not come to praise our fearless leader. They were there to co-opt the event, and enhance their own fame. One of them was Howard's cybersex partner Rubberbaby. She looks like a suburban house-frau — a veritable Erma Bombeck replete with a garbage pail vocabulary. Rubberbaby reminds me of a soap-opera-watching, load-in-the-dryer, romance-novel-reading, gossipy old washer-woman. Connecting her to cybersex is a major turn-off.

Howard Stern's book *Miss America* contains a color picture section of unused book cover designs. One design was for a scratch and sniff cover. Readers could scratch and sniff the ass of a fat woman with cellulite. Even this fat "stray cat" exploited her dubious claim to fame. She actually believed that fans would want her to despoil their treasured copies of *Miss America* with her foul chicken scrawl. I was pretty bored from all the standing around and needed some amusement. I told the fat lady that I didn't believe she was the heifer from Howard's book. I suggested that she show the fans her cottage cheese butt to prove she was the authentic scratch and sniff lady. Everyone was horrified when she complied. She was the genuine article. I was afraid that the crowd would be turned to stone from the horrid sight. My Ben's hot dog and onions shot up like a space launch. I threw up. It was spontaneous combustion to rival the Challenger shuttle mishap.

Howard's most loathsome stray cat is Melrose Larry Green. He is a sandwich board toting exhibitionist. His daily activities involve parading about on Melrose Avenue in Los Angeles, displaying sandwich boards that usually contain Howard Stern related writing. Fortunately for Melrose, his sandwich boards are well-constructed and very sturdy since they have to perform double duty as shields against the garbage hurled at him. Fans were yelling at Melrose. They told him to go back to Los Angeles and to take his "smelly-melly" odor with him.

Melrose is completely oblivious of the extent to which he is hated. He kept telling anyone foolish enough to listen that he was loved by the majority of fans, all the while trying to grab copies of *Miss America* in a pathetic effort to sign them. I am surprised he was able to get out alive. Melrose lives in a fantasy land of his own design. He has somehow convinced himself that people love him. Talk about denial!

Even Joey Buttafuoco's lawyer Dominic Barbara made a brief appearance. Howard refers to Dominic as a bloated attorney. I'm hard pressed to come up with a more appropriate description. Dominic looks like a fat, spoiled, little boy. His gut hangs over his belt like a spare tire filled with jelly. I find his personal friendship with Howard Stern mind-boggling. Deep down, I'm certain Howard is just using Dominic to gain access to his sordid but newsworthy clients. For his part, Dominic is manipulating his clients' infamy to enhance his own pseudo-celebrity status.

I don't know what Dominic was expecting when he came out to give the fans a once-over. Perhaps he thought he would be cheered. Howard's stray cats just can't accept the fact that the fans are there to see Howard — not them. Despite this fact, a few dozen fans, myself included, surrounded him. I wanted to give Dominic a hard time. I planned on asking him if Joey Buttafuoco had gone to any prostitutes lately. We were making great sport of shoving our books as close to Dominic's face as possible. He was frantically signing the picture of himself while sweating like a pig. The situation was overwhelming him. I shoved my open book within a half inch of his face. I was tempted to

Nicole Bass & Joey Buttafuoco

snap the book shut on his fat nose, but Dominic quickly signed my book. His signature is barely decipherable.

I suspect my aggressive actions were the straw that broke the elephant's back. Dominic tried to escape, but he was impeded by the cocoon-like envelopment of Stern fans nipping at his feet. The scene resembled a *National Geographic* wildlife film. Dominic was the sickly wildebeest about to be felled by a pack of wild hyenas. Several security guards rushed to Dominic's rescue and gathered him in their protective fold to rejoin the herd inside the bookstore. I admit that I'm jealous of Dominic's nearly unlimited access to Howard, which is why seeing Dominic run for his life was a high point of the book signing.

My fellow fans represented a cross-section of society. I spoke with computer programmers, advertising experts, and hospital workers — people from many walks of life. Although these fans all shared an appreciation of Howard, they were hardly the one-dimensional dregs of society the media likes to portray. We discussed a large variety of topics while waiting in line including the significance of the Internet in society, the upcoming presidential election, peace in the Mid-East, late term abortions, the literary merits of various books, and the role of DNA in future court proceedings. And this is just a small sampling. I only wish the media had captured, and appreciated, the depths of knowledge and sincerity of the average Stern fan.

After several hours, the cold, damp weather was getting to me. My feet were frozen. I shifted from foot to foot in a vain attempt to stay warm. I asked a fellow fan to save my place in line and ran to Ben's Deli to warm up. I was not alone. At least a hundred other fans had the same idea. The place was a madhouse. The line for the bathroom rivaled the book signing line outside. I dubbed this line the Yellow River (Huang Ho) after the famous waterway in China. At least here in the restaurant I was safe from frostbite. Then I bought another cup of tea and reluctantly reclaimed my spot in line.

The people in front of me were extraordinarily friendly and considerate. They shared their pizza with me. I offered to chip in some money, but they wouldn't hear of it. I know some people may consider their generosity to be insignificant but to me it was touching. I think this act of kindness was exactly the unnamed ingredient I was searching for. This is what I had hoped to find when I decided to join my fellow fans and get my book signed. I felt so warm inside that I even forgot about my icy feet for a while.

No matter where one goes these days, favoritism and corruption exist. Two men several yards behind me happened to be personally acquainted with one of the security guards. They signalled the guard and were quickly escorted to the front of the line. My fellow fans and I were outraged and vented our anger by shouting obscenities at the traitorous duo. Howard always rants against favoritism when it doesn't include him. We were no different.

Before I knew it, six hours had passed. The line was still very long. People were starting to drop like flies, done in by the cold. Some had to drive home before nightfall for work or family commitments. I wasn't sure that I could last either. My cold was really bothering me. My whole body ached. I was tired of breathing the damp air. It seemed as though the line was hardly moving. Many people wondered whether or not Howard would really be able to honor his word to sign all the books. What if he got writer's cramp? I was expecting the worst. It was starting to get dark. I had no desire to remain in line when the temperature plummeted after the sun went down.

The mounted police didn't improve the situation. They kept patrolling the line like mean and angry Gestapo guards. It is hardly reassuring to have a huge horse with a club-carrying policeman heading your way. The police looked ready to bash a few heads. Despite this, I don't think a single warning was issued to any of the well-behaved fans, much less an arrest. The only rabble rousers were at the head of the line, and they were long gone.

Truth be told, after a day of hell we had become a downtrodden mass as we shuffled along like a chain gang. After close to eight hours, I was finally within fifty feet of the bookstore. I spotted a couple with a young baby in a carriage. Several fans, including myself, cajoled and embarrassed our brethren into letting the family move to the head of the line. I couldn't believe that anyone would subject a tiny baby to such abuse. If a Nassau County social worker had been present, the couple probably would have been taken into custody and the baby placed with a foster family. Part of me admired the parents for their die-hard loyalty to Howard Stern. Yet as a future Howard Stern fan-in-the-making their baby needed to be protected. Therefore, until their child is old enough to say "Baba Booey," I think that Howard Stern book signings should be strictly forbidden! Then again, the baby neither moved nor made a peep. Perhaps it was really a fake designed to help the "parents" cut the line. Now *that's* something I definitely could sympathize with.

The clerks at Barnes and Noble were so cruel. They were allowing fans who had not purchased books to enter ahead of others, out of turn. After half an hour, I decided not to put up with it. I charged ahead and declared myself to be one of the fans needing to purchase a book. I was becoming quite ill. I felt like a creep for deserting the people next to me in line. They now looked at me with total contempt. I felt terrible. I told them to come join me. Eventually some did. I took comfort in the warm air as I stepped across the threshold of the store's doorway.

Once inside I was frisked by a huge African-American woman security guard. It was an up-close, and very personal, invasion of my privacy, to say the least. My shoulder bag was taken from me, and put on a table to be retrieved on my way out.

I was so angry at Barnes and Noble that I foolishly resisted purchasing a second copy of *Miss America*. Little did I realize how much it would be worth in the future. The Barnes and Noble people were very strict. Only purchasers could get a bookmark souvenir of the signing.

Finally, I was within twenty feet of the King of All Media — Howard Stern. A store clerk-cum-acolyte took my copy of *Miss America*. Mere fans weren't allowed to hand books to Howard. The store clerk then rapidly placed the book in front of Howard, and he signed it. Then I was hurried along, and handed my signed book by yet another clerk. This was the procedure, and there were no exceptions. Howard is fond of saying that he makes eye contact and usually says a few words to each fan. I guess Howard had to abandon this noble goal after eight hours. Besides which, I doubt that Howard could make eye-contact with anyone due to the impenetrably dark glasses he was sporting.

Dominic Barbara was standing behind Howard, rubbing his shoulders and speaking words of encouragement to him. Howard looked much thinner than he seemed on television interviews. His hair was tied back in a pony-tail, his right arm was resting on a towel. I had planned on making a silly wisecrack in order to make a personal connection that I could later regale and impress my friends with. When I saw how hard Howard was working, I abandoned such plans. As bad as I felt physically, I could tell that Howard felt even worse. I can't think of any other celebrity who would put himself through such an ordeal. Howard was there to please his fans and give something back. I doubt that it increased book sales very much because fans would buy the book anyway. I was learning a lot about Howard, my fellow fans, and myself that day — and I knew it.

The moment of truth arrived. Howard signed my book with a red felt tip marker. His signature was beautifully clear and easily identifiable. It all happened too quickly. Howard didn't look at me or say a single word. Neither did I. The clerk handed me my book, I picked up my shoulder bag, and before I knew it, I was back outside.

There were still a few hundred people in line. It was completely dark. The temperature had fallen about ten degrees. I managed to find my car and as I left the parking lot, I honked my horn in tribute to the remaining fans. They looked back at me, too cold and weary to respond. Then I drove home. Along the way, I reflected upon my experiences. It had been a long day, but a day I will always remember. It was a day that I felt proud to get through, but reluctant to repeat. When I got home, I took some cold medicine, made myself a hot bowl of chicken soup, and climbed into bed. I was totally exhausted. I started to reread my copy of *Miss America*. I kept flipping to the front of the book to admire Howard's signature and to remind myself that the day's events had actually occurred. I fell asleep about an hour later. When I woke-up the following morning my head was on top of my open, spread-eagled *Miss America*. Hey, not every guy can say he has slept with Miss America!

Epilogue: Not long after the book signing, I started to feel very ill. I was short of breath and had trouble swallowing. I'm not the sort of person who runs to the doctor every time I feel bad, but eventually it became apparent that such a visit was in order. My doctor diagnosed me with pneumonia. An x-ray revealed that I actually had a serious case of bronchitis. Even with a strict regimen of antibiotics and rest, it took over six months for me to regain my pre-book signing health. My medical bills exceeded $300. Such is the price one pays when one decides to become a die-hard Howard Stern fan.

What To Take To A Howard Stern Book Signing	What Not To Bring To A Howard Stern Book Signing
1) Insulated hiking boots	1) Don Imus tee shirts
2) Catheter	2) Jackie Martling tee shirts
3) Adult diapers	3) Jackie Martling sweat shirts
4) Thermos filled with hot chicken soup	4) Jackie Martling CDs
5) High energy candy bars	5) Jackie Martling coffee mugs
6) Cough drops	6) Jackie Martling hot dog relish
7) Pain killers	7) Jackie Martling *Joke-in-a-box*
8) Steroids	8) Jackie Martling comedy club videos
9) Brandy	9) Melrose Larry Green caps
10) Cattle prod (to keep the line moving)	10) Melrose Larry Green tee shirts
11) Foldable chair	11) Melrose Larry Green cassettes
12) Dental records	12) Melrose Larry Green buttons
13) Portable CD player with King Norris's *Animal* CD	13) *"Melrose" Larry Green, Everybody!*
14) Riot gear — helmet, shield, and club	14) Your mother
15) Lesbian friends	15) Inhibitions of any kind
16) Last will and testament	
17) Plenty of money to bribe security guards and bookstore personnel	
18) Wack Pack pepper spray / pest repellent	
19) Chocolate treats for Gary Dell'Abate	
20) Crotch-less panties	

CHAPTER 3

PROPER MODULATION–
SCORES PARTY!

In early 1996 Howard Stern announced a new promotional contest. Contestants were to submit 30-second interpretive readings of excerpts from *Miss America.* Listeners were encouraged to send in multiple entries. One winner would be selected from each listening market across the country, resulting in a total of twenty-five winners.

Howard had created a novel prize for the lucky 25, who would be invited to one of Howard's famous Scores parties. Scores is a well-known New York City strip club — a veritable monument to the twin wonders of silicon and thongs. The party would last approximately three hours. There was a great deal of on-air debate whether women should be allowed to enter the contest.

Howard is indeed a genius at generating publicity. His radio show, his book, and even Scores would clearly profit from the promotion, though I wasn't sure how the listeners would fare. It seemed like a lot of effort. I doubted if the average listener could compete with the people who had amateur recording equipment in their homes. I predicted that New York City and Los Angeles would be extremely difficult markets to win in, due to the high caliber of the competition.

I have never liked contests. I don't even play Lotto. Besides, I didn't believe that Howard's book lent itself to "interpretive" readings. I was so wrong!

Slowly, but surely, I was sucked into a whirlpool. Howard had found yet another way to stimulate my creativity. First there were faxes, then Howard Stern webpage surfing, followed by on-line fan club bulletin board postings and chat room conversations. Now, I was about to become a recording artist.

I started to read my copy of *Miss America* with an eye (and an ear) for inspirational contest material. I found several passages with potential. Soon my copy of *Miss America* was littered with dozens of Post-it notes.

For my first two contest entries I chose the chapter on Howard's producer Gary Dell'Abate. Howard always disciplines Gary on-air. When Howard reprimands people he sounds like a dictator. Gary constantly screws up. Yet even when he is clearly in the wrong, he argues. Gary doesn't respond well to constructive criticism. Eventually, Howard resorts to making him "repeat after me." At this point, Gary repeats, word for word, whatever Howard says. Personally, I'd prefer a firing squad. *Miss America* contains one of these hilarious on-air "repeat after me" sessions.

The fascist nature of Howard's reprimands reminded me of an Adolf Hitler speech. The more I thought about it, the more I was convinced that I should read the passage in German and with a Hitleresque voice. I decided to read Howard's lines in German and Gary's lines in English. Howard would sound loud, sinister, and intimidating, while Gary would sound scared and whiny. I could hardly wait to record my contest entry.

I enlisted my German speaking brother-in-law's help with the translating. My brother-in-law holds a doctorate in history. He knows all about fascist dictators, having completed his dissertation on French collaboration with the Nazis. He has a great sense of humor, and he was tickled pink with my idea. Here's the "script" we came up with.

Hitler:	Schweinhund! "Ich..."
Gary:	"I..."
Hitler:	"Werde mitteilen..."
Gary:	"Will tell..."
Hitler:	"Alle wichtige Rufe..."
Gary:	"All important calls..."
Hitler:	"Das Sie die fallsche Nummer haben."
Gary:	"That they have the wrong number."
Hitler:	"In meine Freizeit..."
Gary:	"In my spare time..."
Hitler:	"Ich werde lernen.."
Gary:	"I will learn..."
Hitler:	"Zu sagen..."
Gary:	"To say..."
Hitler:	"Ich weiss nicht..."
Gary:	"I don't know..."
Hitler:	"Ich werde so schwer wie moglich versuchen..."
Gary:	"I will do my best..."

Hitler: "Nicht auf dem Empfänger zu subbern."
Gary: "Not to drool on the receiver."
Hitler: Dummkopf!
Sounds of machine-gun fire.
Cheering Masses: "Sieg Howard! Sieg Howard! Sieg Howard!"

A few weeks later, after I had submitted my contest tape, a funny coincidence occurred. Some German djs appeared on Howard's show. Howard tortured these Germans unmercifully! He even played recordings of Hitler's speeches, complete with machine-gun fire sound effects. Then he asked his guests to translate Hitler's words. I couldn't believe my providential wisdom. My perceived chances of winning the Scores contest had just increased a hundred-fold. I was tempted to shop for a party outfit.

Gary was also the subject of my second contest entry. Gary Dell'Abate, has dozens of nicknames. In addition to Boy Gary, he answers to Baba Booey, Fafa Fooey, Mama Monkey, and many others. Reading some of these silly names out loud sounded like a mantra. Suddenly, I began to hum the Hare Krishna mantra to myself. Then with the chant still fresh in my mind, I composed my "Ba Ba Buddha Stern" mantra:

The Mantra

Ba Ba Buddha Stern
Ba Ba Buddha Stern
Ba Ba Buddha Stern — Gary, Gary!

First Chorus:

"Boy Gary. Baba Booey, FaFa Fooey,
SaSa Smelly, GaGa Gooey,
RaRa Retard, and MaMa Monkey."

Second Chorus (repeat endlessly):

"What a dummy."

I was really stretching the contest parameters with this entry. But it paid off. Although this entry didn't win, it did get played on-air. Robin's favorite part was my use of the words "Gary, Gary!", in place of the traditional Krishna mantra's "Hare, Hare!". As I've said before, Robin really appreciates it when I turn a phrase.

To research and perfect this entry, I needed a tape of the actual mantra being performed. I located a temple on the Lower East side of Manhattan. The temple is in a small, narrow storefront in a neighborhood known for its many drug addicts. I wanted my "Hare" in a hurry! This was no place for a suburban white boy—either the resident addicts would notice me or the Hare Krishnas would try to recruit me. All I wanted to do was buy a tape, and get out fast.

Upon entering the temple, I had to remove my shoes, which I noted would delay my exit. The floors were made of beautiful golden, freshly varnished wood. The air was fragrant with the scent of lotus blossoms. The devotees were a small group of young adults — all attractive, soft-spoken, and clean-cut. This was not what I had expected. Until now, my Hare Krishna experiences had been limited to solicitations for money in airports and train stations.

But I digress. My cult leader is Howard Stern, and I had a mission. I purchased my tape and beat a hasty retreat homeward. Satan was in the driver's seat, and my tape was in the glove compartment. Little did the Hare Krishnas suspect that I had been sent on a nefarious evil mission to satirize their beloved mantra. I could hardly wait to record my entry. If the Indian man at my local 7-11 ever finds out, he will probably terminate my supply of "slushies". Such is the price of being a Howard Stern fan.

I decided to go "operatic", and honor Robin for my final contest entry. Howard and Robin are like Yin and Yang. Usually their on-air personalities compliment and balance each other. From time to time this precarious relationship hits a bump in the road. When this happens the crap can really hit the fan. From a listener's perspective the ensuing collision is like watching a train wreck in slow motion. The listener is powerless to affect the outcome of the collision and can only witness the event in horror or evil glee. Robin can really bare her teeth when provoked, and Howard doesn't like to back down from confrontation. This is one of the things I find most amusing and entertaining about the show. It really is like an Italian opera.

Because Howard perfectly captures this operatic quality in one passage of *Miss America*, I experimented with some Verdi (*Aida* and *Rigoletto*), imagining that Robin would approve. She is an opera fanatic. Like any rabid fan, I was eager to try any angle that might secure me a seat next to Howard at Scores. Too bad I can't sing. Here then, is the score for my Scores contest entry:

 "Howard, Howard. Ahhhh, the sweet voice of my on-air partner for years, the beautiful Robin Quivers. I know that confident voice belongs to a true broadcast professional. No doubt she is ready to do the morning's shtick."

I performed my aria to the tune of *La donna é mobile* — the perfect choice for an opera about Robin! Like a ham, I totally embellished each syllable with ridiculous rises, falls, and vocal quivers. I sounded like Tiny Tim on steroids.

Once I had all my material organized, it was time to record it. I tried using a small walkman-type tape recorder. The results were terrible. My voice really needs a lot of help. I needed to beef up its sound with echo, sustain, and compression. I needed professional help (acoustic and psychiatric). In short, I needed proper modulation! Howard's father ran a recording studio. I'm sure Howard would understand.

I went to Sam Ash's flagship store in Manhattan. I needed to buy a tambourine for my "Ba Ba Buddha Stern" rendition, and some machine gun sound effects for my Hitler entry. I also decided to buy a recording of Hitler himself to mimic.

I like to dress all in black from time to time. While so attired, I asked a chubby salesman if he had any Hitler recordings. I guess I must have looked like a Neo-Nazi. It's very difficult to make such a request sound natural and innocent. The salesman looked very uncomfortable. He said they didn't carry that kind of stuff.

Eventually, I wandered into another area of the store. It was there that I met and befriended a salesman by the name of Marc. He works in the sound effects and recording department. I couldn't believe it. Right in front of me were hundreds of sound effect CDs. Marc was unfazed by my Hitler requests. He even had several selections for me to choose from. Turns out that Marc has a punk band, Yankee Doodle Blietzkreig, which makes him no stranger to Nazidom.

Marc later informed me that his fellow salesman really thought I was a Neo-Nazi. I don't even have blond hair or blue eyes. I look more like Patty Duke than David Duke! What a riot. I love practical jokes. I told Marc to tell his fellow salesman that I was very angry about being lied to about the store's stock of Hitler speeches. The salesman was scared stiff. For a whole week his mother drove him home after work. Marc finally had to fess-up.

It turned out that Marc has a twenty-four track professional quality recording studio in his New Jersey apartment. Coincidentally, Marc even knew many of the Howard Stern show's personnel, who shop frequently at Sam Ash. Marc thought it would be cool to have something he helped record played on Howard's show. We arranged to meet after Sam Ash closed for the night. I wake up for work at about 6AM every morning. By 6:30PM, I'm beat. Yet there I was, ready, able, and willing to embark upon a late night interstate recording session with a relative stranger.

Marc and I walked to the Port Authority bus terminal, to catch a bus to East Brunswick, New Jersey. Marc is as tall as Howard Stern (6'5"). I am almost 5'8" tall. I had recently twisted my ankle and was walking with a slight limp. There we were on 42nd Street in New York. We must have looked like a modern-day version of Dustin Hoffman and Jon Voight in *Midnight Cowboy*.

Finally, we were on the bus leaving Manhattan. Marc is a really great guy. He is a long-haired, fashionably dressed musician. He looks like the kind of person that must have had a great time in school hanging out with the cool crowd.

I had never before recorded myself attempting a humorous radio bit. In fact, my recording "career" had thus far been limited to leaving prank messages on my friends' answering machines. I was nervous about my non-existent voice. I didn't want to make an ass of myself in front of Marc. All I could think about during the trip was how terrible it would be to completely screw up. I was embarrassed to be such a coward. Eventually, I rationalized that even if I did make a total ass of myself, I would never have to see Marc again.

Marc's apartment was cozy, and the equipment looked first-rate. After an hour of adjusting microphones and wires we were ready to go. We decided to try the "Hitler" entry first. I had hoped that we could record it in two parts — German and then English. Marc said he couldn't do this because he lacked a click track. I would have to read the whole thing without pause, varying my voice from a stern, authoritative German voice to a whiny, scared American voice. It wasn't easy. I had to modify my "two" voices so the levels would be close together. Fortunately I had practised my German at home. It all hinged on achieving the proper modulation. After about ten takes, we finally got it right. Then we added the machine-gun sound effects. This was Marc's favorite part. I would have recorded the gun-fire in a haphazard manner. Marc was a perfectionist. You'd have thought he was recording Richard Wagner rather than Dan Wagner. Howard would've been proud.

Our next effort was "Ba Ba Buddha Stern". I had thought that this would be an easy one. I was dead wrong. My Hitler imitation had strained my recording-challenged voice. I could barely get enough air. My voice kept failing. But we persevered. Finally Marc had me repeat the mantra on five different tracks. He told me to listen through the headphones and try to repeat myself exactly each time. I closed my eyes and hopped about like a real Hare Krishna (or drugged-out idiot.) Marc said I looked like Ravi Shankar. At this point, with my voice going and exhaustion setting in, I was willing to try anything. It was obvious that I wasn't going to get any better, so we decided to mix the tracks together. We added a few tracks of my tambourine playing and called it a day. We were both pleased with the final outcome.

That night I got home at four in the morning. I was exhausted but happy. I told myself that even if I didn't win the contest, or get to have my entry played, I was still fortunate. After all, if it wasn't for Howard Stern, and the tape contest, I never would have had such an adventure. I wonder how many other fans were having similar experiences? What would Howard Stern have thought about the repercussions his show was having with his listening audience?

I met Marc a week later to record my final operatic entry. I wanted to get a real opera singer to do it justice, but Marc told me it would be too expensive. So I gave it a try. Even the dogs in Marc's neighborhood howled in protest. My operatic voice was like a Siamese cat in heat. Now I was truly embarrassed. I eventually submitted my tape entry under a pseudonym — Andy Nominus. Hey, even I didn't want my real name attached to this stinker! The only reason I sent it in was to sadistically torture the interns assigned to screening entries. Still, I kept listening, secretly hoping Howard would play it. However, try as I might, it is impossible to hear all five hours of Howard's show, five days a week. Maybe it aired. Maybe it didn't. It definitely didn't win.

Marc played a copy of our previous efforts for some of his friends. He said they got a big kick out of it. He even thought I might be able to launch a new career writing bits and suggested that I create a tape of all my comedic efforts. Who was I to argue? Marc was the professional. Maybe I could start out small and do commercials for mom and pop shops. I've heard enough commercials and comedic bits to believe that I could do no worse.

Marc likes recording several bits during a session, so he asked me to bring some extra material. I was only too happy to oblige. At the time, Howard's celebrity interviewer, Stuttering John had just announced his upcoming engagement to his pregnant girlfriend. I had already heard Howard perform an interpretive reading of my faxes. What I really wanted to hear next was my own voice on the radio. Perhaps if I submitted a funny tape about Stuttering John I could realize my goal.

Thoughts of Stuttering John eventually made me wonder what it would sound like if the tables were turned. Suppose he was the one being interviewed. His album helped me turn wondering into reality. I came up with a script for a satirical interview, complete with replies from Stuttering John, courtesy of his album *Stuttering John*. I played his part of the obnoxious stutterer. It doesn't get much more poignant than this:

Stuttering John

Dan: Stuttering John! Stuttering John! Can I interview you for my college radio station? I'm a big fan! Just a few questions. Please!

John: Do you want the truth? Or do you want only lies! *(His lyrics are so deep!)*

Dan: How many times have you cheated on your fiancé in the last week?

John: 1-2-3-4!

(John's counting out a song intro.)

Dan: Stuttering John, what will people say if your baby looks like you?

John: The kid don't look pretty. I hate to break it to you.

Stuttering John

(I can't believe my good luck in finding such perfect lyrics. And on John's own album!)

Dan: What did your buddies say when they heard you were getting married?

John: My friend died today.

(Howard Stern equates marriage with death.)

Dan: What will people say about you after you become a father?

John: The dude's going bald, he should quit the guitar!

(I think John should become a fortune-teller!)

Dan: Stuttering John, can you really be as stupid as you look? Why don't you take Howard's advice?

(Howard told Stuttering John not to get married. He said it would destroy his life! Good advice! Howard's got John's number.)

John: You're asking too many questions!

(This is a commonly heard complaint during Stuttering John's celebrity interviews.)

Dan: John, stop f—ing pushing me! I don't have a gun! It's a microphone!

(This is what Stuttering John actually said when an angry subject of one of his interviews started slapping him around.)

John: It doesn't matter who you step on in a fight!

(One has to admire Stuttering John's code of ethics.)

Dan: Yeah, well have a nice life, man.

(Another typical Stuttering John quote!)

Marc was howling. I had all

Stuttering John

of John's answers marked and timed out on his CD. Marc was doing a great imitation of the game show host from *Family Feud*. After each of my questions, he would say "And the answer is?" We had a great time with this bit. It almost made up for the pain involved in recording my operatic satire. The best part of this skit was that it was so true to form. Should Stuttering John ever get laryngitis I would be an excellent choice for a substitute.

The contest deadline was 5PM on Friday, January 12, 1996. I submitted my entries by hand. I was not willing to trust the post office with my precious cargo and I wanted to guarantee that my tapes would arrive before the deadline for submissions. Plus the idea of seeing the entrance to Howard's lair was enticing. Over the course of the contest I made three trips to drop off my entries in person, figuring that my chances of winning were better if each entry arrived separately. Unfortunately, I was never able to catch a glimpse of Howard. Perhaps he was hibernating.

On my last trip to Howard's building (600 Madison Avenue), January 12, 1996, I was dressed like a terrorist. This was not intentional. It was snowing that day, and I was wearing a shiny black full-length coat with a hood, black leather gloves, and black boots. When I thought about how I was dressed I was surprised that the security guard allowed me into the building. All I had to do was sign-in. They didn't even ask for identification which I thought was pretty amazing considering this is New York.

I took the elevator to the fourth floor home of Infinity Broadcasting. During my ride in the elevator, I imagined what it would be like if I worked for Howard. As an employee, this elevator ride would be a routine event. Howard, Robin, Stuttering John, Boy Gary, Jackie Martling, Fred Norris, and countless celebrities had made this same trip. Perhaps they even stood exactly where I was standing. This was getting too weird. I was starting to scare myself. I resolved to make this my last uninvited visit to Infinity Broadcasting. It seemed like a good idea to nip my behavior in the bud. What would come next? Would I show up at 5:30AM to greet Howard as he entered the building? Would I wear a sandwich board with Howard's name on it? Sometimes, where Howard is concerned, my mind really leapfrogs too far ahead of itself.

The Infinity Broadcasting reception area is plush, with slate gray walls, sleek modern furniture, and a neon sign with Howard's name. Three elevator banks lead to this outer sanctum. To one's left and right are glass partitions with electronically controlled doors. To the left, and in front, is a glass-enclosed reception area.

I wanted to hand my *Miss America* tape contest entry to the receptionist for safe-keeping. Evidently she is instructed not to accept any packages from strangers. The lack of security precautions downstairs were more than made up for with the first-class measures upstairs. The receptionist buzzed open the glass door on my right. I was instructed to place my submissions on top of a pile of packages and mail. I was surprised that there weren't more contest entries. Howard had given the impression that they had received thousands.

I am a nosy bastard. I started looking at the packages. The package area is surrounded by cinderblock walls on three sides and is probably bomb-proof. I am absolutely positive that the packages are rigorously inspected, tested with a metal detector, and x-rayed. Finally, the receptionist took notice of my loitering and asked me to hurry up. Although I was still entertaining hopes of bumping into Howard and the gang, I did manage to tear myself away. I think Howard's security dossier on me doubled in size that day. I forgot to look for the hidden cameras. I wonder if Howard would be willing to send me a few 8x10 glossies of myself dressed in my terrorist regalia?

I felt like an expectant father. The seeds of my efforts had been deposited at Infinity Broadcasting. I hoped that they would take hold and grow. I kept a close vigil by my radio listening for the sounds of my creative offspring. I was a nervous wreck. During the time that I was making my tape contest entries, I tried to convince myself that winning didn't matter. I told myself that the journey was the true reward. I was wrong. I desperately wanted to party at Scores with Howard.

One day was particularly painful. Howard played an entry from a listener doing an interpretive reading from the chapter in *Miss America* where Howard talks about Rodney Dangerfield. The listener sounded exactly like Dangerfield himself. I kept waiting for Howard to announce that the tape was a hoax. I strongly believed that it really *was* Rodney Dangerfield. It didn't seem fair. This entry was an impression of Rodney Dangerfield, not an interpretive reading. I realized that my chances of winning were ruined if this is what Howard was looking for. Howard even said he wouldn't mind partying with this listener at Scores!

I always worried that the tape contest would be reduced to a popularity contest. Who would Howard rather party with? Hitler, Buddha, Pavarotti, or Rodney Dangerfield. A dumb question. Rodney won hands down. It wasn't even close. I should have tried submitting my entries to a smaller, newer, and less competitive market. Perhaps I would have had better luck in Florida or Texas. My disappointment was so hard to swallow.

It was even worse on the day of the Scores party, which was held less than a week after my own birthday. I had entertained fantasies of having Howard and my fellow winners toast my birth. Howard invited the winners to his show prior to the party. They sounded positively gleeful. Why wouldn't they? They'd just spent the night ensconced in a luxury hotel at Howard's expense. They'd even been given airfare and limos. It was first-class all the way. Howard really knows how to do things right.

Howard led his merry followers in a series of loud chants. They sounded like wild men. "Scores, Scores, Scores! Girls, Girls, Girls! Howard, Howard, Howard!" The chants went on and on. I was glued to the radio. I felt terrible, yet I was unable to tear myself away.

Howard made sure that the winners knew the rules of the road. No staring at Howard. No talking to Howard. No spending all your Scores' lap dancing chits and then trying to hang out with Howard. Howard really wanted to keep the winners at a distance. Anyone of legal age can go to Scores any time. As far as I'm concerned, the real prize is getting to hang out with Howard.

Despite the "No fraternizing with Howard" clause, I still would have loved to go to the party. I am such an ungrateful child sometimes. Over the course of the contest, I had been given an opportunity to learn and appreciate opera, German, and Indian culture. My life was enriched with new experiences (24-track-recording). I made a new friend (Marc). My hum-drum existence received a much needed boost of excitement. My creative juices were revitalized. But still, it would have been nice to be a winner.

Tips For Entering One Of Howard Stern's Contests

1) Avoid foreign languages, especially German.

2) Be natural. Be yourself. Try to sound like Rodney Dangerfield.

3) Sing only if you have talent.

4) Submit your entries to the smallest radio markets that carry the show.

5) Pretend to have a speech impediment.

6) Pretend to have an orgasm.

7) Claim to have been abducted by aliens.

8) Claim to have had sex with a farm animal or inanimate object.

9) Become a Hare Krishna member.

10) Bribe a Scores worker into letting you stowaway inside the club.

CHAPTER 4

GREAT EXPECTATIONS— CHAT PARTY LOSERS

Despite the disappointing failure of my contest entries to score a Scores party invitation for me, I was still ready to get down and boogie. And I knew where to head. Several times each year the people from Prodigy Howard Stern on-line chat rooms organize get-togethers called Chat Parties, which are attended by chat room denizens. Howard's own occasionally disparaging references to these gatherings as "loser parties" did little to dampen my determination to give one a whirl. I may have been a contest loser, but I knew I could be the life of a Chat Party.

Going to a Chat Party requires a leap of faith. Why would I *really* want to see what someone with the nickname* Halitosis (bad breath) looked like? How about Braindead, Flagellater, Cadaverlover, MissingLink or Valiumgirl? Come to think of it, going to a Chat Party should have been not only against my nature, but against my common sense and instinct for self-preservation as well. But then, who am I to pre-judge others by their screen names? After all, my screen name at the time was Bambicakes.

Predictably, my party going personality won out. On Saturday July 13, 1996 I attended my first, and no doubt last, Chat Party. It was held at a "sports" bar in New York City called The Polo Grounds. The party was organized by Uzo, one of Howard Stern's stray cats. Uzo spends hundreds of hours in the Prodigy Howard Stern Chat Rooms. For that reason alone, she is an ideal candidate to organize a Chat Party.

On learning that the Chat Party would be held at an establishment located on the Upper East Side of Manhattan, I was filled with great expectations. The

◄ *Uzo*

* *Nicknames changed to protect the "guilty."*

Upper East Side, especially the low 80's, is an affluent, upscale area. On warm summer evenings hordes of the young, the beautiful, and the well-dressed grace the roped-in sidewalk areas in front of fashionable cafés. The air is filled with a buzz that gives audible testimony to the optimistic vibrancy of the weekend revelers. (Warning: $10.00 vocabulary at work!) The youthful crowd is full of vim and vigor. Every eye twinkles with the anticipation of the sexual adventures and hijinks that cap alcohol-driven foreplay.

Such was my state of mind as I made my way to The Polo Grounds, which was ground-zero for the Chat Party. Each

Polo Grounds

time a beautiful restaurant or bar loomed ahead, my heart beat faster. Was this the spot? One place had an elegant red awning with yellow trim, lots of ornate wood paneling, and curbside tables given an air of exclusivity by a perimeter of polished brass tubing. It was with a heavy heart and deflated hopes that I left this jewel behind.

S uddenly, I woke from my day-dreaming to discover that I had passed The Polo Grounds. How could this have happened? I was walking on the correct side of the street. I carefully retraced my route. The address numbers drew me closer and closer to my destination. Calling The Polo Grounds "ground-zero" is very appropriate. Before me was a narrow, weather-worn, dark, seedy and derelict edifice that had unfathomably managed to escape condemnation.

The color scheme was forest green and fungus brown — the fungus no doubt real. The interior lighting made me long for the days of whale-oil lamps. The only thing competing with the low wattage of the lighting was the low mental wattage of the help. The few people seated at the bar looked like extras who failed to make the grade for the Mickey Rourke / Faye Dunaway film *Barfly* (a film remarkable for its portrayal of destitution). I wondered what perverse manifestation of nature had allowed this establishment to remain in business.

With great trepidation and a hand on my wallet, I ventured deeper into the abyss. Though only about fifteen feet wide, the place was quite deep. At the rear, secluded in a dark gloom whose sole source of illumination was the dull glow of a large-screen projection-television, sat the huddled mass of Prodigy Chat room denizens. A wiser man would have turned tail and fled screaming like a character from an Edgar Allen Poe or Lovecraft horror story. However, the site held me captive by its very grimness. Time slowed, twisted, and retracted. Eventually, my pupils dilated to the point where I was conscious of a number of eyes focused upon me.

Most of the chatters knew each other from previous Chat Parties. They regarded me cautiously, like a pack of wild wolves encountering a strange wolf in their midst. After I exposed my vulnerable throat and identified myself by my unintimidating appellation, Bambicakes, they visibly relaxed. The lead wolves of this canine matriarchy came forward to sniff me. Rubberbaby and Uzo fully appraised me from head to toe and in between. Evidently I passed muster. With a quick business like lack of decorum, and an Olympian gymnastic agility, I was separated from the two twenty dollars bills that I had secreted in my left shoe. This was the price of admission, my appeasement of the wolf pack. Once this formality was dispensed with, I was decorated with a yellow and black Chat Party identity button. I also received a K-ROCK key chain. The $40.00 admission fee included an open bar of non-premium drinks and some very suspect warm party food that I was too scared to try.

The last time I had seen Rubberbaby had been at Howard Stern's Long Island book signing for *Miss America*. Rubberbaby received her fifteen minutes of fame in Howard's book as a result of her on-line, licentious, and titillating cybersex escapades with Howard. Humorously, Rubberbaby's close encounter with Howard Stern had worked as many wonders for her appearance and sense of self-importance as Kato Kaelin's encounter with the Los Angeles judicial system had worked for him. Since the book signing Rubberbaby had shed a few pounds, gone blonde, restyled her coif, and bought some new duds. She still reminded me of a thick-legged hausfrau, but this time she looked more urban than suburban. Gone were the homely K-Mart prints. Now Rubberbaby was wearing what appeared to be a Filene's Basement urban power outfit — a black skirt and white blouse. She had transformed herself into a *cinema verité* version of Melanie

Uzo

Griffith's character in the movie *Working Girls*. I almost went to the jukebox in search of an appropriate Carly Simon tune.

Uzo, the primary organizer and financial beneficiary of the event, floated amongst the Chat Party attendees like a hostess at a society soireé. She was very nervous about the Chat Party's success because she knew that the party would be subjected to an exhaustive critical review in the chat rooms. As concerned as Uzo was about throwing a good party, she was even more concerned about throwing a profitable party. There were approximately thirty partyers paying forty bucks each for a total of $1,200.00. Uzo was also videotaping the party, offering the fruits of her labors for sale on her Internet web-page at $30.00 for two tapes. To augment her finances, Uzo later gave pretend, no-penile-contact, blow-jobs to fully-clothed male party "members" willing to part with another $40.00! I witnessed about five members availing themselves of this for-profit service.

Uzo and I eyed each other skeptically. Neither one of us was willing to turn our backs on the other. Our movements must have resembled a strange circular dance. Uzo and I had skirmished in the past on the Howard Stern Fan Club Bulletin Board. I wondered if she had anything evil planned for me. (As it turned out she did. She placed a picture of me making a silly face with my tongue sticking out on her Internet page — how creatively devious.) At this point I renewed my vows to monitor my alcoholic intake and keep my wits about me.

It is said that water always finds its own level. How true. The party goers were restless due to the long wait for the basement to be vacated. Evidently a bachelor party was in its death throes, and the various celebrants were doubtless too inebriated to get up the necessary enthusiasm for locomotion. In other words they were shit-faced, plastered, destination-less assholes. They were the prognosticators of our own future condition. Uzo became increasingly agitated. Perhaps she feared that some people might ask for their money back. After some furtive conversations with management, we were assured that the basement would be made available momentarily.

While we waited, another infamous chat personality by the name of Cinnamon arrived. She seems to make more bulletin board posts than anyone else. Her particular delight comes from being the first person to scribble a badly written and hasty one-line comment regarding something occurring on Howard's show, while it is occurring. She must listen to the show, fingers poised and ready at the keyboard while logged-on to Prodigy.

Like Uzo and Rubberbaby, Cinnamon has been on Howard's show. The reason for her appearance was to promote the Prodigy Howard Stern chat rooms after their opening, at a time when Prodigy was an advertiser on Howard's show. Cinnamon, Uzo, and Rubberbaby form the nucleus of the self-anointed "chat room elite".

From the beginning, it was painfully obvious to me that these three were close. However, never in my wildest imagination could I have imagined how close! As soon as Cinnamon entered The Polo Grounds Uzo ran over to her and jammed her tongue in Cinnamon's mouth. They soul-kissed and fondled each other as though they were participants in one of Howard Stern's Lesbian Dial-a-Date games! One of the chat partyers told me that this happens all the time. Ultimately, an employee of The Polo Grounds had to separate the hormonal duo. I was worried that he might end up needing a bucket of cold water and a crow bar to get them apart. The funny thing is that even a low-life establishment such as The Polo Grounds doesn't want to sink even lower in their rankings as a party destination! I couldn't help but wonder and marvel at the effect of Howard Stern's show on the lives of others. Would these two have behaved in such a manner if they hadn't sought to identify with Howard's love of lesbian hijinks? Howard knows it's a show, but do they?

I waited until Cinnamon's skin color returned to normal and she managed to fix her hair and straighten her clothing before going over and introducing myself. Cinnamon told me that it is impossible to say no to Uzo. In fact, I saw Uzo make numerous attempts, with varying degrees of success, to repeat her earlier performance with Cinnamon. I half expected Cinnamon to be very fat and ugly on the basis of remarks made to me by her nemesis and Stern Show regular Melrose Larry Green. I told her this and she laughed. (Physically she was far above and out of Melrose's league. I guess it was just sour grapes on Melrose's part.)

After about half an hour of waiting, the Howard Stern Chat Partyers were invited to proceed to the basement. Some of the bachelor party celebrants, having refused to leave, were still in attendance. It was weird watching the two groups mix at the bar. It reminded me of a muddy river (the bachelors) mixing with the ocean (the chatters) in a tidal delta. The chatters were easily identifiable by their yellow buttons with black chat names. I wonder what the bachelors thought of us. I felt like a thirsty salmon swimming upstream towards the bar in a futile effort to get my gills around a cold one.

The basement was a hot, humid, sweltering jungle. The air conditioner was broken, and the reek of urine from the nearby bathrooms permeated the place. I viewed the conditions as an evil omen. Even the floor was sticky. Saying that the basement was past its heyday would be a colossal understatement. Much of the floor space was a repository for cheap, cheesy, quarter-guzzling, amusement machines way past their prime. It was a museum devoted to machines that had enjoyed very brief popularity as distractions for the intoxicated. Too bad Howard Stern didn't make an appearance. I'm sure the "King of All Media" would have enjoyed seeing how his loyal peasant subjects entertained themselves.

The more I write about this Chat Party, the more I identify with the character of Harriet, in the *Harriet The Spy* children's book. On one hand, I am an observer, chronicler, and eye-witness to the follies and foibles of my fellow chatters, and on the other hand I enjoy interacting with them and share some of their short-comings. In that sense, we are bound together in a symbiotic relationship that defies explanation. We are a group that owes its creation and continued existence to a shared interest in Howard Stern's radio show. In fact, Robin Quivers and Howard Stern have commented that people in the chat rooms "satellite the show" and base all their friendships on being a Howard Stern Fan.

Now that this has been said, let me get back to the business of exposing the truth, and thereby further trashing my fellow Sternites. Fluffystuff is the sort of person Howard Stern would expect to see at a Chat Party. She is the overweight epitome of a Chat Party loser. From time to time, the media runs footage taken at various non-Stern Chat Party gatherings. Without exception the primary focus of the footage is on people who meet and marry their fellow chatters. Fluffystuff and quite a few other people at the Chat Party seemed to have this agenda in mind. However the basement of The Polo Grounds was so depressing that I'm sure any hopes of finding romance were rapidly shattered, despite ever-increasing blood-alcohol levels.

Cadaverlover was our youngest attendee. He spent most of the evening sitting in the shadows of the basement bar illegally drinking beers and bumming Capri cigarettes from Fluffystuff. I strongly doubt that Cadaverlover has seen his seventeenth birthday. He is in the midst of a rampant fascination with necrophilia and an even more rampant case of acne. His body is lumpy and betrays an absolute aversion to physical activity. Most of his bulletin board posts are made after midnight. I can only marvel at his being able to function through such sleep deprivation. The black tee shirt he wore had some sort of writing about corpses and appeared to be related to a heavy metal band. Visually, Cadaverlover reminded me of one of those suburban teenagers one reads about who are arrested for cruelty to animals or for being members of a Satanic cult that writes racist graffiti. Cadaverlover's sole redeeming attribute was his embodiment of the misfit teenager trying to find his place in society. How much was real and how much was false bravado was hard to tell.

If I were to have played matchmaker, I definitely would have paired Fluffystuff up with Halitosis. During the Chat Party, Halitosis told me all about his penchant for and knowledge of strange diseases and deformities. I even coined a disease for him — travelitis — a disease that makes a person travel from California to New York for a Chat Party in a decrepit basement full of losers. Too bad Halitosis and Fluffystuff failed to hook up.

Halitosis was clearly intelligent and pleasant to speak to, but nonetheless, he gave me the heebie jeebies! During the course of the party I continually spied him lurking in the shadowy outskirts of the bar. Beer in hand, he appeared to be calmly surveying the scene. Halitosis is a tall, heavy man. With his somnolent expression he reminded me of a lizard on a log. If a vote had been taken for "guest most in need of having his basement searched for missing bodies," then I'm sure Halitosis would have won.

Throughout the course of the party I hoped that someone from Howard's program would show up. I felt confident that in a social setting with drinks and such,

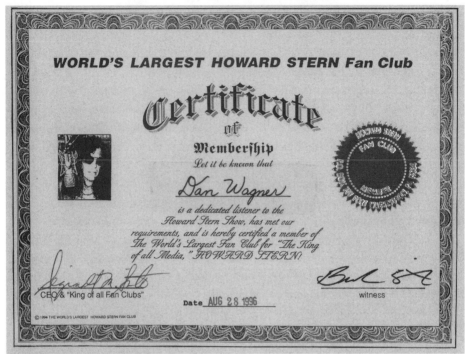

WORLD'S LARGEST HOWARD STERN Fan Club

Certificate

of

Membership

Let it be known that

Dan Wagner

is a dedicated listener to the
Howard Stern Show, has met our
requirements, and is hereby certified a member of
The World's Largest Fan Club for "The King
of all Media," HOWARD STERN!

CEO & "King of all Fan Clubs"   witness

Date AUG 28 1996

© 1994 THE WORLD'S LARGEST HOWARD STERN FAN CLUB

Howard Stern Fan Club Membership Certificate

I could loosen tongues and get some material for my book. As it turned out, I was not disappointed. Eventually, one of the members of Howard Stern's "Wack Pack", Elephant Boy, materialized. Elephant Boy's real name is Fred Schrieber.

His claim to fame is his speech impediment combined with a unique way of expressing himself that can be extremely difficult to understand. Nonetheless, I was determined to chat with him. During our conversation Elephant Boy asked me to guess his age. I guessed twenty-eight. Elephant Boy showed me his driver's license. To my astonishment, he was born November 9, 1958.

Howard Stern

When words failed me, I had a Polaroid picture taken with Elephant Boy, which he graciously signed.

One of the people at the party was an Imus fan. He had been brought there by a friend of his named Scarecrow who had met up with him by chance at Penn Station. Due to his allegiance to Imus he was immediately named Zero. Zero was loaded with money and alcohol. He purchased at least one of Uzo's fake blow jobs. Perhaps in his inebriated state he thought it was the real thing. I was preparing to leave when a commotion erupted from the other side of the basement. Evidently, Zero had passed-out from drinking too much. A few people tried to revive Zero, but without success. Management came down and carried Zero to the front entrance of the place, handling him like a sack of potatoes.

Some of the Chat Party participants wanted to carry Zero to Rockefeller Center and deposit him in a phone booth. They thought that this would be appropriate treatment for an Imus fan since Howard Stern has said that Imus was an alcoholic who used to be found passed out inside phone booths around Rockefeller Center. Elephant Boy thought a better idea would be to paint Zero's fingernails and toenails pink. He told me that

Dan Wagner, Elephant Boy

this was a common prank to play on drunk people during his college years.

Ultimately, the police and an ambulance were dispatched to the scene. The management put a slant on Zero's condition which was partly true. They told the policemen that Zero had arrived at the party slightly drunk to begin with. They also said that it was a private party. Uzo was as nervous as a guppy in a pool filled with piranhas. I think she had dreams of lawsuits and vanishing party profits dancing in her head. Zero's friend Scarecrow seemed to enjoy the whole proceeding. As far as he was concerned this was just an exciting way to cap an evening of debauchery. My lasting visual impression of the night is of Scarecrow happily waving good-bye to his fellow chatters as an ambulance whisked him and Zero off to New York Hospital.

CHAPTER 5

ELEPHANT BOY

Howard Stern loves to refer to himself as a "King-maker", who can make a star out of anyone. To prove his point, Howard uses members of his "Wack Pack" as examples. Crackhead Bob is a young man who overused crack to such a degree that he suffered a stroke which resulted in permanent physical and mental damage. His speech is barely understandable. His singing voice is even worse. Despite Crackhead Bob's handicaps, Howard has made him into a quasi-celebrity who can command as much as one thousand dollars per appearance. Amazing! If this is not proof of Howard Stern's king-making skills, then I don't know what is.

The prototype of all "kings in the making" is Fred "The Elephant Boy" a.k.a. Fred Schreiber. Fred, too, has a speech impediment. Fred is the Jackie Robinson of speech defect sufferers. He opened the door so that other similarly afflicted individuals may follow. People with speech defects are essentially circus performers for the ear. Since they're entertaining and play well on the radio, Howard likes to have them on his show. Fred Schreiber also gets paid for appearances. His specialty: hosting wrestling events. I can just hear it now: "My name is Fred The Elephant Boy and I'm proud to introduce Murderous Mad Dog The Murderer versus Toro Tanaka The Japanese Kamikaze Killer!" Wow! I just love up-scale cultural events.

Howard is a genius at defining the cornerstone of a person's marketability. When it comes to Fred The Elephant Boy, Crackhead Bob, and Stuttering John, Howard focuses on their speech problems. Howard's producer Gary Dell'Abate gets ridiculed for having horse-sized teeth. For intern Steve Grillo, it's a lack of intelligence and Brooklyn accent. Fred Norris's unique view of the world catapults him into the sphere of being an alien from Mars — in other words, a complete weirdo. The list goes on and on. Obviously, Howard has been blessed with a divining rod for deviations and deformities.

All of Howard's "king-making" talk had made me curious. What was a recipient of Howard's Midas touch really like? I decided to find out. I had met Fred The

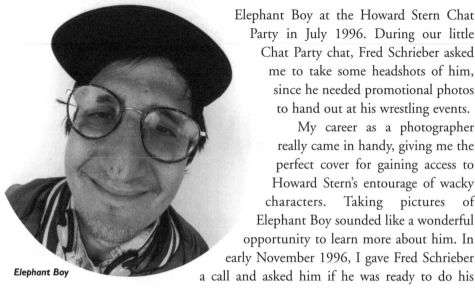

Elephant Boy

Elephant Boy at the Howard Stern Chat Party in July 1996. During our little Chat Party chat, Fred Schrieber asked me to take some headshots of him, since he needed promotional photos to hand out at his wrestling events.

My career as a photographer really came in handy, giving me the perfect cover for gaining access to Howard Stern's entourage of wacky characters. Taking pictures of Elephant Boy sounded like a wonderful opportunity to learn more about him. In early November 1996, I gave Fred Schrieber a call and asked him if he was ready to do his headshots. My timing was perfect. He agreed to meet me on Veteran's Day (November 11th) at my studio. As a government employee at the United States Customs House in lower Manhattan, he had the day off.

Call me naive, but I actually expected someone named "Elephant Boy" to remember his 10AM appointment. When a half hour had passed with no sign of him, I decided to call his home. Fred answered in a sleepy voice. He was very apologetic and assured me that he would immediately leave his house and be at my studio within an hour. Clearly, elephants *do* forget. I regretted not following my inclination to give him a reminder call the day before. I bet Gary Dell'Abate has learned this lesson too. True to his word Fred arrived in less than sixty minutes — breathless and disheveled. I had advised Fred to bring a few extra shirts for the shoot. However, I never expected that he would transport them in a small plastic garbage bag. The shirts were wrapped up in a tight ball and completely wrinkled.

I have a peep-hole in my studio door. When I heard Fred knocking on my door, I checked the peep-hole first. Fred was really hamming it up. A regular laugh riot. Luckily for me, my camera was nearby and I captured Fred's antics for posterity.

I always give a person a chance to relax and get used to my studio before I begin a photo session. Fred and I chatted for about half an hour. Fred isn't very photogenic. This is fine with me. I prefer photographing quirky-looking people. I think Fred was nervous about having his picture taken. He asked me if we could retouch the two cuts on the tip of his nose. I couldn't help asking how he got them. He told me it happened while he was shaving.

Fred talked non-stop. The subject of conversation was, of course, Howard Stern. I asked Fred how much he had been paid to be a judge and featured guest on Howard's pay-per-view 1994 New Year's Rotten Eve Pageant, which had grossed about forty million dollars before videotape sales. Howard is reported to have cleared a cool six million or so for himself. Therefore, I fully expected that Fred must have earned thousands of dollars. I almost passed out when Fred informed me that he had been paid a measly two hundred and fifty dollars. I asked him if he had been paid for the videotape sales and he said, "No".

Luckily for Fred he managed to parlay a friendship with the management of Scores strip club into a five hundred dollar payday for wearing a "Scores" cap during the taping of the pageant. Never one to miss a trick, or a dollar for that matter, Howard even removed Fred's hat at one point during the taping. Fred told me that he is the person responsible for introducing Howard to Scores — Howard's favorite topless girly party venue.

Daniel Carver of the KKK also worked the pageant as one of the judges. Fred told me that he refused to be in the same greenroom prior to show time with Carver. I was impressed by his principled stand.

Elephant Boy

I asked Fred if the pageant had been on the level since I thought it might have been fixed. It seemed to me that some of the contestants were more deserving of winning the pageant and the fifty thousand dollar prize than Elaine Marx. I was suspicious that Elaine Marx's involvement may have been predicated on being guaranteed a victory, since she had been featured in *Playboy* magazine. Therefore, I doubted that she would jeopardize her marketability by risking a loss in what was essentially a spoof on beauty contests. Fred told me that he, too, had always been suspicious about the voting. He

Elephant Boy

All photos, Elephant Boy

said, "The show was only two hours long, and I didn't see how they had time to count the votes. I thought Debbie Tay should have won."

It's always fun to take pictures of people as they look when they first arrive at a photo shoot. Fred had come dressed in a stained light blue denim shirt, black *Private Parts* cap, tinted wire-rimmed glasses, shiny blue baseball-type jacket, loose fitting slacks, and fanny pack (for his walkman). He sported headphones with yellow ear covers. Howard's show was done for the day. I wondered what he was listening to. Probably the *Symphony No. 2 in B minor* by Alexander Borodin. He reminded me of an old lady.

I knew that I had my work cut out for me. I hoped that removing Fred's cap might improve things, but his hair was a mess. It looked as though it hadn't been washed in quite a while. Normally, I would let someone use my hairbrush. In Fred's case it would have been a waste of time. Besides which, I didn't relish the concept of having my brush in Fred's hair. I know this isn't nice, but his hair really didn't look very clean.

Fred didn't smell that great either. At first I attributed this to his having overslept. Perhaps he hadn't had time to shower before the shoot. On the other hand, Howard regularly makes fun of his odor. Prior to smelling Fred for myself, I had thought that Howard was only joking. Hopefully, Fred's smell was due to wearing his clothes too long between washings. Even the guy at my photo finishing lab asked me if Fred smelled as bad as Howard says. Talk about the power of radio! King-making, indeed!

Fred Schreiber is truly a nice person. He's sincere and has a heart of gold, which makes him a very cooperative subject. We did a variety of poses. It's always difficult

to photograph someone who wears glasses. I kept having to remind Fred to keep his eyes as wide open as possible. Fred's facial expressions remind me of a cross between Pee Wee Herman, Gomer Pyle, and Jerry Lewis.

Quite often I talk to people as I'm photographing them to help them lose some of their self-consciousness. During the course of the shoot I learned that Fred, who still lives at home, is in love. You might ask what sort of gal a guy who goes by the appellation "Elephant Boy" could attract. I certainly did. Her name is Mary, and she lives in Cleveland, Ohio with her two children from a previous marriage. Fred met her while appearing with Howard at a mock funeral for a Cleveland disc jockey who had the temerity to share the same airwaves as Howard. Fred is so serious about Mary, that he is even considering moving to Cleveland. I'm sure Howard and his crew would kill for this information.

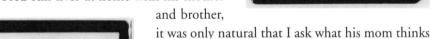

Fred plans to go to Cleveland for a month or so and see how things work out. Seeing that Fred still lives at home with his mother and brother, it was only natural that I ask what his mom thinks of his plans. Fred said that she advised him to "take it slow". Since Fred will soon be forty, he'd better not take it *too* slow.

Fred has a realistic and humorous self-image. He told me that he loves playing video games with Mary's children. In fact, Fred has many child-like qualities himself. (Warning: Literary pretension ahead.) Sometimes Fred reminds me of Dostoeyevsky's Prince Mishkin — a sincere spirit adrift in a world of charlatans. Anyway, Fred painted a picture for me of what a typical evening at home with Mary might be like with this dialogue:

Mary: "Fred, I'm in the mood."
Fred: "I can't come right now. We're in the middle of a video game and I'm on the third level!"

I asked Elephant Boy who his favorite person on Howard's show is. Elephant Boy told me that he likes Fred Norris the best. I wasn't surprised. Fred Norris is humble and down-to-earth, seemingly without conceit. He's considerate and easy to get along with. I guess Freds of a feather flock together. It was pretty easy to guess which member of Howard's entourage Elephant Boy likes the least — Stuttering John. Elephant Boy's take on Robin, "she's a bigger instigator than Howard".

Elephant Boy

Elephant Boy

It was about two o'clock and Fred and I were getting hungry. We decided to wrap up the shoot and go out for some Chinese food. Howard frequently makes fun of Fred's eating habits. I was curious and a little bit scared to see if he was accurate. Fred ordered General Chow's Chicken and fried rice. Howard has obviously made Fred very aware of his manners. Fred ate carefully and slowly. I was impressed. In fact, Fred's table manners are far superior to my own. I happen to love fortune cookies. What writer doesn't? Fred's fortune cookie was right on the money vis-a-vis his plans to relocate to Cleveland: "A new environment makes all the difference in the world. Lucky numbers 8, 15, 23, 1, 18, and 4."

After lunch we returned to my studio so Fred could get his shirts. Fred didn't want to leave. He asked me if we could use my computer to cruise the Internet for pornography. It seemed journalistically imprudent to deny Fred his request. Seated before my seventeen-inch monitor we began our quest. I asked Fred what keyword I should search for. "How about adult entertainment?" No go.

U.S. Customhouse

"How about Hustler?" No go. Finally we tried "Playboy". Bingo. I asked Fred if he wanted to try the listing generated by typing Playboy — "Sex, pornography, and nudity sites"? Fred said, "that's good enough for me!" Unfortunately, I was having trouble with my Internet browser and we were unable to view the pictures. All we saw were empty boxes with lines around them. Perhaps this was just as well. I didn't relish the idea of seeing Elephant Boy hyper-ventilate. We called it a day.

I thought that my time with Elephant Boy had been well spent. Fred's comments shed new light on Howard Stern. Consequently, I decided to expand my knowledge of Elephant Boy by visiting him at work and at home. I was curious to see how someone called Elephant Boy survived in the real world. I found it fitting that Fred works as a clerk in the food and drug division of the United States Custom House. Evidently there is a government job for everyone. Fred's job is to approve various forms and applications for business people. I pity these poor applicants. It takes a long time and a great deal of concentration to get used to Fred's speech impediment. I bet the businessmen regard having to deal with Fred as a cruel joke.

Seeing Fred at his workplace exceeded my wildest expectations. Fred was dressed like a slob. I thought he would be wearing a suit. Instead Fred was wearing a black sweat

Elephant Boy at work

Utopia Parkway

shirt, and loose fitting trousers. I know readers may not believe me, but Fred's fly was wide open. I didn't want to learn if the rumor for how Fred got his name Elephant Boy was true, so I immediately told him to zip it up. Fred just laughed. I imagine this is a daily occurrence for him.

Fred still had his fanny pack and headphones with the yellow foam covered earpieces on. Spread before him were the day's newspapers and a large radio

tuned to Howard's show. What a job. During the half hour or so that we spent looking at contact sheets from our photo shoot, Elephant Boy had absolutely no work at all to perform. Not even one businessman in need of approved applications showed up. The place was a ghost town. Before I left Fred suggested that I take a picture of him with his feet on top of his desk. He's such a ham.

Fred's ability to maintain a clear-eyed perspective on his status as a Stern anointed pseudo-celebrity is impressive. I doubt that I could achieve the same equanimity. Even having my anonymous faxes read on-air had swollen my head to the size of a prize pumpkin. Fred told me that Howard had asked him to be in a few

Elephant Boy at home

scenes for his movie *Private Parts* several weeks earlier. I would have been a nervous wreck. Fred, however, took it all in stride. He told me that although he wanted to be in the movie, he refused to ask Howard or Gary Dell'Abate to cast him. Most of *Private Parts* takes place prior to Fred's involvement with the show. Fred reasoned that not asking to be in the movie led to his being invited to be in it. Dealing with Howard Stern can be as convoluted as a soap opera plot. Personally, I think he was cast because Howard loves speech impediments, and Felliniesque freaks.

I asked Fred how much Howard was paying him, and he told me he had no idea. Fred desperately needs an agent. Without one, Fred will probably just earn another two hundred and fifty dollars. What an outrage. I've heard Howard berate his frequent guest Jessica Hahn for making bad deals. He always tells her that she

Elephant Boy at home

works for too little. Considering the degree to which he underpays Elephant Boy, he's really one to talk.

So far I had observed Elephant Boy at my studio and at work. To complete my anthropological investigation, I knew that I'd have to visit Elephant Boy in his lair. I loaded up my Subaru and headed west on a Whitestone (Elephant Boy's home town) safari. The land of the Throgs Neck Bridge, home of Elephant Boy beckoned me. What a rugged landscape. Fortunately, my vehicle was equipped with four-wheel drive. I kept my windows tightly shut in case of attack.

Fred had given me excellent directions to his abode off Utopia Parkway. I was curious to see if Fred's home really was a "utopia". I had chosen a beautiful day for my safari. Sunday, November 17th 1996 was unseasonably mild and sunny. The trees still had many of their fall leaves.

Fred's home is in a cluster of two story brick "garden" apartments. His ground level apartment is set back away from the street and opens onto a courtyard. I'm sure Howard and his crew have never visited Fred at home. Too bad. It would be very educational for them. I know it was for me.

With a sense of trepidation I rang Fred's bell. I had no idea what to expect. I wondered whether Fred's mother and brother would look and speak like him. I would know soon enough. Fred's mother answered the door. She is a small woman with a thinning head of completely whitish-gray hair. She

Elephant Boy at home

summoned Fred with an ear-piercing yell. Apparently Fred always looks like he has just stumbled out of bed. He came to the door *sans* shoes, wearing slacks and a "Howard Stern for Governor" tee shirt. I commented on the resemblance between Fred and his mother. Fred turned red and tried in vain to deny it. Evidently he's heard this before. His mother, however, agreed with me by stating that Fred resembles her, and that his brother Philip resembles his father.

While I spoke with them I surveyed the apartment. The Elephant Boy domicile has three main rooms. One bedroom for each brother, and a larger living room with a twin bed that serves double duty as his mother's bedroom.

Elephant Boy

The apartment was over-heated and dark. Even though I had been inside the place for only a few minutes, I was already longing for a breath of fresh air.

Fred gave me the fifty-cent tour. First stop, Elephant Boy's lair! All I could think when I saw Fred's bedroom was that this was a complete disaster area. His bed was unmade, there were clothes on the floor, and junk was piled high on every available surface. Even Fred's mother made apologies for the room's appearance. Fred's proudest possessions are his stereo, twenty-seven-inch television, and videotape player. The worst part of my visit was inhaling the air in Fred's room. It smelled like a laundry hamper.

Prior to visiting Fred's bedroom, I used to believe that photojournalists covering wars had the hardest jobs. Now I know better. The hardest photojournalistic assignment is going on an Elephant Boy safari. However I had come to photograph Elephant Boy, not to shoot him. Keeping

Elephant Boy at Dan Wagner's photo studio

this in mind I had Fred pose next to his bar-mitzvah photo.

After bagging this shot, I suggested we do a shot for Fred's paramour in Cleveland — Mary. Fred was gung-ho for my idea. With Elephantine agility he leapt onto his bed and struck a suggestive pose.

Just as I was starting to feel woozy from the stale air, I was saved by the bell: a phone call for Fred. While I waited for him to return, his mother showed me Philip's room. She wanted to show me a photo of Philip that would illustrate how much he resembled her husband. Fred's mother couldn't resist commenting on how neat and orderly Philip's room was. Neither could I. The Schrieber brothers make quite an odd couple.

Philip's room looked like it belonged to a thirteen-year-old. One wall was lined with floor-to-ceiling Star Trek memorabilia. Whereas every available surface of Fred's room was covered with junk, Philip's had Star Trek dolls and spacecraft. How appropriate. Visiting the Schreiber household really was like a "mission to explore strange new worlds." I mentioned to Fred's mother that I thought Philip was older than Fred. She said, "Yeah, he's a year older — thirty-nine."

FRED, *The Elephant Boy*   Howard Stern Show

I'd seen enough. Elephant Boy and I made arrangements to meet at my studio the next week so he could pick-up his headshots. He asked me to have the words "Fred 'The Elephant Boy' — Howard Stern Show" printed on them so he could sell them at wrestling events. Having heard Howard Stern boast of his king-making skills made me wonder how much Elephant Boy could earn for a typical wrestling appearance. Fred told me he usually gets fifty bucks. Quite a king's ransom! I beat a hasty retreat, but not before leaving the Schriebers with the following words: "Live long, and prosper."

CHAPTER 6

KENNETH KEITH KALLENBACH:
"I'M NO WACKO!"

You can't fight fate. When something is meant to be, it's meant to be. Or so I told myself when I spied a familiar looking gentleman a mere five feet in front of me on the same New York City block as my photo studio. The gentleman in question was none other than the famous Howard Stern Wack Packer, Kenneth Keith Kallenbach. What are the odds of that happening — a million to one?

Kenneth was with his girlfriend Rebecca. They were on their way to pick up some promotional materials for Kenneth's new CD *Yeah!* from the trunk of Kenneth's car which was parked at a neighborhood parking lot. The last time I had seen Kenneth was approximately ten months earlier on Howard Stern's forty-third birthday. He had just left Howard's birthday party, and was standing outside in the freezing cold waiting to hail a cab with his fellow Wack Packers, Elephant Boy and Captain Janks. Despite the frigid January temperature, I had managed to get them to pose for a few photos.

At first Kenneth didn't recognize me. Maybe it was because I wasn't blue with cold and bundled up in arctic gear. In fact, he thought I had followed him and Rebecca from the flea-bag motel where they were staying. I pointed out that *he* was the one who chose to park on my block. My flawless logic convinced him.

Fate had handed me an opportunity for adventure which I couldn't refuse. I invited Kenneth and Rebecca up to my photo studio for a chance to hear and perhaps buy a copy of his new CD. The thought of making a quick ten bucks appealed to Kenneth. However, the real deal-maker was Kenneth's urgent need of a bathroom. Hey, I'm humble, whatever works is fine by me.

I have to admit that I was a little nervous about letting Kenneth use my bathroom. Kenneth is skinny to the point of appearing anorexic. The way he looks, behaves, and carries himself suggests nothing less than your stereotypical junkie — even though I don't know whether Kenneth uses drugs or if his behavior is just an act. Howard Stern loves to talk about his own former drug-related experiences and relishes making fun of Jackie Martling's pot smoking. Therefore, I'm never surprised when Wack Packers such as Kenneth choose to adopt druggie personae. But with Kenneth it seems real. Kenneth was in my bathroom for at least ten minutes. During this time Rebecca and I heard him produce some bizarre noises. Kenneth was moaning, groaning, and clearing his throat with a loud and prolonged hacking sound. Rebecca and I traded nervous glances. Rebecca even rolled her eyes and made an expression that let me know that this goes on all the time. Be that as it may, I wished that it wasn't going on in *my* bathroom. Could getting a story really be worth this sort of abuse? I was starting to doubt it. I turned up the volume on Kenneth's CD to block out the dreadful bathroom sound effects.

Kenneth & Rebecca

Eventually Kenneth completed his mission and emerged from the bathroom looking pale, but proud. Despite the fact that we were gathered at least thirty feet from the bathroom, and that the door was closed, a stench rivaling the open sewers of Bangkok enveloped us like a malevolent cloud. It was truly terrible. I thought someone had died. In order to survive, I opened all the windows and set my air conditoner's fan to maximum exhaust. Despite these measures my eyes continued to tear. Next time Kenneth visits I'll be sure to have a few gas masks on hand.

Kenneth was impressed by my studio. Most people aren't used to seeing professional photographic equipment such as light stands, camera platforms, backdrops and such. The tools of my trade can be pretty intimidating. The object that fascinated Kenneth the most was a framed 8x10 publicity photo that I'd taken of Elephant Boy. I imagine that Kenneth must've thought that I had to be a good photographer to make Elephant Boy look handsome.

While Kenneth and Rebecca made themselves at home I concentrated on Kenneth's CD. I was surprised by how great it sounded. His guitar work and vocals fit his inspired lyrics to perfection. Over the next few weeks I frequently found myself humming some of his tunes. It's rare for an album to have this effect on me. Howard and Robin frequently say that they can't wait for one of the bands they showcase to make it big. If they're serious about this, I wonder why they haven't made a better effort to promote Kenneth's band. In my opinion, Kenneth's completely shameless and honest personality is reflected in his music. Even Kenneth's song titles accurately sum up his outlook on life:

1) *I Got Beers*
2) *40 Ouncer*
3) *Doggy, Doggy, Ruff* (My fave)
4) *Do You Think I'm Dumb*
5) *I Have Never Dated A Stripper*
6) *You Better Dress Up Like A Ho-Bag*
7) *You Better Give Me Booze*
8) *One Short of Nothin'*
9) *Don't Hand Me That Crock*
10) *Nothin' But Drunk*
11) *Surfboard Odor*

The only thing dishonest about Kenneth's CD is what he wrote above his autograph, "I'm no wacko!" Wack Packers constantly make feeble attempts to portray themselves as being normal. In my opinion they're all so obviously defective that I believe they should save their breath and stop protesting. As far as I'm concerned, Kenneth traded any claim to normalcy during his first Howard Stern WOR television appearance in the early 1990's, when he was booked on the show after writing Howard a letter stating that he could blow smoke through his eyes. Prior to attempting this spectacular feat Kenneth pointed his butt towards the television cameras, grabbed the sides of his ass and produced a feeble string of farts into his microphone. Then Kenneth whipped out a large funnel

Kenneth Keith Kallenbach

— the same kind that one would use to fill a gas tank — and proceeded to ingest about a gallon of water. He referred to this as, "Doing a funnel." Howard and the gang loved it and howled with laughter. Kenneth was a hit! By the way, despite his protests to the contrary, Kenneth was unable to make smoke come out of his eyes. In fact, the only thing he managed to expel was a prodigious quantity of vomit. Howard promptly declared that this was a show precedent — no doubt reassuring his revolted audience immeasurably.

The phrase "I'm no wacko!" is one of Kenneth's favorites. He has an entire repertoire of catch phrases that he uses to spice up his on-air dialog with Howard, much as a chef relies on seasonings to add flavor to a recipe. Kenneth's current hot list is, "I'm confused!", "Yeah!", "I'm no wacko!" and "Hode on." Fellow Wack Packer Crackhead Bob has an even more famous array of catch phrases such as: "Dat's it!", "Oh, come on, now", "Oh baby!", and "I am torry."

Kenneth Keith Kallenbach

Kenneth is quite the entrepreneur. In addition to selling his own CD, he also markets the following items through the Internet:

1) Four videotapes of Kenneth's antics at $20 each (shipping and handling included).

2) An autographed 8x10 black and white photo for $10 (shipping and handling included).

3) An autographed Fender Squire Stratocaster guitar for $350. "Brand new and still in box." Add $30 for shipping and handling.

4) A Kenneth Keith Kallenbach doll which is currently sold out.

I asked Kenneth how many guitars he had in stock, and he told me, "None." When I asked him how many guitars he had sold, I got the same answer. He told me that he will buy the guitar as soon as someone mails him a check for it. I was curious to know what his profit margins were. Kenneth told me that the guitar costs him $150.00. I guess one should never underestimate a "Wacko."

Even Hollywood recognizes the entertainment value of a Howard Stern "Wacko." Cameron Crowe, the director of the sensational Tom Cruise blockbuster, *Jerry McGuire*, cast Kenneth in his movie. Kenneth played the part of a demented sports fan who asks Tom Cruise's character for an autograph. Unfortunately for Kenneth his part wound up on the cutting room floor. As for Cameron Crowe, he's no dummy — prior to hiring Kenneth he asked Howard's producer, Gary Dell'Abate, if Kenneth was dangerous. Evidently Gary's answer didn't scare Crowe off. Who knows to what lengths Gary went to insure that Kenneth would be a comfortable 3,000 miles away? *Jerry McGuire* happens to be Kenneth's second film. His first was a porno flick called *Pussyman 9.*

Captain Janks & Kenneth

When it comes to whether or not Kenneth is really a dangerous individual, I believe that his girlfriend, Rebecca, is the most qualified person to address this issue. In July, 1996 it was reported in the media that Kenneth had been arrested for allegedly beating Rebecca up badly enough to cause her head to bleed. Of course Howard invited Kenneth to explain his actions on-air. Kenneth tried to excuse his behavior as being merely a "lovers' quarrel." However, fellow Wack Packer Captain Janks was unwilling to let Kenneth off the hook so easily. He called in and told Howard that Kenneth treats Rebecca "horribly." Janks even related an alleged incident in which Kenneth ripped off Rebecca's skirt on the side of a busy highway for no apparent reason. Kenneth responded to the criticism by claiming that Janks is a dwarf who picks up whores, and abuses heroin and cocaine. I should mention that during on-air skirmishes it's difficult to tell how much of the action is true and how much is contrived.

Captain Janks & Kenneth

Kenneth Keith Kallenbach

When Kenneth told me that he had received a $50 parking ticket earlier in the day, I realized that it was the perfect opportunity to ask him about his run-ins with the law. Kenneth told me that he had once been fined for "peeing on a church." When I started laughing, Kenneth added that he had also been fined for "biting off a dog's ear." Rebecca kept Kenneth honest by making him confess that the dog story was a put-on.

One might wonder what makes Rebecca stay with an "outlaw" like Kenneth. I certainly did. My explanation is that Kenneth's predictable unpredictability makes life exciting. Some people like that. Although Kenneth is a fascinating man, I found his manic nature tiring. As for Rebecca, she confided that she always cries when she and Kenneth part. Kenneth overheard this remark and "tenderly" replied, "Maybe I should leave now."

Rebecca has my sympathy. Not only does she serve as Kenneth's emotional and physical (alleged) punching bag, but she also seems to function as a mother figure. Rebecca constantly nags Kenneth to rehearse his music and to stay focused. If Kenneth were left to his own devices, he would probably

Kenneth Keith Kallenbach

sleep all day and party all night. Rebecca, at thirty, is more practical than Kenneth, who at twenty-nine seems to be an emotional adolescent. Despite their differences, I believe that Kenneth and Rebecca are perfect for each other. They even look alike. They remind me of a flaky but likeable 1960's hippie couple stuck in a time-warp. The day I ran into Kenneth and Rebecca they had been planning to visit the Statue of Liberty. Approximately once a week Kenneth and Rebecca rendezvous in New York City and play tourist. Kenneth lives and works in Pennsylvania. As far as I can figure out, he has a part-time job with the post office. Rebecca currently works as a waitress and shares a tiny apartment with a friend who doesn't seem to want Kenneth as an overnight guest for some unfathomable reason. No wonder they spend so much time in motels.

Rebecca asked me how to get to the Statue of Liberty. She seemed somewhat confused by my directions, so I offered to chaperone them. I even volunteered to serve as their personal photographer and document the excursion for posterity. What can I say? I'm a swell guy. Kenneth loved my idea of creating a photo essay of their adventures.

A mere ten minutes later we found ourselves chugging-along on the Number Nine train towards lower Manhattan. Normally such a trip would be pretty humdrum. But nothing's humdrum when it comes to transporting a Wack Packer. Kenneth made me nervous. Despite the fact that I told him it was illegal to put stickers advertising his new CD on the train, he continued to do so. In fact, throughout the day, wherever we went Kenneth marked our route with his two-by-eight inch glossy black and white promotional stickers. Kenneth couldn't keep still. Like a little kid he kept asking, "Are we there yet?" Kiddingly, I suggested that he lie down and take a nap. Imagine my surprise when he did. It made me feel powerful. I decided to test the limits of my powers by suggesting that he hang from an overhead metal pole and swing like a monkey. He complied. I felt like a hypnotist. What should I try next? Perhaps he would pretend to be a chicken, or bark like a

dog. Luckily I didn't have time to find out. The conductor announced the final stop, South Ferry, and we exited the train. Whew! We hadn't even reached the Statue of Liberty and already I was exhausted.

Outside the train station I told Kenneth and Rebecca that it costs

Rebecca & Kenneth

$10 to visit the Statue of Liberty, and that it would require about a thirty-minute wait to catch the boat going there. Once there it can easily take several hours to reach the top of the statue. Due to the tourist season, summer and early fall are the worst times to visit. The amount of time didn't

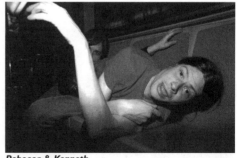

Rebecca & Kenneth

phase my new friends, but the $10 did. I suggested that we take a round-trip on the Staten Island Ferry instead, which is free. Kenneth loved my suggestion, and Rebecca liked the fact that although it's pretty far away, the Statue of Liberty is visible from the ferry.

While waiting for the Staten Island Ferry we held an impromptu outdoor photo session. Kenneth was a regular hambone. He made funny faces and even lifted up his shirt so I could photograph his scars. I think he got them in a bad motorcycle accident. At one point Kenneth spied a Calvin Klein ad in the distance. He told me that he wanted to supplement his post

Kenneth Keith Kallenbach

office income by modeling. Even Rebecca had to laugh. Kenneth said, "No, I'm serious, man." Kenneth asked me to send some of the photos to Calvin Klein. What could I say? I responded, "Okay Ken, consider it done!" Kenneth even gave me the following list of companies he believed might benefit from the Wack Packer look:

1) Calvin Klein
2) Ford Modeling Agency
3) Sassoon
4) Guess Jeans
5) The Gap
6) Versace
7) The New York Post

I was surprised he left out Dior. Then again, heroin chic is in these days, so who knows? Maybe Kenneth is more marketable than I think. I wonder how he'd photograph with Kate Moss or Claudia Schiffer.

Rebecca & Kenneth

At long last the ferry arrived and we boarded. With furtive glances left and right, Kenneth decorated the vessel with several promotional stickers. Kenneth causes a scene wherever he goes. It's so embarrassing. At one point the wind blew a huge stack of fliers out of Kenneth's hands and sent them flying from one

Kenneth Keith Kallenbach

end of the ferry to the other. It reminded me of a ticker-tape parade. People glanced at Kenneth and gave him the kinds of looks usually reserved for smelly street urchins and weirdos. Occasionally Kenneth would become aware that he was being stared at. He thought people were looking at him because he was a famous Howard Stern Wack Packer. Sometimes this was the case, but mostly it was because he was acting like a wacko.

I asked Kenneth what Howard Stern thought about his antics. He answered my question somewhat obliquely by relating an incident that occurred several years earlier in Rochester, New York during Howard's prematurely aborted run for governor. K-ROCK had graciously put Kenneth and Rebecca up at a nice hotel the evening before one of Howard's campaign stops. Kenneth and Rebecca then proceeded to abuse Howard's hospitality by running up a $400 bill for room service. Kenneth told me that he ordered steaks, platters of jumbo shrimp (his fave), bottles of champagne and other goodies. Rebecca described the scene by saying, "We would wake up and the whole floor would be covered with plates from room service." I

Rebecca & Kenneth

found their story hilarious. Unfortunately for Kenneth, Howard wasn't amused. Even though Kenneth tried to redeem himself by waving a dildo at the Libertarian Convention, it was the last time K-ROCK offered to put them up.

Kenneth Keith Kallenbach

Kenneth told me that he once asked Howard Stern for a job. When I asked him what had happened, Kenneth said that Howard had just laughed. I was surprised that Howard didn't offer to make him the show's treasurer. I love hearing the behind-the-scenes shenanigans and inside scoop about the show. Rebecca told me that they occasionally visit Stuttering John at his home. I asked her what he's like. Rebecca said that he didn't stutter and implied that she's suspicious that his on-air stuttering is just an act. Frankly, I'm often suspicious of John's stuttering, too. Kenneth, clearly worried that it might get back to John, immediately replied, "John only stutters when he's nervous." Perhaps.

Kenneth Keith Kallenbach

After our round-trip to Staten Island we decided to catch a train to nearby Chinatown and have lunch. Kenneth wasn't looking very well. I thought that some soup might make him feel better. He was pale and kept having to use the bathroom. Every couple of minutes Kenneth would start to cough and hack like a chain-smoker or cancer patient. During these times he would stand rooted to one spot, teeter back and forth, and cough up a huge phlegm ball which would hang by thin, yellow, viscous threads from his chapped lips until a combination of gravity and vigorous head shaking set it free. I

Kenneth Keith Kallenbach

guess all those years of trying to blow smoke through his eyes had finally caught up with him. Although quite nauseous, I managed to capture the moment on film for future historians and Stern fans alike. Concerned, I asked Rebecca if Kenneth was okay and she told me, "Yeah, this happens all the time."

I'll spare the reader a description of what went on during lunch. It seems like the compassionate thing to do. On the way back to my block to retrieve Kenneth's car I asked Kenneth and Rebecca how they had met. The soup had performed wonders for Kenneth's health, and we actually enjoyed ten spit-free minutes. Rebecca told me that she and Kenneth met about five years earlier at a bar. The following day Kenneth proposed to her, although to my knowledge they have no immediate plans to wed. Ken complained that Rebecca always nags him, and Rebecca complained that they haven't seen a movie together in four years.

I suggested that they end the day by going to a nearby $3 movie theater. Rebecca responded to my idea as though it were the cure for AIDS. Kenneth, how-

Kenneth Keith Kallenbach

ever refused and said that he was tired and wanted to take a nap on the couch in my studio. The thought of having Kenneth back in my studio scared me to death. Suppose he wanted to use my bathroom again? Could the toilet survive another onslaught? Speaking of which, I was afraid to see what my bathroom looked like after his earlier visit there. As far as I was concerned, I'd already sacrificed myself enough for the betterment of my tale. Therefore, I mumbled something about having to attend a fictitious social engagement and bid them a fond farewell. Before parting Kenneth reminded me not to forget to send some of the photos of him to Calvin Klein. "Okay Ken, consider it done!"

Postscript: On October 28, 1997, Ken told me that he and Rebecca were breaking up. After recovering from Ken's shocking news, I expressed my surprise and offered condolences. Though they made a pretty wacky couple, I had thought they were a perfect match. What could've happened to split them up? Ken informed me that during a recent outing with Rebecca and some of her girlfriends he became convinced that one of her friends liked him. Unable to resist temptation, Ken slipped the woman his phone number. Of course, Rebecca found out — hence the break-up. I suggested that he propose to her again. Ken told me that that was what Rebecca wanted him to do. However, despite being depressed at the prospect of a Rebecca-free future, Ken was fundamentally incapable of committing to just one gal. When I asked him if she might be bluffing, Ken replied, "She already bought her one-way plane ticket back to Chicago."

Kenneth Keith Kallenbach

Ken's problematic love life had left him mad at the world. Ken confessed to me that he was annoyed that the *Stern Show* never offers to pay his travel expenses from Philly to New York. That's not all. "They won't even pay for my parking," he griped. I tried to be sympathetic. But, considering Ken's history of $400 room service bills, it was hard to feel too sorry for him. Oh well, perhaps Calvin Klein will offer Ken validated parking.

CHAPTER 7

THE STING!

("Dan Wagner, hero and Emmy winner!")

From first-hand knowledge, I can attest to the fact that Howard Stern fans dream of interacting with their king. Sometimes they manage to reach Howard on the air when he takes listener phone calls. They tell Howard that they've been trying to get through for years. (At which point Howard promptly hangs-up on them.) Other fans try to participate in Howard's show via faxes and letters — my own favorite way to get my two cents in.

The relative anonymity of faxes and letters leave a true Howard Stern fan like myself hungry for more. Howard's celebrity status has made him virtually inaccessible. The ultimate way to get to him is with a scheme that lands you on his show as a guest.

From my first fax I had wanted to be on the show, but I feared this goal was unattainable. Indeed, it remained out of reach until I thought of a way — after returning home from a Florida vacation on Saturday, April 20, 1996 — to make my dream come true.

The next night I watched the 10 o'clock news on *Fox 5*. Penny Crone — who has often interviewed Howard — had just won an Emmy. Their on-air antics always amuse me. Howard never fails to push Penny's buttons, make her jump through hoops, and otherwise make her perform like a well-trained seal. I had even spoken to Penny at one of the *Miss America* book signings. The wheels in my head began to turn.

Since 1988 I've had a real Emmy award gathering dust in the back of my closet. It became mine by default when I photographed the cover of an annual report for the National Academy of Television Arts and Sciences. Despite numerous requests by me, the art director from the annual report chose not to reclaim the award. As far as I was concerned, the Emmy award was abandoned property and therefore mine to do with as I pleased.

◀ *Emmy Award*

I decided to con Howard into believing that the Emmy award was for him. To do this I needed a believable story to present to Howard's people. They would be difficult to fool since they were skilled at playing practical jokes on the unsuspecting public. I would first have to get by the court jesters before I would get a crack at the king.

I rejected numerous ideas that were too complicated or far-fetched. Ultimately, I decided the best way to fool the foolers was to combine truth with fiction, fantasy with reality. I already had the Emmy. Perhaps Howard et. al. would believe their eyes — if not their ears. Like any con artist, I would also have to appeal to their greed and their egos if I wanted to be successful.

All night I tossed and turned in bed while my mind worked feverishly to come up with a foolproof plan. I set my alarm clock for 5AM, reasoning that it would be tougher for Howard's staff to verify my story if I arrived at Howard's broadcasting studio before 9AM. (The Academy of Television Arts and Sciences would not be open that early.) Still, I doubted I had the guts to go through with it all, for if I failed, I knew I would never get a second chance at being on-air. It was a gamble, but the reward would be worth the risk.

Eventually, I decided on a cock-and-bull story of epic proportions. I would tell Howard that I had saved a young boy's life while on a canoe trip in Florida. Since I had just been canoeing in Florida, it would be easy to give truthful answers to any of the questions that might be asked. Once he bought the life-saving concept, I could easily introduce the sting. I would tell him that the young boy's father was an owner of the Emmy awards. Giving Howard an Emmy would satisfy the fictitious father's desire to reward me for saving his son's life. It was a great plan. Short, simple, logical, and believable. Far-fetched and improbable? You bet! But don't forget I had a real Emmy award in my possession. Surely the substantiality of the award would overcome the insubstantiality of my

Steve Grillo, Dan Wagner

tale. Who would they believe? Their common sense or their own eyes? My logic indeed proved flawless.

Sun Tzu said in his book *The Art Of War*, "Know thy foe, and know thyself: In a hundred battles, you will never know defeat." I had listened very closely to Howard's show. I felt that I understood the mind sets of those involved with the show. I decided to trust the wisdom of the ancient Chinese sage and follow my plan through to the end.

I woke up the following morning at 5AM as planned. While showering and dressing, I reviewed the plan in my head. It still sounded feasible. During my hour-long commute to work, I listened to Howard's show. I wanted to see if he would mention Penny Crone and her Emmy award. When he didn't mention it, I got nervous. In fact, I was sweating profusely. This would not do — I wasn't even in Manhattan, and already I was falling apart at the seams.

I searched my copy of *The New York Post* for Emmy-related news. With great relief, I learned that numerous Emmy awards had been presented at the Sheraton Hotel the previous evening. (These were the non-televised Emmys for news programs and such that the general public isn't very interested in seeing.) The daytime and prime-time Emmys were to be held at future dates. I hadn't realized there were so many ceremonies.

Arriving in the city, I took a cab to Howard's offices at 600 Madison Avenue. The front doors were locked. I had neglected to consider the fact that the building doesn't officially open until 9AM or so. A woman came along with a computerized access card and I followed her in. A security guard witnessed my entry and immediately asked what I was doing. Luckily Howard's intern Steve Grillo was returning from an errand. I explained my situation vis-a-vis the Emmy award to him. I had to look Steve in the eye during this recital. It was the first time that I had heard my whopper out loud, but the physical reality of the Emmy won out. Steve believed me. He told the security guard everything was okay and escorted me to the elevators. I'd passed my dress rehearsal.

K-ROCK's offices and reception area are on the fourth floor, where Steve told me to take a seat. I had visited the reception area four months earlier for the purpose of dropping off my Scores contest entries. I wondered if I was being watched by hidden cameras. I even avoided touching the styrofoam

Steve Grillo

box housing the Emmy, lest unseen security guards grow suspicious of my behavior and think I was carrying a bomb or a weapon. I was as paranoid as a low-life criminal. My heart beat rapidly. I forced myself to relax by breathing in and out in slow, even, measured rhythms. My pulse slowly returned to normal.

Before 9AM, the reception area is a dimly lit, womb-like cave. Numerous ceiling speakers blast forth Howard's show. While awaiting further developments, I leaned back and enjoyed the protective embrace of my chair.

Dan Wagner

After an eternity of ten minutes or so, Gary Dell'Abate came out to meet me. First, he examined the Emmy. Then he pre-interviewed me. I got the impression that the decision to have me on the show had already been made. Perhaps my scam would succeed. I tried not to complicate my tale unnecessarily. I didn't want to get caught contradicting myself. Gary told me to wait, but he promised to return shortly. I would have to be patient, as only time would tell if they'd fallen for my story.

My paranoia increased exponentially with each passing moment. The employees at Infinity Broadcasting Management started to arrive in greater numbers. Each time an elevator door opened I flinched. I worried whether the Emmy Award people would be angry, or if they would welcome some free publicity. I also wondered whether anyone would recognize my name from all my previous faxing and tape contest activities. I had been surprised when no one had asked to see my identification, or frisk me, or check my box. Hey, I could be a terrorist, or worse yet, an Imus fan!

Glory, glory hallelujah! At long last I was ushered into the famous "greenroom". Unlike the plush reception area, this greenroom is in desperate need of some remodeling. It looks, and smells, worse than an overused horse stall. The walls and furniture are filthy and decrepit. Howard always gripes on-air that it is next to impossible to get his general manager, Tom Chiusano, to approve expenditures for the most basic necessities of a top-rated radio show. Until that moment, I never could have imagined how reasonable Howard's requests were. I had to park my butt in an ugly, moth-eaten, flea-bag of a chair. If there had been a roll of toilet paper nearby, I would have covered the chair's seat with it! Yet, despite the awful furniture, there was no place I'd rather have been. At least I could console myself with the fact that hundreds of famous people had sat in that same chair. Could this be the most coveted chair in all of New York?

I was tempted to call my wife and tell her to listen to the show, but I was afraid of being overheard and revealing my charade. Besides which, the phone was disgusting. I had never seen a phone in quite that shade of dull brown — or had it been white at one time? I wasn't brave enough to perform a scratch test. There was no table for the phone, much less a note-pad or pen. The phone sat on the floor. The rectangular plastic piece of the phone that fits around the push buttons was detached.

If Howard Stern was trying to instill a bunker mentality into his guests prior to entering his studio, then he was succeeding beyond his wildest dreams. Any of Howard's verbal spitballs would pale in comparison next to the assault upon the senses generated by this so-called greenroom.

My cousin told me that greenrooms are typically stocked with light refreshments. However, none were in evidence at The Stern Show. Nor was I offered anything. (Not that I'd want to consume anything in such a germ-laden environment. Is it any wonder that Howard himself is obsessed with hygiene after years of working in this potentially plague-ridden office?) Management is probably afraid that the interns would drink all the refreshments before the guests could get them.

Maybe there are actually two greenrooms, one for strippers and street urchins such as myself, and one for celebrities — but I doubt it. The room had a sickly sweet smell reminiscent of rotting food matter. This is surely attributable to the interns, who must all eat their meals there. Judging by the rainbow-like colors on the once white walls, I bet they have food fights in there, too.

The show is broadcast into the greenroom. The sound comes from a solitary, beat-up, brown speaker with an ancient green metallic volume adjusting device resting on top of it. There is also a much used and abused multi-colored boom box in the greenroom. The room is only about ten by twelve, with no windows, just a doorway. Passersby are unable to resist this temptation — every single person who passes looks inside. This was the original fishbowl. I wondered what the passersby thought about me. I am clearly not a celebrity or a stripper, but I could pass for an over-aged intern, which is an opinion that was later voiced to me.

Gary Dell'Abate asked me to sign a release and to fill out some sort of contest entry form. Gary told me that I might even appear on an *E!* show segment. They were about to videotape me for the show. I viewed it as yet another dry-run to rehearse my tale. I felt it would be easier to practice my performance in front of a pawn than it would be in front of the king.

Howard's intern Mike Gange (the pawn) operated the video-camera. Mike Gange is a rotund, jovial, and good-natured chap. He was dressed in loose pants, and an overworn, and under-washed, tee shirt. His hair was long, straggly, and greasy. Howard constantly berates and mocks Mike. Now I could see why. But despite the surface defects, I could instinctively tell that Mike Gange was a decent human being. He generated a certain warmth, although I could have mistaken the chemical reaction of fermenting body odor for inner warmth in my distracted state.

Mike Gange asked me to tell my Emmy tale. I did my best to look into the camera lens and look natural. Mike was very close to me. Unless he had a wide-angle lens, he was doing an extreme close-up of my face. If he did have a wide-angle lens, then my face must have been very distorted. My nose probably looked like a foot-long hot dog. I tried to relax, keep my facts straight, and not contradict myself. The last thing in the world that I wanted to do was blow my big chance before it had even occurred. I was so close. Mere minutes away.

Other than loosing my virginity and witnessing the births of my two children, I can't think of too many other events in my life when I was so in the moment and so preternaturally aware of everything happening around me. I was feasting on the mix of reality and fantasy.

Mike Gange seemed to enjoy video-taping me. His eyes twinkled with amusement. I'm sure he never expected

Ronnie Mund, Robin Quivers

to be regaled with such a bunch of baloney the first thing on a Monday morning. I was trying to be animated for the camera, but I think I probably was less lively than a videotape of drying paint.

The moment of "truth" had finally arrived. Gary ushered me into the sanctum sanctorum, the holy chamber from whence his mighty eminence Pope Howard Stern pontificates. I was instructed to put on the headphones and speak clearly and directly into the microphone. The microphone looked like a giant, gray, foam-covered zucchini. Howard told me to maintain the suspense by not revealing what was in my styrofoam box. Evidently, Robin had not been clued in. Howard wanted to make certain that Robin's reaction to the Emmy award would be spontaneous.

In a minute or so I would be introduced to my fellow Howard Stern fans. I used the precious time to survey my new landscape and grow accustomed to it. The broadcasting studio was smaller than I had imagined, about thirteen by twenty-three feet. The studio's lighting was fairly subdued. The atmosphere was intimate and cozy. Of course there were no windows.

Jackie Martling was to my left, about four feet away, at the nine o'clock position. He looked trimmer than I had imagined. Howard always rags Jackie about his weight. Frankly I didn't see it. Jackie looks like a man ready for the golf-links, not sausage-links. He came across as mellow, relaxed, and pleasant. Occasionally he looked up from his note pad with a certain apprehension and shyness — but not too often. Was this the man who had inspired the popular anthem F-Jackie? Wow! Talk about scamming the public.

Ronnie Mund, Jackie Martling

Jackie wore a crisp, freshly laundered, tucked-in shirt. I bet he crackles when he walks. I never saw so many sharply ironed creases in my life. He must spend a small fortune on spray starch. A person could get a paper cut from Jackie's pants' crease. His hair was platinum white and combed for maximum scalp coverage. He reminded me of an overgrown elf. His only visual drawback was the latex "nighties" which adorned the upper half of each finger. I believe he has some sort of bad skin condition. The "nighties" must keep his medicated fingers germ-free.

Fred Norris was seated at the eleven o'clock position, about ten feet away from me. I recently engaged in a fierce debate with a fellow fan. I believe that Jackie's seat is superior to Fred's. My reasoning is based on the metric system. Jackie is a few millimeters closer to Howard than Fred is, or so it seemed to me, without my tape measure. The other fan thinks that Fred has the superior position because he sits on Howard's right side — i.e. he's Howard's right-hand man. I countered with the fact that the guest is on Howard's left, and as such, Howard usually has the right rear portion of his head to Fred, while Jackie enjoys a much more frontal view. I leave it to the behavioral psychologists to decide.

From my vantage point, everything below the upper portion of Fred's face was hidden. He was slouched between the console and the wall to his left. The only part of Fred that I could easily distinguish were his eyes, since he looked like a submerged crocodile. Throughout the course of my visit, he fixed me with what can only be described as a malicious, glazed-over, amphibian stare. I felt as though Fred were looking right through me. I was unable to speak and look at him at the same time. It is very unnerving to be in the same room as Fred.

With regard to my Emmy tale, Fred was definitely the most suspicious person in the room. I never could have succeeded in lying to those eyes of his. That's one of the reasons I looked away. In fact, the memory of them still makes me nervous. He looked as though he were mad at the whole world. I later discovered that he had had an enormous public argument with his wife at the Rainbow Room in New York City the previous Saturday. Therefore, I believe my concerns regarding Fred were probably on target. He was a loaded gun looking for trouble.

Robin was seated behind a partition with a four or five-foot window to my extreme left. The wall behind her is painted an aqueous blue. It is well-lit, perhaps for the benefit of the *E!* show video cameras which are mounted in fixed positions throughout the studio. Robin was on display. Between the blue wall and the glass window she looked like an aquarium exhibit.

I truly love Robin, especially after reading her best-selling book *Quivers: A Life.* I even stood up before my segment began to wave to her. I must have looked like a madman. I don't think she saw me. I wonder what the guys thought of my behavior. But since Robin is so popular, I'm sure they've seen others behave the same way.

Perhaps Robin deliberately looks away so she won't become sympathetic to the guest in the hot seat. Maybe Howard had some on-air humiliation in store for me. Howard's done that before. I always enjoy laughing at his pathetic victims. Maybe the shoe was now on the other foot. Howard can eviscerate someone with his quick wit and sharp tongue. I didn't relish meeting an untimely demise.

Howard sits directly across from Robin. I was approximately four feet to his left. Howard is enveloped by a Star Trek-esque broadcasting board which surrounds him on three sides. His masterful skill with these boards rivals that of a roomful of concert pianists playing *The Flight of the Bumble Bee* in four-part harmony. To exit his techno-lair, Howard must first push his chair back several feet.

I had not seen Howard in person since the Long Island book signing, six months earlier. He looked even thinner than I had remembered. It was common knowledge that he had been losing weight for the upcoming filming of his movie *Private Parts*, but I never expected him to look so gaunt. I hoped the camera really does add ten pounds. He could have used them.

Howard was dressed from head to toe in black. He was sporting a Champion sweat shirt with cut off sleeves, shiny black nylon running pants, and sneakers. The black attire made Howard look even taller than his 6'5" frame. In truth, he looked like a giant. The ceiling seemed too low to accommodate his height. One of the perks of radio is the lack of a dress code. Howard was attired for speed-speaking. He was verbally and visually aerodynamic.

It was a lot of fun watching Howard work the microphone. Whenever he launched into one of his trademark tirades, he tilted his head up to the mike like a giant feeding bird. At this point, I was treated to the rare profile view. His beak-like nose did nothing to dispel the avian imagery.

It was time for my appointment with destiny. I wished that my black swivel chair were equipped with a seat belt. I felt as though I were in for a very bumpy ride. I was a child at the edge of a giant slide. I leant forward and let go. Whee! I would finally get to go *mano-a-mano* with the great one. I was a fool going where angels fear to tread.

Howard: "There's this dude out there. This is the most bizarre story you'll ever hear. Hey Dan, come in here real quick."

Howard is always saying to people, "come in here real quick." It's his way of showing who's boss. As a mere fan, who was I to resist his power? Other minds much greater than mine have been cut to bits by Howard's enormous ego and matchless wit. I'm a mere mouse in comparison to him. Even my voice sounded squeaky and mouse-like.

Howard could see that I was nervous. He gave me some time to get acclimated by postponing my story for the moment and taking a brief side trip to discuss the cartoon characters Rocky and Bullwinkle.

Howard: "Just check this guy's story out. (*To me*) And don't tell anyone what's in the box until the end of the story. It's not the Unabomber. You gotta hear this. Dan, tell everyone where you were this weekend."

Listening to the radio is fine and dandy, but being on-air with Howard Stern is an education. I call it Boot Camp For The Brain. Howard made the introduction to my tale both interesting and suspenseful. That's why Robin is deliberately left out when it comes to planning various parts of the show and writing certain bits. Howard views Robin as his audience's representative. He plays to her. As such he wants her responses to be spontaneous and genuine. It's a great formula for success. Witnessing Howard in action allowed me to appreciate it all the more.

Dan: "I was in Fort Myers, Florida. At Tarpon Bay National Wildlife Refuge on Sanibel Island. I was going on a canoe trip. The people up ahead of me... their three-and-a-half-year-old son fell out of the canoe."

Even though I had rehearsed my story numerous times, I still found it very difficult to bullshit my hero. I only wanted to have the opportunity of meeting Howard. As such, I wasn't prepared for the emotional turmoil that lying to him entailed. However, in for a penny, in for a pound — that's my motto.

Although I was uncomfortable I persevered. I went on to tell Howard that my wife and daughter had been in the canoe, too. For some reason Howard had been under the impression that I was with a bunch of guys cruising down through rapids. I explained that due to the changing tide the current was too difficult to paddle against. This happens to be true. Howard looked at me skeptically. I knew that I was on thin ice — or at least treading water. I was stuck in a whirlpool of my own design. My lies had me by the ankles and were pulling me down. To deflect Howard's skepticism, I began telling him about the mangroves that extend for hundreds of yards towards the shores of Tarpon Bay. By the way, if you ever get a chance to visit Sanibel, don't forget to tour the mangrove trails — they're beautiful.

While I described the tentacle-like structure of the mangroves, Fred Norris played running water sound effects through my headphones. It sounded like a waterfall. I could hardly concentrate. I wanted to laugh, but somehow managed not to. I needed to keep the details of my scam straight. I said to Howard, "it's a very narrow trail, so you can't turn the canoe around, and the mangroves grow all around you." Fred Norris added gargling noises to his barrage of sound effects. I was ready to split a gut, if not my bladder.

The sound effects were so distracting. I meandered all over the place. Howard was losing his patience. He said, "all right, go ahead. So the kid's in real trouble. Like drowning. Screw the mangroves, and the tentacles!" Even Robin piped in with, "I have no clue where he's going." My dream fantasy was quickly turning into a nightmare. I started speaking frantically and making wild gestures.

Dan: "Okay, the kid's underwater. His head's underwater, even though he has a life jacket on. And I pull the kid out. The parents are both screaming, having a complete fit! The father can't get the canoe turned around. He can't get it backed up."
Howard: "And the dad doesn't jump in the water and save the kid?"

Busted! At this point I was sure that Howard was on to me. What would he say next? I bet he was wondering how to extricate himself from my segment. Fortunately I managed to regroup and come back stronger and more confident than ever. I figured, why worry? It's not as though Howard could force me to serve jail time for playing a prank on him. After all if pranks were a felony, then Howard Stern and company would be serving life sentences.

I answered Howard's question by replying, "It was very weird. I guess he felt he could move the canoe back. You know, it was moving that fast. It happened instantly." Robin wanted to know if I had to get out of my canoe to rescue the child. I told her that, "I had to use all my strength in one arm just to hold the canoe steady, and I had to use all my other strength to pull the kid out." Some comeback! Robin merely responded with an, "Uh-huh." It's hard work bullshitting bullshitters.

But with the golden Emmy keeping my feet warm I managed to plod on. I scored a few points by telling Howard that the drowning child's toy binoculars were caught in the mangroves. That seemed to placate Howard and Robin. Howard steered the conversation back on track by reminding me — and his listeners — that I'd saved a kid's life. Robin was getting impatient and curious to learn what was in my styrofoam box. Howard told her to "mellow-out." It was a funny moment. In fact, lest the reader think that things were too serious, despite my bullshitting, Howard and Robin were having a good time. Come to think of it so was I. I even got a few laughs with some of my far-fetched explanations. At least I was out of the mangrove trails.

I told Howard that the drowning child's father was very grateful to me for saving his kid's life. I even volunteered that the child's mother was younger than her husband. Without missing a beat Howard said, "Was the wife hot?" I shot Howard a surprised look. In fact, my entire face was one enormous "O" of surprise. I had forgotten who Howard's audience was. I almost let the perfect opportunity for titillation pass me by. Thank goodness for Howard. His comment brought me back to earth. I discovered for myself, first-hand, just how much fun it can be to discuss boobs with the masses on the radio. If you ever have the opportunity to say boob on-air, do yourself a favor, and don't let it pass you by!

Howard: "Very hot?"
Dan: "I don't know whether she was grabbing her halter top, or trying to grab the kid. She could have floated to him."

It had taken quite a while, but I had finally hit my stride. At long last I was comfortable, relaxed, and having the time of my life.

Howard and Robin loved my imagery. Howard added, "If the wife had fallen out of the canoe, he would have jumped into the water!" I parried with, "I don't think I could've gotten those whoppers back on the boat!" Talk about going tit for tat! My on-air conversation resembled a sword fight with wits instead of sabers. I think I might have scratched Howard with my whopper remark. He leapt back and exclaimed, "All right, so anyway, so the guy. . . Get back to the story. Don't mangrove me!" Touché, point Howard.

It was quite an exchange. I decided to take the offensive and interject a red herring of my own by thrusting with, "Yeah, well, he's an older guy. He said that they had gone to fertility, and that was their last chance. They could never have another kid. And his previous family had died, so you know — this was it." A lesser man than Howard might have called it a draw. In a verbal riposte worthy of Errol Flynn, Howard went straight for the jugular by asking, "Did he kill them? Did they all go canoeing with him one day?" Robin, smelling blood, delivered the coup de grace, "I believe his family was killed."

I checked myself for blood and found that although uninjured my shirt was sliced to shreds. There's nothing that I love more than a spirited conversation. This was exuberance incarnate. I was so excited that I responded brilliantly by saying, "I don't know."

It was time to cut to the chase. I told Howard that during the course of making small talk with the drowning child's father I had mentioned that I was a big Howard Stern fan. So far, so good. The most important aspect of my story was that the child's father was a rich and powerful man. Accidentally, I described the father as being a "big mucky-muck." Howard and Robin love it when guests mispronounce words. In fact, Howard wasted no time whatsoever by immediately replying, "No, he's a big muckety-muck!"

Robin: "Or a mucky-muck!"
Howard: "Yeah, mucky-muck as you say. You know what? You big strong guys are good at saving people, but you're not good at talking! You ain't going to save anybody with words! A mucky-muck! How do you say it again?"
Dan: "Ah, muckety-muck!"
Howard: "Muckety-muck! Okay, yeah, all right, go ahead."
Dan: (*Laughing*) "Don't, don't, edit me."

This was great. I never knew it could be like this. I hoped Howard and Robin would call me the next morning, or at least send me flowers. All kidding aside, I was having the time of my life. The "muckety-muck" talk was a definite high point in the conversation for me.

But back to the story. I described for Howard how the child's father owned a big portion of the Emmy Awards, and that he was clearly quite wealthy. I even fed Howard a line of crap about the man having a chauffeur driven "brand-new white Range Rover." Howard was eating it up. He wanted to know more. I played it coy and fed Howard a ridiculous line of bull by saying, "he (*the father*) wanted to give me some sort of reward, and I didn't want anything. You know, 'cause um..."

Howard: " 'Cause that's not cool."
Dan: "Well, it would cheap... I mean if you save someone's life, and..."
Howard: "It would cheapen the act."

Howard and Robin are professional speakers. They ran sentences around my every syllable. I imagine that it must be very boring and frustrating for them to converse with neophytes like me. I was putty in their hands. Howard simply steered me where he wanted me to go. He stopped me when I needed a rest. He edited me. He even completed my thoughts for me — usually before I'd even thought them.

He was everywhere and nowhere, all at the same time — a verbal ninja! I felt like a frog in a blender. I am positive that Howard's manipulation greatly improved my performance. Listening to my tape of the show makes me half believe that we sounded like friends. I'm probably just projecting my not-so-hidden desires. Anyway, I was in very capable hands. And I knew it!

Robin reminds me of a fat, furry, Cheshire cat trying to look all innocent and sweet. Meanwhile, it's obvious that the Cheshire cat has your favorite, yellow, canary in it mouth. Robin demurely responded to my mealy-mouthed, goody-goody comments by saying, "but you know, I guess he's a good guy because he didn't do it with any idea of getting a reward." Robin is one of those rare individuals with real smarts and street smarts as well. If you're looking to sell the Brooklyn Bridge or some Florida mangrove swamp, then don't expect Robin to buy it. She's too clever. As for cheapening the act, Howard told me that he would've taken cash. And he wasn't subtle about it either. Without missing a beat he said, "Before I grabbed the kid, I'd say how much are you worth?" As if this wasn't enough, Howard added, "How much is this little monster worth to you? Dickface! How much is this worth if I just grab this kid by the head and pull it out?" Howard was on a roll and everyone was laughing hysterically. I couldn't resist putting another log on the fire so to speak and said, "You could have had an auction." It's not easy slipping in a line or two between Howard and Robin, but luckily I was finally getting the hang of it. Howard came right back with, "Yeah right! Keep dunking him!"

Robin: "Get that price up!"
Howard: "Yeah, right! What is that? You're worth three million? I just want a hundred grand. Here goes! What? Fifty grand?"
Dan: "Yeah! The kid was changing colors."

I was tempted to do my imitation of Sally Field winning an Oscar and say to Howard and Robin, "You like me, you really like me!" One has to understand that although listening to the radio makes you feel like you're friends with Howard Stern and that you somehow know him, the fact remains that you don't. That's why it was so gratifying for me to have a chance to share a few laughs with him. On a certain level it made my hero worship less weird. Personally, I couldn't give a rat's ass that Howard Stern is a rich celebrity. I'm not a social climber or a mindless sycophant. What I treasure the most is Howard Stern's on-air creativity and wit. Off-air, I might not even like him. Who knows?

Anyway, I still had the styrofoam box between my legs, and Howard wanted to keep the box rolling — or if not the box at least keep the story moving along. Howard asked me what happened next and I told him that the child's father wanted to give me some kind of reward.

Howard: "And you said to him, how come Howard Stern has never won an Emmy?"
Dan: "Exactly. Especially since I just heard that Penny Crone won one. And the only time she's been good, has been with you"
Howard: "I mean the *E!* show should be up for an Emmy. They won't even nominate it. And it's such hypocritical crap!"

Howard loves to complain. He went into a long rap about Larry King getting awards. Howard even called Larry King a, "little suck ass." For a moment I forgot my place and interjected, "Well if Larry King ever dies, they could always put Charles Grodin in his place because he's just about as dull!" (Howard hates Charles Grodin, too.) Howard gave me an I-can't-believe-you-had-the-nerve-to-interrupt-me-and-say-that kind of look. He even said to me, "Oh please, just go back with your story. Stop making jokes." I felt a little hurt by this put-down, but I couldn't help being a wise-ass.

Howard: "So you said to the guy, 'How come Howard Stern has never won an Emmy?"
Dan: "Right. I said how come he hasn't won one? And, I said you know if you guys were smart, you'd give him an Emmy before the Academy Awards gives him one. At least you could be the first in the bandwagon."

When it comes to Howard Stern, flattery will get you everywhere. I was immediately forgiven for my naughty Grodin comments. Howard proceeded to tell his audience that he expected to win Academy Awards for *Private Parts*. As for me, I plodded on to my final destination — opening the styrofoam box and revealing my golden Emmy.

Dan: "Yeah. So anyway, he (*the child's father*) says he'll have his driver take me from

Fort Myers to Tampa, and put me on a plane. I got into Islip Airport last night at about 10:30. And he said, you go to your work. I'll have a messenger meet you there in the morning, and he'll give you a little something for Howard. And..."

Howard: "And here it is. Open it up. This is my Emmy."

Dan: "I got your Emmy! Am I the best fan or what?"

Howard: "Look at that!"

Robin: "Wow!"

Dan: "I'm King of All Fans! Right, Howard?"

Howard: "This is a real Emmy!"

Howard's face glowed like a child's face on Christmas morning. He looked so happy. I felt sad that he hadn't really won the award. Then I remembered that he earns in the neighborhood of seventeen million per year, and I didn't feel quite so bad. Everyone on the show was thrilled that Howard had an Emmy.

Robin wanted to know if there were any words on the Emmy. I told them that it usually takes a couple of weeks to get it engraved and complete the paper work. As if I knew! Even Gary got in the act. He still didn't know that he'd been fooled. As far as Gary was concerned he had finally done something right.

Gary: "That's a National Emmy! Not some local piece-of-crap."

Robin: "Yeah!"

Dan: "Howard, it's not an F-Emmy, (*Howard gives out phoney F-Emmy's to poke fun at the Emmy awards.*) it's the real Emmy!"

Howard: "Right, that's the real Emmy! I got one!"

Howard said that he would have loved to have received the Emmy Award during the actual Award ceremonies. He told the audience that he would love to "yell at everyone." I bet he would. Howard would probably say something like, "Ladies and Gentleman. I would like to thank the imbeciles at the Academy for finally realizing that I am God..."

Gary actually had the nerve to recommend that Howard display the Emmy prominently in his office where reporters would see it and assume that he'd really won it. He went on to add that, "reporters never do their research. (*Hey, he's one to talk!*) We'll just leave that in the back — and now, every time you get interviewed, people will think you won an Emmy. They won't check." Howard loved Gary's sinister plan. And there I was feeling guilty for scamming Howard.

Howard: "And you know what I'll do? I'll get some dopey reporter in there and tell him I won this Emmy. I promise you this will end up in a newspaper article."

Dan: "Well you did win it! But, I, he didn't tell me what category it was."
Howard: "Well, I won it for you being a fan, and you saving his kid's life."
Dan: "Yeah, that's enough."
Robin: "That's a fan!"
Howard: "Yeah, so here it is, the National Academy of Television Arts and Sciences, ladies and gentlemen, my Emmy."

I figured why not push my luck a little further. I asked Howard if it would be okay to say hello to some of my friends from the Prodigy Howard Stern Fan Club Bulletin Board. Howard didn't mind. The people that I mentioned on-air were delighted and flabbergasted. I was so excited that I almost forgot to say hello to my family. It was pretty funny. Ironically, our on-air chat was beginning to sound just like an award ceremony acceptance speech.

Howard was so happy that he even became giddy. He said to me, "Hey, good work!" and, "Who needs you now? I got my Emmy!" We even engaged in a little on-air small talk about Prodigy and Chat Parties. It was a lot of fun. Howard believes that Chat Parties are for losers. I couldn't agree more. Robin piped in with, "Yeah, I always hear and see that they're having a little get-together here, or a picnic there..."

I can't resist a little idle banter. Without thinking I confessed, "My wife told me that she wouldn't sleep with me if I went to one (*Chat Party*)." Howard immediately perked up and asked me, "Your wife what?" I replied, "My wife said she wouldn't sleep with me. She said I was looking less attractive the more I was getting into it! (*Chat Parties*)"

I was really hitting my conversational stride when Howard changed the subject slightly.

Howard: "Hey, don't your eyes hurt when you're on Prodigy a long time?"
Dan: "Oh they do. I have a seventeen-inch monitor. You have a big monitor?"
Howard: "I got a twenty-something inch monitor."
Dan: "Oh Jesus! You're probably getting radiation poisoning or something."

A more humorous response would've been to say "Wow, I can't believe you have a bigger one than I do. Does this mean you no longer want to meet in the little boys room for a sword fight during the next break?" Howard loves a gratuitous penis reference. My unsaid remarks would have alluded to his constant laments regarding his self-confessed, sub-standard penile size. Then again, perhaps my actual response was best.

Howard: "My testicles glow in the dark! So anyway, thank you for getting me the Emmy."

Dan: "My pleasure Howard."

Howard: "You're a good man. What's your name again?"

Dan: "Dan Wagner."

Howard: "Dan Wagner, hero and Emmy winner."

This was the crowning achievement of my whole scam. *My* hero had called *me* a hero, by name, and in front of his entire multi-million member audience. Who could have guessed? Howard and Robin had five months earlier called my "King of All Prison Librarians" fax the greatest letter ever. Where could I possibly go from here? I am already happily married. So marrying one of his daughters was ruled out. His studio was too small and crowded with great writing talent, so a job on his show was ruled out, too.

I t was quite a moment. One that I'm sure I'll never forget. Robin expressed her opinion that I should get to go to the Emmy's. Howard looked at me with kind benevolent eyes and told me that I should have "held that guy up for a lot more!" Things were getting really weird. If I didn't come clean soon, then I knew that I really would be a liar. It's one thing to play a practical joke on someone. But, if you let it go on for too long it's just plain mean. Therefore I decided to confess. What else could I do?

Dan: "I just have one question, Howard."

Howard: "Yeah?"

Dan: "On a scale of one-to-ten, what was worse? The Ashley potty story, (*A reference to another listener scam. The listener taped his little daughter's voice saying, "Daddy, I pooped on the potty". Then he called Howard on the phone and played the tape. Howard thought it was his own daughter, and started congratulating her. He was so proud. It was a fantastic scam! In fact, Howard was bent when he discovered that his daughter was not really potty-trained.*) or me with my bogus Emmy?"

Howard couldn't believe he'd been scammed. He asked, "This is fake?" I came clean and told him that I was a photographer and explained how the Emmy came to be in my possession. Everyone on the show was laughing and moaning at the same time. Hadn't they ever heard the expression, "Beware of strangers bearing gifts?" Gary quickly covered his fat butt with a little damage control by saying, "He told me the same story he told you guys, and you guys bought it." The trouble with Gary's reasoning is that he's the producer, and it's his job to fact check, not Howard and Robin's — they're busy entertaining on-air. Sheesh! Gary can be so dense at times.

Howard engaged in a little damage/spin control of his own. He inquired, "Is this a real Emmy?" When I told him it was he said, "Oh it is. So I don't care." Howard commented that he thought the show was "having too much interaction with the listeners." He even threatened to put a moratorium on it. What a spoilsport. I asked him, "Are Stuttering John and Gary going to beat me up on my way out for this one?" I was no longer a hero in my own hero's eyes. Things quickly deteriorated to the point where Howard said to me, "You are so annoying, too!" Howard can be such a spoilsport sometimes.

Gary was glad to have escaped blame. He too joined in and said that I was annoying. Robin commented that my mentioning details like the mangroves and such had given my story an air of authenticity. No kidding. I didn't score in the 1,400's on my Scholastic Achievement Tests because I'm stupid. Duh!

Gary: "Did you doubt him at all?"
Howard: "No, I didn't doubt him for a second. Hey Gary, beat him over the head with his Emmy."
Robin: "Yeah, beat him with the Emmy!"
Dan: "No, don't F-Emmy with that Emmy!"
Gary: "Needless to say, we're keeping it!"
Howard: "Yeah, we're keeping the Emmy man! You scammed us. You certainly did, but we have an Emmy, and we don't care."

I couldn't resist saying to Howard, "Hey, look, Howard, you know, I was thinking about being a writer, could like I, submit some, um, ideas for you, like some really good stuff?" I was referring to a string of young male guests who had recently been on the show asking Howard for writing gigs. I even talked in a pseudo-dumb voice as I asked him to consider letting me write for him. I winked at Howard as I said it. He was smiling. People always ask Howard for favors. I think Howard enjoyed having me poke fun at the favor-seekers. Meanwhile, I was laughing inside because I was in the middle of actually writing this book. I wanted to laugh out loud.

Howard: "Oh, is he annoying! Let's get him outta here, Gary."
Gary: "Immediately!"
Robin: "Good-bye Dan!"
Howard: "Good-bye Dan!"
Robin: "Is your name real?"

Dan: "Bye Robin. Yeah my name's real, and I really love the show, and I think you're both great and..."

Howard: "— and I believe he's really on Prodigy! That part I believe."

Dan: "I'm Bambicakes."

Howard: "Okay Bambicakes!"

Dan: "That's my name on Prodigy."

Over the past couple of months, I had taken to calling myself Bambicakes on Prodigy. However, the regulars knew who I really was. I chose the name for the funny responses it always seemed to generate from my fellow cyber-fiends. I also reasoned that it would appeal to Howard, and perhaps get me noticed. I liked the attention.

After I said my name was Bambicakes, Gary replied, "Oh, that's you?" Even Howard said, "I can't believe it!" I was very pleased to discover that they were aware of some of my Prodigy postings. One of my goals when I first started to post messages on the Howard Stern Fan Club Bulletin Board, was to interact on some level with the show. I think the post that must have caught their attention, was the post about Howard's pal, Joey Buttafuoco's lawyer Dominic Barbara. In this post, I publicly confessed my desire to have Dominic's out of-wed-lock child. I even professed to be physically attracted to him. Dominic is fat and visually unappealing, to put it mildly. I knew that it would be amusing to my fellow bulletin board members to post a claim that I had a crush on him. I'm sure it must have been amusing to the people who work on Howard's show.

As long as I was confessing I decided to come clean about my faxes as well. I said to Howard, "You know that letter you got from the inmate? That was me. And you know the woman who could play the kazoo with her privates? That was me, too."

Howard: "That was you, too?"

Robin: "That was you?"

Dan: "That was me."

Howard: "We don't care if it's real or fake, as long as it's good."

It was foolish of me to confess to so many things in one fell swoop. Howard looked as though his head was about to explode. I bet it's been a long time since anyone has so completely pulled the wool over his eyes. I knew I had committed an unpardonable sin when my hero said to me, "I thought you were gay quite frankly. Sphincter says what?" Despite the fact that I'm an obsessed fan, I saw no reason for Howard to get abusive. Therefore I decided to come back with the following:

Dan: "I would be (*gay*) if I could stay on the show a few more minutes." (*I bet Howard has never heard that one before.*)
Howard: "Sphincter says what?"

Howard is as impressionable as I am. The "Sphincter says what?" line is from the movie *Wayne's World.* I have no clue why it took several years for Howard to see the movie, and adopt this routine as his own. Some people play along, and say "What?", and some don't. Perhaps it's Howard's way of testing his domination over people — those who say "What?" are friends, and those who refuse to play along are enemies — or so I would guess.

I took a very long pause. I was trying to think of a wise-ass comeback. I decided to be a good sport. After all, I got to play my little prank on Howard and company. It seemed only fair, that I should play along with them. Howard and I were locked in eye-to-eye contact while he waited for my reply. It was a tense moment. I doubt that Howard tolerates any challenges to his authority. Hey, if I worked for him, I'd behave like a little lamb! I think I might have taken too long in saying "What?". Howard could tell that I had foolishly tried to resist his powers. Would there be a price to pay later on?

Howard Stern and "his" Emmy Award

Dan: "What?"
Howard: "There you go. All right! We'll be back right after this."

My fourteen minutes (13 minutes, and 51 seconds.) of fame were up. Hopefully my faxes, which were read on-air by Howard and Robin will count towards my remaining minute. I don't want to miss out on having a full fifteen minutes of fame in my lifetime!

I hated to leave Howard's studio. I knew that I would feel this way from the moment I set foot in the place. Being there was an exciting once in-a-lifetime experience. I still can't believe it actually happened. It's like the way the first day of vacation feels — you're excited and happy but also very conscious of the number of days left.

I had done everything possible to prolong my stay but I didn't want to overstay my welcome. Howard was very polite. Still, I couldn't help picturing a Vaudeville performer receiving the famous hook and getting hauled off the stage while an angry audience pelts him with rotten vegetables. The commercial break saved me from the vegetable pelting and rescued Howard from my continued presence.

I had just experienced one of the most unreal events of my entire life. By virtue of my wits, imagination, and resourcefulness, I had found a way to get on-air with Howard and company. I had stormed the Bastille armed with only my raw courage and a golden Emmy.

After Howard broke for commercial, he congratulated me on my appearance. He even told me that I had done a good job. I was so relieved. I wasn't sure how he would take to being the victim of a scam. But I guess it's like Howard said on the air, "We don't care if it's real or fake, as long as it's good."

Even Robin came over to congratulate me and shake my hand. She also said that I had done a good job. I was dumbfounded. I was keenly aware of the fact that by leaving her own glass enclosed studio and coming out to greet me, Robin was paying me an enormous compliment. She could just as easily have ignored my departure. As far as I'm concerned, it was a very generous act. Just as I suspected, Robin's on-air personality exactly matches her off-air persona. She's so nice! I enjoyed shaking hands with her.

Unlike Robin, Howard's off-air persona is diametrically opposed to his on-air one. Howard isn't one for idle chitchat. He has a great deal of responsibility, and there are too many demands placed upon his time. The whole show seems to rest upon his shoulders. Perhaps that explains why Howard is as subdued off-air as he is vivacious

Dan Wagner, Howard Stern

on-air. Howard knows that if he gives an inch, people will demand a mile.

Once I left the studio, Mike Gange videotaped Howard, the Emmy award, and me for the *E!* show. Then he conducted a post-show interview. He asked me what it had been like to be on-air with Howard. I think I said that it was a great experience. I was still walking on cloud nine, so it's hard to remember. I hope I'll get to see the videotape one day. Then I can perform a post-show analysis.

I was about to leave when I remembered that I'd brought my amateur Snappy camera. I wanted to have my picture taken with Howard. Fortunately, the show was still on a commercial break. One of the interns summoned Howard. I handed Steve Grillo my camera, and he took the shots. I was holding the Emmy award and standing next to, and slightly in front of, Howard.

From my position, I couldn't see Howard's face. I assumed that he was smiling just like I was. When I got the pictures developed later in the day at a one-hour photo lab, I was shocked. Howard was vogueing for the camera. His cheeks were sucked in and he was projecting a ton of attitude. It looked as though he were trying to imitate a male model from a Calvin Kein ad. Truth be told, he looked like a man in pain with a huge stick up his butt. Although Howard is always making self-deprecating comments on-air, it is now clear to me that this is just an act. He actually fancies himself to be a black-haired, taller version of Fabio! At least he didn't give me donkey ears in the photos. Then again, that would have made for a very unique and collectible photo. Howard's expression isn't that important to me. What really matters, is that I had been photographed with my hero.

Before I left, Gary Dell'Abate told me that I would receive a $522.00 check for my appearance in seven to ten days. When I asked him why, he informed me that it was union scale. I was flabbergasted. I had to pinch myself. Who would have thought it possible? Gary's back was turned towards me as he delivered what I consider to be an insult. He said, "$522.00, that's not bad for doing nothing!" I guess all the years of working on a number one radio show have made Gary blasé. I'm sure that being in a powerful position with people constantly sucking up to him has done wonders for his humility. Luckily Gary couldn't read my mind. Maybe I'm overly sensitive, but I was pretty pissed-off at him. Perhaps that's why he didn't look me in the eye when he made his comment. I would hardly call perfectly executing a plan to get on the Howard Stern Show, and then giving a reasonably decent interview "nothing". Not to mention the fact that radio time is worth hundreds of dollars per second. If being on-air is nothing, then why does the Howard Stern Show charge their advertisers such high rates?

At 9:07AM I found myself back on the street in front of 600 Madison Avenue. My incredible journey had lasted less than ninety minutes from start to finish. My time in the sun had flown by very quickly. It was strange to be outside. Most of the people passing by were on their way to work. I felt like going home and taking a nap. I was tired and emotionally spent from my brush with fame. Despite my drained condition, I knew that I had an important job to perform.

The job in question was that of post-show promotion. From my point of view, marketing and properly positioning oneself for a future appearance was almost as important as the appearance itself. I rushed back to my studio and quickly called all my friends and acquaintances with fax machines. I requested, begged, and cajoled them to fax letters to Howard regarding my on-air performance. They all agreed. I even asked them to tell Howard to hire me as a writer. Talk about gilding the lily! By 10:00AM Howard would receive at least twenty faxes applauding my efforts. Robin is the fax-master of the show. She loves to read the faxes that listeners send in. I'm sure she was impressed by the quantity and quality of my fan mail.

I asked my friends to send me copies of their faxes. My favorite one came from a woman friend of mine who works as a photo-stylist and production coordinator. She is not a Stern fan. In fact, she told me that she was only sending the fax as a favor to me. However, once she applied herself to the task, she really seemed to get a kick out of it. This is what she wrote:

Howard!

This morning my Virtual Spouse gave one of those triumphant yells that announced that even Mondays can be worth waking up for. "Hey! They're giving Howard an Emmy!"

Ok, so it was a scam. But a funny one. Where'd you find that Wagner guy? He was so good at pulling one over on the public that either you've got to hire him to do it full time, or somebody will have to nominate him for public office where those talents can really be put to use.

Any chance you'll re-run this? Virtual Spouse says the guy had some whole fantastic shaggy dog story worked out, only I missed the very beginning. (I admit it, I was in front of the bathroom mirror working on my corporate costume, and pissed off because your hair looks better than mine.)

So, how about a repeat performance, Howard? I'd send you my bra in gratitude, but I'm afraid it would short out the fax machine.

Sincerely, Joanne

I never knew Joanne was so funny. Even the cover letter that she enclosed with a copy of her fax was hilarious:

Hi Dan-

Here's the fax I sent Howard Stern; hope it helps. Personally, I don't like the man, but that could be due in part to my ex's habit of setting the clock radio to his program and chortling all the way through (Yet Another Irrevocable Rule of Divorce: Everything your ex-husband adores in the way of media automatically sucks, particularly if sexist.)

I've figured out the appeal of the Emmy to Stern...it's phonetic. "M-E!!!" - the all-capital lettering of the self-centered megalomaniac's favorite phrase. Anyway, I lied about the bra. And I adamantly refuse to discuss any of my anatomical parts or sexual preferences with him should he attempt to contact me.

And frankly, I honestly do wish I'd tuned in that morning to hear you help him make an ass of himself. So there.

Sincerely, Joanne

Several of my friends and business associates called to congratulate me on my appearance. I never realized I knew so many dedicated Howard Stern fans. I asked them what I had sounded like on the air. I am well aware that my voice is not radio material and I imagined that I had sounded like a nerd. However, everyone assured me that I sounded fine, and I had handled myself very well. I let out a huge sigh of relief. Before I left the show, I asked Gary to send me a tape of my appearance (which he never did). I admit it, I'm vain and self-conscious. Many people told me that they didn't even know it was me on the air until I said my name.

Canoe accidents played a prominent role on Howard's show over the next week and a half. Although Howard didn't mention my scam, he did say on numerous occasions that a good way to kill one's wife was on a canoeing accident. Were these canoe references sub-conscious? Perhaps Howard was avoiding any mention of my Emmy-tale until the day of the Emmy Awards for daytime television (soap-operas and talk shows), which were less than a month away. I was betting that he would do something outrageous with the Emmy award I gave him. Even the national news had gone canoe crazy. Super-spy William Colby was reported missing and presumed dead in a canoeing accident. His empty canoe was found on a sand-bar in the Potomac River.

The people on Prodigy were very impressed with my scam. Due to my confrontational and acerbic nature, I had never been very popular with my fellow Prodigy members. After my appearance everything changed. People congratulated me and included me in activities and discussions. I felt like a teenager who had discovered a wonder drug for pimples. I was no longer the pariah of Prodigy. In fact people would rush to my defense, saying "I was one of them", if anyone said anything even slightly critical to me.

New York City Hawks mascot & Gary Dell'Abate

During one chat room discussion I mentioned Gary Dell'Abate's statement that I would be paid $522.00 for my appearance. Evidently some of the people in the chat room had either been on the air in Howard's studio themselves, or knew others who had. They told me that they hadn't been paid any money. I had opened up a can of worms. What exactly was going on here? Gary had told me I would get a check. I started to believe that I had been tricked. I decided to label the whole issue of payment as one big scam to save face in case I had been deceived. I was happy to have been on Howard's show — check or no check.

I was worried that appearing on the show might become an addiction. Would one taste of fame be enough? Each post-show day brought new withdrawal symptoms. I wondered how long it would be before I contrived another scam to get on the show. In the meantime I had to satisfy my longing to return to the show by repeatedly playing the tape of my appearance sent to me by a cyber-friend. Without this tape I think I would have been tempted to believe that I had never really been on Howard's show. The whole episode had been that surreal.

CHAPTER 8

ONCE STUNG, TWICE SHY

There's a saying that goes: Fool me once, shame on you. Fool me twice, shame on me. I'd successfully run Howard's fact checking gauntlet once with my Emmy award scam. I wondered if I could do it again. An encore performance would be fun, but making another attempt within a week of my first scam was risky. On the other hand, the boldness of such a move might just throw Howard's people off balance. Perhaps they would think: He would never try to scam us again so soon, especially with such a bald-faced lie. This time he *must* be telling the truth.

When I left Howard's offices after my Emmy scam, I promised myself that I wouldn't turn into one of those nut cases who incessantly hounds Howard. Thus far, my behavior had been exemplary. After my scam, I resisted the urge to linger. I got in and out quickly, without being ejected by security. I went back to my photo studio and put in a full day's work.

As far as anyone was concerned, I was a fan with a cute scam. Nothing more, nothing less. If I continued with my good behavior, perhaps I would be invited back for a follow-up segment. The daytime Emmy Award ceremonies were taking place within a month's time. That would be the ideal opportunity for Howard to give me a call. If I wanted this to happen I would have to behave myself, but I wondered how long I could last.

A mere three days after my Emmy scam, fate once again tempted me. During a photo shoot for an article on imported beers, I learned from a friend that one of my clients, *Cigar Aficionado Magazine* owner and publisher Marvin Shanken, had just purchased the humidor given to J.F.K. in 1961 by Milton Berle at the Sotheby's Jackie Onassis auction for $574,000. I'm not one to let moss grow under my cigars. I immediately called the creative director at *Cigar Aficionado* and demanded that I be given the first crack at photographing the famous humidor. He laughed, and said, "Okay, if we need any photos, I'll call you." As it turned out, I didn't have long to wait.

The next day the creative director called me on the phone and gave me the assignment of a location shoot at Sotheby's. I was to photograph the humidor alone as well as with its new owner, Marvin Shanken. To ease my way past security, the creative director messengered over a few official black and gold *Cigar Aficionado* caps. These caps came in very handy when my freelance assistant, Josh and I arrived at Sotheby's later in the day.

My freelance assistant, Josh, frequently works in the film industry. I was pleased to learn that Josh had worked on Howard Stern's New Year's Rotten Eve 1994 Pay-Per-View Special. During the cab ride uptown to Sotheby's, I asked him about it. The special had taken place at a theater in Newark, New Jersey. It received tons of bad press due to all the alleged debauchery that occurred between the cast and crew. Josh confirmed the press reports. What a small world. We each had Howard Stern tales to tell.

We got to Sotheby's early, which was a good thing, because even with our silly *Cigar Aficionado* caps, and liaison arrangements, it still took quite a while to clear security. Eventually we were ushered into a large room above the auction floor which was decorated with ornate tapestries, paintings, antiques, and vases of white tulips. A massive-large screen television and several high-volume speakers were broadcasting the sights and sounds of the auction taking place below us.

Josh and I decided to use one of the nicer paintings as a background for the photographs. We would place the humidor on a large, circular, ornate, green felt-covered table which rested on a thick Oriental rug that in turn rested on even thick-

er wall-to-wall carpeting. By moving the table in front of the painting we created several folds in the Oriental rug. We would need to watch our steps. Once the lights and camera were set-up, we took a few Polaroid proofs. Everything looked fine.

A few minutes later the Sotheby's people brought in the world's most expen-

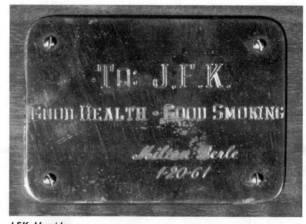

J.F.K. Humidor

sive humidor. Josh and I exchanged "you-must-be-kidding" looks. The humidor looked as though it was a gift from Jack Benny, not Milton Berle — it looked that cheap. The brass plaque on the humidor was smaller than an index card. The inscription ("TO: J.F.K. GOOD HEALTH - GOOD SMOKING Milton Berle 1-20-61") looked as though it had been engraved at a dime store. It was hard to read and pitted with age and abuse. The humidor itself was in even worse shape. Some of the wood on the front of the base was missing, and the edge was jagged. The wooden back of the humidor was cracked from lack of proper care. As far as I was concerned, this was a garage sale item, not an international auction house *objet d'art*.

My Emmy scam paled next to the scam that was being played on an over eager public desperate for Jackie O. memorabilia! Josh and I joked that the humidor looked as though it were a victim of a Ted Kennedy bender. To make matters worse, the humidor was empty and devoid of Cuban blockade cigars.

Finally, Marvin Shanken, owner and publisher of *Cigar Aficionado*, and proud new owner of the J.F.K. humidor arrived. Over the years Mr. Shanken has cultivated the mien of a wealthy and fabulously successful publishing magnate. He is never without his trademark stogie, and glass of fine wine. His magazines (*Cigar Aficionado, Wine Spectator, Food Arts*, etc.) are devoted to living the high-life, and he is the high-life's finest proponent. Even his waistline communicates indulgence. He shaves with one of those special electric razors that maintain the randy appearance of a three-day beard growth. Marvin also has a swarthy complexion and walks with a swagger. He reminds me of a middle-aged pirate in pinstripes.

Marvin can be very intense. When he enters a room, heads turn — sometimes out of curiosity, and sometimes out of fear. I've been in meetings with him and have personally experienced both of these reactions to his presence, and more. Once during a meeting with magazine staffers Marvin tried to convey to me how he wanted a photograph to look. Eventually he said, "I want it to look like a big hard-on!" I was the only one in the room to break up with laughter. I knew what he meant. He wanted the viewer of the photo to experience physical lust over the objects depicted in the photo. The particular objects in this case were among Marvin's most prized possessions — Venetian glassware.

As intense as Marvin can be, he can also be equally generous. While photographing the Venetian glass, I accidentally broke a small piece off one of the glasses. I wrote Marvin a letter and gave him my insurance company information. Marvin wasn't fazed. He never mentioned the broken glass to me or asked me to replace it.

Howard loves to lampoon the Kennedys and Jackie Onassis. When it came to the Sotheby's auction, Howard said words to the effect of "What's next, her old tampons?" I have to agree with him. The prices commanded by the junk at Jackie's auction were beyond reason or good taste. The biggest bidders were the *nouveau riche* such as Marvin Shanken and Arnold Schwarzenegger (He made the winning three-quarter-million-dollar bid on J.F.K.'s golf clubs).

Even the Sotheby's people confided to me in snickering tones that they were flabbergasted by the ridiculous prices and carnival-like atmosphere of the auction. Jackie's fake pearls had just sold for $200,000. The Sotheby's employee acting as my liaison told me that she would prefer real pearls worth $200,000 to fake ones that can be had anywhere for $65. She also informed me that Sotheby's had received numerous phone calls from bidders interested in knowing if the pink dress that Jackie O. had worn when J.F.K. was assassinated was for sale. Wow. I bet Howard would have had a field day with this information.

When the time finally came for me to photograph Marvin with his new toy, I couldn't resist saying, "Hey, good job snagging the humidor." In the most transparent acting job this side of Lou Ferrigno as Macbeth, Marvin grimaced and said, "Yeah, now I got to pay for it!" The rich are always pleading poverty. I couldn't prevent the edges of my mouth from vibrating in mirth. I said, "Oh well, at least it's a tax deduction."

In my opinion the people in the art department at Marvin's magazines are some of the most overworked and underpaid people I know. They are barely one step above the interns on Howard's show. I was slowly coming to the conclusion that Marvin and Howard were more alike than not. They both are self-indulgent and have more money than they can ever spend. Howard pathetically tries to downplay his wealth. Since he hadn't wanted to comply with standard financial disclosure rules, Howard had even aborted his short-lived run for governor of New York. Howard also hides from the tradesmen who make repairs to his Long Island abode lest they be tempted to jack up their fees. As for self-indulgence, one has only to consider Howard's home-away-from-home basement wonderland. A room crammed with the latest in high-tech electronic gadgetry, it's an adolescent fantasy brought to life.

Contents Of Howard Stern's Basement Wonderland

1) 100-inch television and broadcast quality VCR
2) Digital Satellite reception
3) Communications center with over a dozen phone lines
4) Top of the line IBM computer system with 20-inch monitor and ISDN high-speed modem
5) Leather couch
6) Top-of-the-line sound system

7) Climate control system
8) Enormous floor-to-ceiling 700 gallon saltwater fish tank
9) Security camera monitoring system
10) Extensive music, video, and pornography libraries
11) Private bathroom
12) Electronic door lock

My Emmy scam had left me so obsessed with Howard Stern that I was starting to find parallels to him everywhere. I was like a ravenous dieter who thinks everything he sees is made of chocolate. But in my case, everything I thought, saw, or heard was potential Howard Stern material. Then again, the J.F.K. humidor was national news, and Howard really does like to rag on the Kennedys.

It required a conscious effort for me to concentrate on the job at hand. I was at Sotheby's to take beautiful photographs of Marvin and his humidor, not to daydream or think up Stern stunts. Ultimately, I managed to create dozens of photographs that fulfilled my assignment to perfection. One particularly nice photo was given a full-page in *Cigar Aficionado*. The publicity value of the photos was enormous. In fact, many of them were distributed around the world.

During the shoot, I had the opportunity to look inside the humidor. I was hoping to find a rough draft of a love letter written by J.F.K. to Marilyn Monroe. I even flipped the humidor upside down for a better angle to shoot the commemorative plaque. I couldn't believe that the Sotheby's people allowed me to manhandle the humidor. Whenever I had photographed valuable objects before, only a bonded representative or the object's owner were allowed to touch the goods. It was fun to hold the humidor. It's worth more than anything I'll ever own.

Suppose I dropped it? I almost did. After the shoot was done I was moving the humidor back to the cart that it had been wheeled in on. As I carried the humidor, I stumbled and almost tripped over one of the folds we had inadvertently created in the Oriental rug. The people at Sotheby's gasped in horror. Fortunately, I managed to regain my balance. I breathed a huge sigh of relief when the humidor was wheeled away. The Sotheby's people couldn't take it away fast enough. I bet that's the last time I'm invited there.

During the cab ride back to my studio, Josh and I chuckled over my having almost ruined the humidor. Josh said that it would have made me a national celebrity. I countered by saying that at least I would have had the last photographs of the intact humidor. Even the cab driver joined in the fun. He said, "Kennedy kindling!" I answered him, "Why cry over split wood!" We laughed so hard, that I thought the cab driver might sideswipe someone.

All our clowning around made me think. I told Josh that in a way I wished I really had dropped the humidor and that it had broken into a thousand pieces. Then I could tell my story on Howard's show. Josh stopped laughing. He looked at me with sober, intelligent eyes and gave me some of the best advice that I've ever received. Josh said, "Don't let Howard Stern take you down." Great advice but several months too late. My Howard Stern disease had progressed too far and was consequently inoperable. Like a candle, it would burn out when all the wax was gone. By my estimation, my Howard Stern fixation was a pretty large candle. I doubted that it was even halfway used up.

Once again the wheels in my head began to turn. Sure I was obsessed, but I was also inspired. The same creative urge to scam Howard also drove me to take photographs. Watching a scam unfold is as exciting to me as watching a photographic print develop. Either your creative concepts are validated, or they're not. It's that simple. But scamming Howard is less predictable than photography. There are so many variables to consider, and a great deal more strategy is involved.

Finally I came up with what I believed to be a foolproof scam. I would tell Howard's people that I had broken the J.F.K. humidor. If Howard's people asked me why they hadn't heard about the humidor being broken on the news, I would tell them that there was a press conference scheduled for later in the day. There isn't a media person alive who can resist a good scoop. Or I could tell them that Sotheby's was doing a cover-up over the whole incident due to their being embarrassed about it. A cover-up would definitely garner Howard's interest. He loves to catch people with their pants down. There were so many possible excuses to choose from. I would also tell them that I was giving them the news scoop because I was a Howard Stern fan, and that I was worried that my name might be dragged through the mud before I had an opportunity to give my own version of what had happened. In short, I wanted to make sure that Sotheby's didn't put all the blame for the broken humidor on my shoulders.

I set about putting together an evidence package to support my scam. I already had polaroids of both the humidor and the commemorative brass plaque with Milton Berle's inscription. These would be exhibit "A". I also had my *Cigar Aficionado* black and gold caps, and issues of the magazine with my photo credits — exhibits "B" and "C".

The next piece of evidence I obtained was my *pièce de résistance* — an authentic letter from my insurance company addressed to Sotheby's. I called up my insurance agent and told her that I needed to file a claim. She was momentarily speechless after I informed her that I had broken the J.F.K. humidor. Then she started laughing. Afterwards she started apologizing for having laughed, but before she knew it she was laughing again. In fact, everyone at the insurance office had the same reaction — laughter. Here they were, facing a claim of over half a million dollars, and all they could do was laugh, and say "Dan, Dan, Dan, you've really done it this time!"

I told my insurance agent that I was waiting to hear from Sotheby's. I further told her that Sotheby's was in the process of estimating the damage to the humidor and ascertaining whether or not it could be repaired. She loved my story. I knew that she couldn't wait to get off the phone with me and call her friends. Perhaps the media would get hold of my fake story before I could spring it on Howard. Then he would really believe it. I informed my insurance agent that I needed a letter proving that I had an insurance business liability policy to give to Sotheby's. She asked me to dictate the letter to her over the phone. I picked up the letter later in the day. Here it is (exhibit "D"):

Sotheby's
1334 York Avenue
New York, New York 10021

To Whom It May Concern:

We are the insurance broker for Mr. Dan Wagner. We understand that the J.F.K. Humidor was damaged by Mr. Wagner during a photo shoot on 4/25/96 during which Mr. Wagner was the photographer. Mr. Wagner has liability insurance with "Acme" Insurance for up to one million dollars.

Please contact us with an estimate of repairs for the damaged item. We will be happy to process any necessary paperwork.

Kindly include Mr. Wagner's policy number in all your future correspondence. The policy number is: JMW 1213 87-PHW 617 92.

Thank you for your attention to this matter.

Sincerely,
Etcetera, Etcetera

My last piece of evidence (exhibit "E") would be a copy of Sotheby's Jackie O. auction catalog. I intended to tell Howard that while photographing the humidor, I ran into J.F.K., Jr. Furthermore, I would tell Howard that I tricked the young heir into autographing the catalog for him. The scam would be that I had an older brother named Howard, who was in the hospital recuperating from third degree sunburns sustained during a recent vacation to Florida. My poor older brother rented a convertible and forgot to use sunblock. Hence the third degree burns. This fancy explanation would justify the guaranteed-to-amuse personalized inscription on the autographed catalog.

The bogus inscription read: Howard, get well soon! By the way, steer clear of convertibles — they're too exposed. Hardtops are much safer. —John Kennedy. (An obvious reference to Kennedy Sr. being assassinated in a convertible.) This would surely appeal to Howard's warped sense of humor. To fake J.F.K., Jr's signature, all I had to do was look at the Letter From The Editor Section in his magazine *George*. I knew that J.F.K., Jr. was really in Milan, Italy, but I could always tell Howard's people that the Milan story was only a cover. Leaving the country while earning thirty-four million dollars at a trumped up garage sale doesn't make sense to me, anyway.

I planned to deliver my evidence package in a blue and white Sotheby's shopping bag. I was counting heavily on real props lending credibility to my fantastic tale — just as I had with my Emmy scam. I planned to stage my encore performance on the one week anniversary of my successful Emmy scam. The Jackie O. auction was ending on Friday, April 26th. Therefore Monday, April 29th would be the ideal time for me to strike — when the J.F.K. humidor would be at it's most newsworthy.

I was very excited the night before my scam. I even fussed over what I was going to wear. I knew that it would be much more difficult to fool Howard a second time. The scheduling concerns that I had during my Emmy scam still applied. If Howard had too many activities planned for Monday, then I would miss my chance to scam him a second time. Any delays would give Howard's producer Gary Dell'Abate the opportunity to call Sotheby's and perhaps see through my shenanigans.

A wiser man would have given the scam to someone who was unknown to Howard and Gary. It would have been fairly easy to use another person's name and make it look less suspicious. Also Howard had already had almost fourteen minutes of me. Would he want more? Having someone else carry out my plan would still be satisfying. But of course, like Howard, I wanted it all.

Monday was cold and rainy. I cabbed it to 600 Madison Avenue. This was beginning to feel familiar. I waited in the rain for a few minutes. I was hoping to run into one of Howard's interns and thereby get brought up to the reception area. After a little while I decided to call from the corner phone. An intern answered on the first ring. I explained my situation and was put on hold. Unfortunately, Gary was too busy to come to the phone himself. The intern came back and informed me that I should drop off my material an hour and a half later at 9:00AM. This was a bad sign. I told him that I had to go to work, but he wouldn't budge. I decided to head to my studio and replot my strategy.

As I rounded the corner of 57th Street and Madison Avenue I was nearly run down by a madman with a sandwich board. This madman turned out to be none other than Melrose Larry Green — Howard's most annoying fan. He was carrying a sign that read "Howard Stern for President". After my Emmy scam Melrose had called to congratulate me and complain that I hadn't mentioned him during my show appearance. Coincidentally, Melrose was scheduled to appear on Howard's show the following day (Tuesday, April 30th). I said, "Hey Melrose." He stopped running and came over. The first words out of his mouth were, "Who are you?" Once I told him my name he was glad to see me. He said that my show appearance the previous Monday had been "brilliant."

Melrose asked me what I was doing near Howard's offices. I told him about the J.F.K. humidor but not that it was a scam. He said, "Wow, that's amazing. I'm sure Howard will be interested." He then asked me where I was headed. I said I was going to my studio. Melrose proposed that we hang out in front of 600 Madison Avenue for a few minutes and then get breakfast. His treat. Melrose is renowned for his cheapness. I figured if worse came to worse, I would at least get a funny story to tell the people on Prodigy. They all hate Melrose. I eventually wrote about my little breakfast with Melrose. I called the post "Breakfast at Tiffany's". (Since we dined a block or two from Tiffany's, I couldn't resist.)

The reason Melrose wanted to wait in front of 600 Madison Avenue for a few minutes was to see the famous stripper Amy Lynn who was being interviewed on Howard's show. In a minute or two she would exit out the front door. I agreed that it might prove interesting. While we waited, I spoke to Amy Lynn's bodyguard and chauffeur. He was a funny guy. He told me that contrary to public opinion, being a chauffeur for strippers was not all fun and games. Without waiting to be asked, he even confessed that men in his position didn't "get a lot of pussy." He had, however, once been married to a female bartender who worked at a strip club. He described this marriage as one of the worst experiences in his life. I thought that meeting this guy was worth the cost of a cab ride uptown. In fact, I think he should have been the one on-air, not Amy Lynn.

Amy Lynn came outside a few minutes later. She was dressed in a pure white pants suit with a low-cut white blouse showcasing her impressive cleavage. She was at least a 38D. Howard's intern Mike Gange followed her carrying her luggage. One thing was for sure — she didn't travel light. Mike was puffing and sweating like a pack mule.

Once Mike unburdened himself, I took the opportunity to present my scam. While I spoke to Mike, Melrose was standing next to me. He was eager to get Mike's attention. Through body language and by rolling my eyes

Mike Gange, Scott Einziger

in Melrose's direction, I let Mike know that I wasn't with him. I knew that being with Melrose — an acknowledged nut job — could only work against me. I gave Mike all my "evidence", with the exception of the auction catalog. I wanted to keep that as a surprise. Especially the phoney inscription. I did, however, tell Mike that I had the catalog, and that it was inscribed by a celebrity. When he asked me who had signed it, I coyly said he would just have to be patient. This seemed to amuse him.

Before Mike returned to Howard's offices he said to me, "You realize of course that with a few phone calls we can check out your story?" I said, "Sure, call anyone you like." I knew that Sotheby's wouldn't be open for a few more hours. I also knew that it would take a million calls, and a great deal of effort, for Stern's flunkies to find someone at Sotheby's willing to answer their questions. I doubted that they would even try that hard to verify my story. Besides, the people at Sotheby's would probably think that Howard was trying to scam them. That's why I decided to call Mike's bluff.

Mike told me he would give my package to Gary. A few minutes later another intern named Sean came downstairs. He was a gangly, pimply-faced kid who looked about seventeen. For an instant my heart skipped a beat. I thought he had come to fetch me. Big mistake. Sean told me that Gary needed one of my business cards. I asked Sean if I should wait, and he said he didn't think so. With nothing left to accomplish, I joined Melrose for a cup of java at a nearby diner before heading back to my studio.

I was busy working on a shot when the phone rang. I answered with the typical photographer's greeting, "Hello, studio." Gary was on the line. He said, "What's up?" I asked him if he wanted to put me on the show. He said that he was waiting to speak to someone at Sotheby's. I said, "Good, then you'll finally believe me." Gary said, "Well Dan, after last week... I mean, we have to consider where this is coming from."

I mentioned the "signed" auction catalog. Gary wanted to know more. I told him that one of my clients is in the same building as J.F.K., Jr's magazine *George*. I also informed him that I had shared an elevator with J.F.K., Jr. on several occasions. In fact, I went on, I had even told J.F.K., Jr. that "My father in-law drove his father from the Baltimore airport to Washington College in Chestertown, Maryland to give a speech while he was running for President." The funny thing is that all the stuff I had told Gary about J.F.K., Jr. so far was true. But this didn't last long. I then told him that because of this history with J.F.K., Jr. he now would always say hello to me as though we were old friends. So far so good. Gary was buying it. Then Gary said, "So what you're saying is J.F.K., Jr. signed a copy of the Jackie O. auction catalog for Howard?" I said, "That's right." Unfortunately I didn't know when to quit. I said, "He signed it for Howard, but he didn't know it was for Howard Stern." Gary was confused.

I told him that the inscription read "Howard, get well soon! By the way, steer clear of convertibles — they're too exposed. Hardtops are much safer. — John Kennedy." Gary said, "How did you get him to write that?" Wow! Gary was going for the bait. This was great! I started in with my bogus brother getting sunburned in a convertible story. When I mentioned the word "Florida" something clicked in Gary's brain. In fact, his brain even seemed to make an audible popping sound. At that instant we both knew that I had boldly, stupidly, overplayed my hand. Gary said something about getting back to me, but we both knew that the game was over. What was wrong with me? Talk about repeating myself. I should have said my bogus brother was driving in California, Hawaii or Ethiopia. Anywhere but Florida. During my Emmy scam Howard had said, "Don't mangrove me!" Sound advice — I should have followed it.

In retrospect, the most amazing part of this stillborn scam was that I was even willing to try it. Not because it might fail, but because it might succeed. What would have happened if Marvin Shanken had heard me besmirch his priceless humidor? Would he tell his art directors not to hire me again? Would I be sued for humidor libel? For ten years I had worked on his magazines. They represented about thirty percent of my income. Was I really willing to gamble all this away in exchange for a few minutes on-air with Howard? Was I that bored? Or was I going through a very early mid-life crisis? Perhaps my assistant Josh had said it best, "Don't let Howard Stern take you down."

CHAPTER 9

MEL-O-DRAMA

When Howard Stern was a little boy his father gave him a puppet theater to encourage his creativity. It was one of Howard's favorite toys. He loved to play God with his puppets, making the puppets do whatever he desired. The puppet theater let Howard act out his strange fantasies which were already in full bloom. It's been said that his parents were unaware of the extent of Howard's macabre imagination.

During Howard's grade school years, his Roosevelt, Long Island hometown took center stage in America's experiments with integration. The stress of being a lab rat accentuated Howard's less socially acceptable personality traits. In the sixties, kids like Howard Stern vented by making their toy puppets fornicate. Today, the troubled youths of this cauldron of neuroses are not so easily placated. The sweet puppets of yesteryear have been replaced by the vicious pit bulls of today, a phenomenon which has resulted in daily displays of dead dogs along the tree-lined streets of Howard's boyhood burg.

You can take the boy out of Roosevelt, but you can't take Roosevelt out of the boy. Howard frequently admits that he loves to hear people fighting like pit bulls, that he loves to listen to two guys fighting, and that he could listen to such fights all day.

My fanaticism as a fan, coupled with my impressionability and eagerness to entertain my hero, Howard Stern, resulted in a real life melodrama of my own. It began innocently enough, but quickly became a nightmare. Looking back on the whole affair, it is easy to compare the events to a tragi-comedy fit for the Broadway stage. Since the central character in this non-fiction tale goes by the stage name of Melrose Larry Green, I have titled this chapter *Mel-O-Drama*.

Over the past several years, I have laughed along as Howard has mocked Melrose on-air, characterizing him as a "mental patient" worthy of contempt.

Whether or not Melrose really deserves this treatment is almost beside the point. The fact of the matter is that Howard's show treats guests in one of three ways. If the guest is a celebrity who supports the show, Howard rolls out the red carpet, knowing that his own stock goes up when he rubs elbows with a big name. On the next rung of the evolutionary ladder of guestdom sits the beautiful stripper — or any beautiful woman for that matter — who lets Howard display his trademark sense of naughty humor, treating her with equal parts of affection and lust. Anyone who does not fall into these guest categories is deemed an annoying idiot. This is Howard's formula for successful radio. And Melrose is at the bottom of the entertainment ladder.

THE HOWARD STERN GUEST LADDER

Top rung — Celebrity Guests
(Howard wouldn't like to have sex with):

Alec Baldwin
Jim Carrey
Ivan Reitman
Arnold Schwarzenegger
Male Rock Stars

Middle rung — Strippers
(Howard would like to have sex with):

Elaina Beastie
Jenna Jameson
Amy Lynn
Tempest

Below the middle rung — Famous Women
(Howard would like to have sex with):

Carol Alt
Pamela Anderson
Nicole Eggert
Jessica Hahn
Teri Hatcher
Heather Locklear

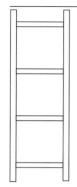
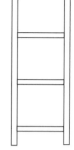

Bottom of the ladder —
(People Howard wouldn't like to have sex with):

Marv Albert
First-time callers
Melrose Larry Green
Annoying Idiots
Dan Wagner

My first direct exposure to Melrose was on the Prodigy Howard Stern Fan Club Bulletin Board. Melrose, in an effort to attract attention, had chosen the path of unrelentingly obnoxious behavior. The more he bragged about his on-air relationship with Howard Stern, the more his Prodigy brethren responded with aggression. Melrose needs attention to such a pathological degree that he is willing to take it in whatever form he can get it, and he will do *anything* to prolong his exposure to the limelight.

Sometime during the month of February, 1996 Melrose posted his home phone number on Prodigy. The management at Prodigy advises against doing this for obvious reasons. Eventually, I decided to see if the phone number was the real thing. It was.

Melrose announced in his Prodigy post that he was in the early stages of writing his life story. When I first spoke to Melrose I told him that I, too, was writing a book about my experiences as a Howard Stern fan. Even though Melrose had been forewarned, his colossal ego prevented him from taking my efforts seriously.

I once asked Melrose if his behavior was a conscious effort to get people to hate him. Melrose told me that this was not the case, and yet he freely described himself as being one of the most hated Howard Stern Fans.

Melrose Larry Green

Melrose constantly contradicts himself. This is what he said to me at a later date: "They're (the Prodigy Fan Club members) just a miserable group of people. They hide behind the anonymity of the keyboard. You don't have to reveal your true identity. It's kind of like driving on the freeways! The reason why I'm doing all this fucking attacking is to get stuff for the book. That's why I'm doing all these insults to people. Telling people to change their tampons, squat on me, kiss my ass.... That's the reason. They're all falling for it, those dumb asses. The best thing to do is just ignore me." In fact, when Melrose was told that everyone hates him while on-air during the Howard Stern show, he responded "I'm a loser that the whole country knows. A loser known all over America!" I rest my case.

Melrose is at his best when under attack or threat of attack. Howard Stern recognizes this, which is why he allows his employees and interns to hassle and otherwise torment him. Melrose always plays into the hands of his tormentors. The funny thing is that his tormentors need only tell the truth and make accurate assessments of Melrose's odd behavior, to set him off.

Melrose Larry Green

I had always entertained the hope of taping Melrose while he expressed his true feelings about Howard Stern. After talking with Melrose on an almost bimonthly basis I eventually struck gold. On June 6, 1996 I finally got my chance. Melrose was in a foul mood. His anger was due to fact that the *Howard Stern Show* wasn't returning his calls. After years of being on Howard's show and holding up signs about Howard on Melrose Avenue, Melrose had come to feel he deserves V.I.P. treatment. He needed to vent — and not just about Howard Stern.

Unfortunately for me, the first thing he wanted to discuss was his sex life, which according to him consists primarily of watching pornographic videotapes. Melrose informed me that he recently rented one of Howard Stern's personal favorites, a blockbuster called *Breast Torture*. I asked him how many times he pleasured himself to this tape and he proudly replied, "twice." Melrose's honesty encouraged me to delve further. I fearlessly inquired what sex act he liked to watch best. Melrose responded with, "That's an excellent question. That's almost as good as Lenny Bruce." I was flattered. As for Melrose's favorite position, the answer is — "doggy-style." Woof-woof!

There is such a thing as too much information. Melrose was on a roll. He could hardly wait to reveal his fondness for a cum-shot on a girl's face — especially if her eyes are open. Melrose was making me nauseous. He even coined an expression for this sex act — "a corneal abrasion of cum." Seeing as he was such an expert, I asked him if he had ever experienced this himself. Evidently, he hadn't. He made me laugh when he replied, "My sex life is limited, believe me. It's mostly based on what I've rented from the video store." This is one voyeur who makes Pee-Wee Herman look squeaky clean.

I began to believe that Melrose was pulling my leg — if not his "pud." Perhaps Melrose was just trying out some new comedy material on me. He occasionally opens for Jackie Mason, so my thoughts were not that farfetched. Nonetheless, I decided to press on by asking him the following questions:

Q) How many videos does Melrose rent per week?
A) Two per day. "It's like vitamins."
Q) Does Melrose have a girlfriend?
A) Yes, "But girls in L.A. are too concerned with their careers."
Q) How many "loads" does Melrose drop a week?
A) "I don't do it that often. I swear to God!"
Q) If Melrose got divorced in California, would his video machine get half his assets?
A) "I think so! For me group sex is three videotapes!"
Q) Has Melrose ever gone to a hooker?
A) Once, "sixteen years ago", and it was "terrible." He doesn't even remember her name. And no, he didn't kiss her on the mouth. But on the good side, it only cost "$50.00."

After listening to Melrose discuss his pathetic sex life I advised him to "talk to Howard about that on the radio. It would be interesting." Well, it would.

Melrose has opinions on everything, even wives. Melrose believes that Fred Norris's wife Allison is the cutest *Stern Show* wife. He's smitten with her. As far as

Melrose is concerned, the other wives aren't even in her league. To put it bluntly, Melrose told me, "Allison is "a piece-of-ass! She's got a great body! Oh yeah!"

As for Fred Norris, Melrose compares his reclusive nature to that of Bob Dylan. To hear Melrose tell it, Fred is Jesus Christ incarnate. Melrose loves to lay it on thick. He proceeded to inform me that, "Howard Stern knows that if Fred left him, he'd have no show."

To the same degree that Melrose loves Fred, he hates Jackie Martling, even though he's been known to label Jackie a genius. Melrose continued his diatribe about Jackie's extra large ego. At this point I knew what was coming next. Melrose invoked the *Stern Show* anthem and loudly exclaimed, "F-Jackie!" It was quite a speech. I wonder if Melrose had been the class valedictorian at Brandeis.

Loyalty is a frequent topic on Howard's show. Melrose claimed to "love Howard" but could hardly wait to bash him too. "I don't think he wears a wig. He might have a little weave." Talking to Melrose is worse than a bad hair day.

When it comes to Melrose's sexual orientation things are slightly less confusing. I asked him if anyone thought he might be gay. Melrose responded, "Yeah, people say I'm gay. People are fucking disgusting! You're one of the few nice guys I've met on the show." On the one hand, I was relieved that Melrose isn't gay, but on the other hand I was slightly worried that he might be coming on to me.

Eventually, we got to the subject that Melrose really wanted to discuss — Gary Dell'Abate, a.k.a. Baba Booey. Melrose was incensed that Gary wouldn't return his calls. He'd even written up what he would do if Gary didn't behave. Without my having to ask he said, "If I don't get a plug or a mention before the book signing, and within five working days of the show — I'm going to try and get on Imus!" Ever the troublemaker, I suggested that he put his ultimatum in a letter and send it to Gary. Unfortunately, Melrose didn't want to send a letter because he felt that Gary would think he was just kidding around.

Melrose seemed to be getting angrier by the second. In fact, it wasn't long before I managed to record the following:

Melrose: "That's my plan B, you see. If they diss me on this book. Which they might. I know how Howard is."

Dan: "Well, they didn't let you use his name, so..."

Melrose Larry Green

Melrose: "Good, all right. How do you spell Imus? I-M-U-S. Hello, good morning Don. How are you Don? It's an honor to be on. Melrose Larry Green, how are you? I'm a big fan of yours, Don. You know, you're the original. Everybody stole from you Don. Don Imus, Donkey Kong forever. (*Singing*) Imus in the morning. Hahahahahahaha!"

Dan: (*Laughs*)

Melrose: "Believe me, I have no allegiance to anybody. As quickly as I went from Peter Tilden (*another radio personality*) to Howard, I can go to Don Imus in a heart-beat. If Don Imus gives me air time, I'm there for him. Jackie Mason goes on Imus all the time. So does Clinton..."

Dan: "Oh, right."

Melrose: "...as in President."

Dan: "Yeah."

Melrose: "Howard gets Roger, and Don Imus gets Bill!"

Melrose Larry Green

Melrose can be such a turncoat. He went on to tell me that despite abysmal ratings, Don Imus airs in more cities than Howard Stern. All Melrose wanted to do was bash Howard. He even mentioned that people on the street have said to him, "Imus rules! and Stern sucks!" As if this weren't enough, Melrose committed the ultimate blasphemy and said, "Imus has got an incredible following." Sheesh, someone ought to give Melrose a urine test. I think he may have been smoking something.

Melrose can be so delusional. He actually believes that Howard would fire Gary if he interfered with his relationship with Howard. The threats went on unabated.

Melrose: "Am I going to start begging for air time? I'm going to give him (*Gary*) a week after my book signing. If I don't hear my name on the show by the following Friday after my book signing — that's a whole week later — (*singing*) 'Imus in the morning!' That's going to be the greatest story of 1996. What happens is Melrose Larry Green goes on Imus. I guarantee you it's crossed Howard's mind. I guarantee you Howard's thinking 'Is there any shot at all of Melrose going on Imus?' — he would fucking die! That would make him angrier than anything in the world. Because Howard is the only one that ever gave me a break in the beginning. But now, I don't need Howard anymore. I want to go back on Howard. You see I can't possibly lose. I'm trying to get on Howard's air-time. I'm not a schmuck. What am I supposed to do? Sit around like one of Howard's useless girls if I don't get air time?

And another thing, is that Howard told me I'm in the movie (*Private Parts*). If I don't get in the movie, you know what that means? *60 Minutes*! I'll go on their show. It's brilliant! It's brilliant! It's fucking genius."

Wow! What a grip on reality! The next thing I expected to come out of Melrose's mouth was that if he didn't get on Howard's show he would discover the cure for AIDS just to spite Gary. My chat with Melrose was pure dynamite. I was proud of my interviewing skills. After all, they were modeled after those of my hero — Howard Stern.

Melrose Larry Green

Later the same day Melrose called me back. Evidently, he hadn't gotten all of his frustrations out of his system. He proceeded to tell me that Howard's assistant Ralph Cirella had taken some sort of "monastic vow" of loyalty to Howard, and that together with Steve Grillo they provide all the friendship that Howard requires. At this point Melrose got ugly. He told me, "These two guys are the most despicable guys in humanity! They are parasites. Gorilla is a fucking douchebag! Gorilla goes around refereeing things."

I didn't know what to say. The only thing I could think of mentioning to Melrose was his friendly relationship with Jackie Mason. This usually calms him down. I think Melrose was grateful for the change of subject.

Melrose: "Jackie's (Mason) the greatest guy of all time. Mason is the fucking funniest guy in the world. You know what he calls Stern? — The Meshugana! He says 'You still going on the Meshugana's program?' By the way, Jackie Mason and Imus are good friends. He can get me on Imus in a second. That's how I can get on Imus. Jackie Mason. That's my contact."

Melrose's emotional outbursts had taken their toll. I thought he should lie down or take some medication. However, Melrose had a better idea. When he needs to relax he does the thing that he enjoys most in life — holding up signs with Howard's name on them. What a character. Even though he was mad at Howard, he still wanted to hold up signs. I couldn't resist baiting him a little bit.

Melrose: "Listen, I got to go out and hold up signs."
Dan: "For who?"
Melrose: "I'm out on Melrose (Avenue) at 7:30AM every day."
Dan: "What's your sign say today? Does your sign say Howard on it?"
Melrose: "No. No."
Dan: "So you're not holding Howard signs up anymore?"
Melrose: "No! I'm not holding Howard signs up until I get some air time! I can't believe Howard. Fuck Howard! Fuck Howard! And fuck Gary! Unless I get on the show I'm never going to hold up another sign for Howard. I mean really, I don't need that. I'm not a retard! If Howard gives me some mentions, I'll hold up a sign — but that's the way I am with my signs. I don't put that in my book, but that's the way I am. If they boycott me, I boycott them! I could start tomorrow with an Imus sign if I wanted to. And you know something? — I think I will. It's easy to write. I-M-U-S. It's easier than Stern! I may just do that. Imus signs. Maybe I'll do that right before my book signing. That's a brilliant idea. Maybe at my book signing I'll have Imus signs all over the place. If I don't hear from Baba Booey — Imus rules! (*singing*) Imus in the morning."
(*Take it from me — Melrose is no Mel Torme!*)

I couldn't believe that Melrose had actually said, "Fuck Howard!" And not just once, but twice. Melrose was having a bad mental health day indeed. Even his "girlfriend" was giving him troubles. He confessed to me that he had been considering breaking up with her. When I asked why, he told me that she's not really his girlfriend. I was confused. Melrose clarified the matter by explaining that his "girlfriend" was avoiding him. I couldn't imagine why. Melrose told me that he pays her monthly rent to the tune of

Melrose Larry Green

$750.00. I immediately replied, "That sounds like she's a mistress? Or a kept woman? She's a concubine!" Melrose tried to debate the issue, but ultimately, even he had to concede my point by saying, "She's going to be ex-concubine pretty soon." I found Melrose's comments hilarious. With an inquisitive mind and noth-

ing better to do I pursued
the issue.

Dan: "Do you have sex?"
Melrose: "Well, a little bit,
but not much. Just blow-
jobs."
Dan: (*Trying to hold back
tears of sympathy and laughter.*) "And how many times
does she give you oral sex a
month?"
Melrose: "Oh, it's not your
business, man."

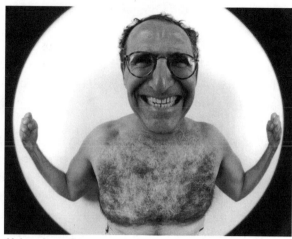

Melrose Larry Green

Dan: "I just wanted to know how much it was costing per (blow) job!"
Melrose: "I see, that's a good point — too much!"

I couldn't believe all the amazing things Melrose had just told me. My head was spinning. After months of laying the groundwork, Melrose finally spilled the beans. From time to time in the past Melrose had made various comments that gave me inklings to his inner workings, but nothing like this. This was the mother lode! Too bad Melrose isn't always this honest. If he were, he could get on-air twice a week.

During this conversation Melrose had complained about not being able to get on Howard's show. Melrose believed there was a diabolical plot afoot to deny him access to Howard. Truth was, Melrose didn't have anything new to say. Howard takes his job and his listeners too seriously to risk boring them for the sake of pla-cating his regular guests.

Thinking about all this gave me an idea. Perhaps I could help Melrose and Howard at the same time. If I gave Howard the tape of Melrose bad-mouthing him, then Howard would have something to talk to Melrose about, and in the process Melrose would be truly entertaining. I didn't think Howard would get mad at Melrose because he already knows that Melrose is a nut-case and expects this kind of behavior from him anyway.

After a lengthy deliberation (ten seconds), I decided to give the Stern Show a call and see if they were interested. Stuttering John answered the phone. He asked me to play him some of the tape over the phone, which I did. Then he told me that the tape was great and that it would probably be a great angle for getting Melrose on the show.

Viewed in this light, I decided to give the tape to the *Howard Stern Show* and see what would happen. Within a few days I received a call from Howard's producer, Gary Dell'Abate.

Gary: "So, I listened to your tape. I thank you very much for sending it."
Dan: "You're welcome."
Gary: "Now, how do you come to chat with Melrose? Do you chat with him on a regular basis? Or is this like a one-time thing?"
Dan: "I chat with him on a regular basis. Sometimes he posts things on Prodigy, and I respond. But Melrose got really angry when Stuttering John called him and told him he'd heard part of the tape. He called up my house and pretended he was from the Howard Stern Show, and spoke to my wife and my daughter. And he started going really cuckoo. He started yelling at her and stuff. Then he called me up at work and started yelling at me."
Gary: "Here's my question. There's two big favors I want to ask you. A: Can I have permission to play it on the air? B: Can you not mention that you sent it to me? Or, if he calls you, don't mention that we spoke. I was listening to the tape the whole way home in my car on Friday afternoon. I was going to call you over the weekend. **I was totally fucking fascinated!** The only problem with the tape is that it's not — the quality of it isn't that great for broadcast, but I'll pull enough clips from it to make it work. Don't say anything to him, and I appreciate it, Dan. Thanks a lot."

My fantastic voyage along the path of Stern enlightenment had come far indeed! First there were my faxed contributions to Howard's show, then came my Emmy scam and live performance with Howard. Now, I had finally reached the stage where I was not only performing on-air with Howard, but I was also contributing material, and pointing out new ways to use old guests to Howard's staff.

Thanks to my excellent undercover work, I got a second opportunity to appear with my hero — Howard Stern on June 26, 1996. However this time it was on the phone instead of in the studio. Gary Dell'Abate had been busy getting

Melrose Larry Green

Melrose Larry Green

things organized for the perfect Melrose ambush.

Robin: "It's time to clean house. We need a new set of kooks."
Howard: "Put him on the line. Yeah, we need a new set of kooks. All right. Here we go. Are you ready? Is that Melrose? Is someone going to get him on?"

From previous conversations with Gary and Melrose, I knew that today was the big day. For this reason I arrived at work early, loaded a fresh tape in my stereo, cooked up some microwave popcorn, sat in my favorite chair, and waited for the fun to begin. When I heard Howard start to introduce Melrose I immediately called the show. From this point on, I was connected, live, via phone to the show. I deliberately remained quiet until the opportunity to contribute to the on-air mayhem presented itself.

Robin: "He doesn't really have much to say. He's gotten a lot of air time for somebody who has very little to say."
Howard: "Yeah, and he's not funny or anything, but he runs around California with signs that say 'Howard Stern is God!' and stuff. And it was always kind of funny, so we let him come on and say some stuff."
Gary: "He's always been bad-mouthing me and John, but now you!"
Howard: "Yeah, this is your final appearance Melrose, for real!"
Melrose: "Oh, really?"
Howard: "Yeah. You're done with the show."
Gary: "Banned for life!"

Of all the people on the *Stern Show*, I think Gary hates Melrose the most. Although Melrose is entertaining, he's also exhausting. As

Melrose Larry Green

the producer of the number one radio show in America, Gary's plate is overflowing. Consequently, he seldom has enough time to administer to Melrose's needs. From the sound of Gary's voice it was clear that he was relishing Melrose's downfall. Of course, Melrose could never really be banned from the *Stern Show*. What Wack Pack would be complete without Melrose?

Melrose tried to pretend that he didn't know why he was being banned. When Howard informed him that he had tapes of Melrose bad-mouthing him, Melrose feigned innocence and asked, "What tapes?" Howard was enjoying listening to Melrose squirm.

Melrose Larry Green

Howard: "You know what tapes."
Melrose: "I don't know what tapes."
Howard: "Did you do an interview with a guy? And did you bad-mouth me?"
Melrose: "No. No."
Howard: "All right. Are you ready to hear it? I'm going to play it for you. Let's see how you respond to the charges. Here's Melrose Larry Green being interviewed for some magazine or something."

At this point Howard played a few segments from the tapes I'd sent him of Melrose bad-mouthing him. As soon as the tapes were finished Melrose lied to Howard and said, "That whole thing was a set-up! It was a sting." Robin laughed and asked Melrose if the F.B.I. was involved, too. Gary put in his own two cents by telling Howard that there was much more damaging material on the tapes. Howard asked him what else Melrose had said. Gary replied, "Well, the quality of the tape wasn't that good. But basically he says that he has no allegiance to you, he's using us for air time. That he just created this character so he could get on, and he could go somewhere else — no problem. I'm an idiot. You're an idiot. Imus is the king."

It looked as though Melrose was trapped. Luckily for Melrose he's a resourceful and excellent liar. Melrose told Howard that he had set me up with what he called, "bobbeh meissehs" (pronounced, BOH-beh My-seh in Yiddish). Bobbeh meissehs are made up stories. Evidently, Melrose expected Howard to believe that he wasn't serious when he had bad-mouthed him. Unfortunately for Melrose, Howard wasn't buying any of it. The funny thing is that it's actually possible. Maybe Melrose wanted air time so badly that he deliberately bad-mouthed Howard. Melrose is clearly capable of anything.

I could tell that Howard was enjoying the conversation immensely. In the days and weeks that followed, the word "bobbeh meisseh" became a part of Howard's vocabulary. He even used it during a press conference. Howard likes to throw out non-sequitors to test his audience's intelligence and to see if they're paying attention.

Gary didn't want to let Melrose off the hook too easily.

Melrose Larry Green

Gary: "And then also you (*Melrose*) said that Howard had a hair weave!"
Howard: "Did you say I had a hair weave? You're not supposed to tell anybody that!"
Robin: "When you're in on such inside information, you're supposed to keep quiet."
Melrose: "I didn't know that Howard had a hair weave."
Howard: "But then again, Melrose is kind of retarded. Don't you expect this kind of behavior?"
Gary: "He talks to a lot of wackos, and they think that he's an authority on you."
Howard: "All right. Go ahead. I don't know why you (*Melrose*) amuse me, but you do."

Melrose continued to plead with Howard and claim that it was all a set up. Howard let it go on for quite awhile. Melrose tried to polish his tarnished image by saying, "Howard, I love the show!" But Howard was not so easily placated. Acting regally he told Melrose, "You had better prove it." Poor Melrose. Things went from bad to worse. Foolishly he had been quoted in *The Daily News Book Review* saying that he hardly listens to the *Stern Show* anymore. Talk about bad-timing.

Howard loves to have people call in to the show whenever he is crucifying someone. This time was no exception.

Howard: "Here's Captain Janks. He wants to yell at you."
Melrose: "Screw Captain Janks!"
Captain: "Melrose, you know what? You are a piece of crap!"

For the next few minutes Captain Janks tied Melrose to the proverbial mizzen-mast and whipped him mercilessly. Melrose fought back valiantly and managed to score quite a few points. His best point was when he told Janks that he pumped gas for a living. Janks tried to counter attack with some demeaning remarks about Melrose's mother's skeleton. Howard and the gang enjoyed the fight so much that Captain Janks was even rewarded with his own *Stern Show F-Emmy Award* at a later date.

Melrose: "Janks, you and Dan Wagner can float off a boat together."
Howard: "Well, here's Dan. Let me put Dan on. Dan is the guy who spoke to you on the phone. Dan, are you there?"
Dan: "Yeah, I'm here, Howard."

I proceeded to inform Howard that Melrose, in a desperate attempt to find out if I gave Gary the tape of him bad-mouthing Howard, had called my home and told my wife that he was from the *Stern Show*. Melrose tried to deflect the truth by falsely announcing on-air that my wife wanted to leave me. This made Howard nervous. The last thing he wanted was to be sued for defamation of character. I put the matter to rest by telling Melrose, "Oh sure! Keep on making up stuff."

I decided that if Melrose was going to fight dirty, then so would I.

Dan: "Melrose told me that he has some woman and he pays her rent and stuff."
Melrose: "Yeah."
Dan: "He has a concubine!"
Gary: "Melrose and his imaginary girlfriend."
Dan: (*edited from live broadcast*) "Hey Howard, Melrose told me that he watched porno movies throughout the writing of his book, and he wacked-

Captain Janks

off after every chapter!"

Melrose: "That one's true. That's the first thing that you said that's true! I love porno!"

Howard and his crew were laughing like madmen. After a few moments Captain Janks decided to rejoin the fray and get in a few more licks at Melrose's expense. Earlier in the conversation Melrose had complained that Captain Janks had told everyone about his mother's death several years earlier. According to Melrose his mother left him over a million dollars. Howard loves dead mother humor. Therefore, I judged that the time was ripe for introducing the topic of Melrose's bad mother related behavior on Prodigy.

Dan: "Melrose, you can't complain about mothers and stuff. I mean, what did you say to that Prodigy member whose daughter died? You wished her a Happy Mother's Day and made fun of her."

Melrose: "She was making fun of my mother's dying for months, and months, and months. So finally her daughter died, and I told her to call the show. That's all."

Howard: "It gets so fascinating that I can't hang-up."

Melrose believed that my on-air comments were deliberately cruel and mean-spirited. Too bad Melrose, a self-proclaimed fan of the show, doesn't understand that this is how Howard's show operates. Controversy and on-air fights keep Howard's ratings in the stratosphere. Melrose on the run is fun. I truly believe that this was his best appearance ever.

Fortunately for Melrose, I was there to act as a tummeler and keep the ball rolling whenever Howard was about to hang-up on him.

One of my favorite moments of the conversation was when Captain Janks called Melrose a loser, and Melrose replied, "I'm a loser that the whole country knows. A loser known all over America!" How true. Revealing too. Melrose doesn't care if people like him — he just wants to be

Melrose Larry Green

famous.

I was having a great time kibitzing with Howard. Unfortunately, I could tell that Howard was ready to end the conversation. For this reason I played my trump card and told Howard that I believed Melrose's inheritance might be a big scam. This really got Melrose's dander up. Howard howled when Melrose told the audience to call Paine Weber if they didn't believe him. Silly Melrose even gave out his lawyer's name on-air. Melrose mentioned that although he hadn't received the inheritance yet, he had somehow paid the taxes on it. This sounded fishy to me. Even Gary was suspicious.

At the time of our conversation O.J. Simpson was about to host a benefit party at his Rockingham Estate. Melrose told Howard that he was going to buy a $1,000 ticket. Howard requested that Melrose call the show if he was able to get into O.J.'s house. I found it amazing that Melrose had managed to weasel his way back on the show. It was the shortest banishment that I've ever witnessed. Melrose was thrilled. However, his glee was not to last long. I was not through with him yet. It was time to get even for his saying that my wife was planning on leaving me.

Dan: "Hey Melrose, if we exhumed your mother's body..."
Melrose: "Hey Dan, Dan, Dan.
Howard: "Wait, let Dan finish."
Dan: "...and gave her tests for arsenic, would we find out that you killed her?"
Captain: "I already did. She's right here!"
Dan: "Did you poison your mother, Mel?"
Howard: (*Laughing in hysterics*)
Jackie: "Ohhhhhh!"
Gary: "Wow!!!!"
Captain: "I already exhumed her body. She's right here!"

Melrose tried to change the subject. He told Howard that he got a bit part in Whoopi Goldberg's movie *Eddie*. Howard was incredulous. Robin piped in with, "You put it over the top!" I love Robin's dry wit. As for Howard — he wanted to return to the topic of Melrose's mother. I think Jackie Martling must have passed him a few mother jokes during the *Eddie* talk.

Howard: "Hey Captain Janks, you got Melrose's mother in your house?"
Captain: "Yep! She's right here. The skeleton and bones are in my basement!"
Howard: "Really? Is her skull on tight?"
Jackie: "Oh!!!"
Melrose: (*Laughs*) "Ah, Jesus!"

Dan: "We're bringing Melrose's mother to the next Chat Party!"
Howard: (*Laughs hysterically and pounds on his desk!*)
Robin: (*Laughs fit to loosen her high colonic tubes!*)
Melrose: (*Laughs*) "Oh, you guys! Dan, you know you're actually amusing me now, Dan!"

I was very proud of my Chat Party crack. Melrose continued to amuse Howard by mentioning that he was videotaping himself talking on the phone. Evidently Melrose was hoping that Howard would use the tape on his *E!* show. Hey, I wish I'd thought of that.

Howard: "All right. Good-bye."
Melrose: "Hey, Howard, you rule! How was my segment? Okay?"
Howard: "All right. Thank you."
Robin: "Good-bye."
Howard: "How was my segment! Well... Janks claims to be having sex with Melrose's mother's skull!"
Jackie: "Wow!"
Howard: "I wonder if you need lube with that?"
Jackie: "Why do you call them the Wack Pack?"
Howard: "That's a little glimpse. So for those of you who are new listeners, those are some of the guys who, just like — they sort of satellite the show. They hang around the show and have different things going on."
Robin: "Yeah. Their lives revolve around the show."
Howard: "Yeah. They're very committed to listening to this show, and they're always falling out."
Robin: "All their friendships have to do with this show."
Howard: "And from time to time they bad-mouth me, and then they come back. How could you be mad? These guys are all wacky! If they're not wacky, then why would you have them on the show?"

Wow, what an experience! I felt as though I'd just run a marathon. I can't imagine how Howard does it. Dealing with so much emotion on a daily basis for four hours or more at a clip must be unbelievably exhausting.

I knew that Melrose would call at any moment. I wondered what his take on our joint Howard Stern appearance would be. I didn't have to wait long. Melrose was furious. He felt that I had ruined his radio career. I tried talking some sense into him with no success. As the day wore on, Melrose got angrier and angrier. My ears were sore from fielding his calls. Eventually, he blew his stack and threatened to kill me. I was really freaked out. I've never had anyone threaten me with death before. I know being a Howard Stern fan has its price, but as obsessed as I am, I'm not willing to risk my life for Howard — especially if I'm not drawing a paycheck. I felt like Salman Rushdie.

Sometimes the chickens come home to roost. My advice to fellow Howard Stern fans and wannabees is: When dealing with nut cases use an alias and get an unlisted phone number. As for Melrose, I think that his reaction was way out of proportion to the situation. My interactions with him were completely Howard Stern-like in nature. He should have recognized the fact that I helped him contribute to the show, and in the process gave him what he craves the most — a chance to be the focus of attention while on-air with Howard.

After getting the death threat from Melrose, I called up Howard's show and tried to speak to Gary about it. Gary never returned my phone calls. I tried getting through to him for several days in a row. Eventually, I realized I was on my own. When Gary needed my permission to air my tape of Melrose, he was instantly reachable. Once Gary's needs were satisfied, he was through with me. I was beginning to sympathize with Melrose's appraisal of Gary's lack of character. Frankly, I'm surprised that I was surprised. However, what really hurt was the fact that once my hero (Howard Stern) got what he wanted from me, he just left me high and dry without so much as a thank you or tender word.

To facilitate a truce, and possibly help reestablish our previous friendly relationship, I decided to apologize to Melrose on-air. Truth was, oddball or not, I missed Melrose's unique take on life and Howard Stern. Perhaps the expression birds of a feather flock together is really true. This thought gives me the chills.

Thanks to my uncovering the fact that Melrose was paying the rent for his girlfriend / "concubine", he was able to get back on the air. Gary

Melrose Larry Green

always needs an angle to get Melrose on the show. On July 25, 1996 Melrose was invited to the studio. Howard, utilizing my information, ambushed Melrose with a surprise call-in by Melrose's "concubine", Kim. It was an entertaining segment. Howard quizzed Melrose at length about his sex life. By the time Howard was through with him I started to believe that Melrose would have to leave the country to get a date.

Melrose Larry Green

Howard: "Kim wants to go on record and say that she and Melrose Larry Green have never had sex! Kim, have you ever kissed him?"
Kim: "Of course."
Robin: "Like a friend?"
Howard: "And have you ever had sex with him?"
Kim: "We are the best buddies."
Howard: "But you don't give him sex?"
Kim: "No, hun."
Gary: "And does he pay your rent and stuff?"
Kim: (*Laughs*) "He helps me out." (*That's it Kim. Good girl. You don't want to rock the boat and mess up a good thing! But just for the record - we're on to your little scam.*)
Melrose: "I pay her rent. Yes."
Gary: "Exactly!"

Howard was clearly in his element. The thing that seemed to impress him the most was the fact that Melrose, a reported millionaire, couldn't get a woman to have sex with him. Howard kept repeating, "That is pathetic!" He even asked Kim how much Melrose was paying for her company.

Kim: "He gives me about a thousand."
Howard: "A thousand a month?"
Kim: "Uh-huh."

Robin: "Wow!"

Melrose: "A cell phone also."

Gary asked Kim if she'd ever been in *Hustler* magazine. Kim admitted that she had been. That Kim is a class act all the way. I thought that the word "hun" was a dead giveaway. Gary summed up everyone's thoughts when he said, "What's more degrading? Getting nude, or taking money from Melrose Larry Green for your rent?" Gary's also very practical. He asked Melrose, "Do you realize that for a thousand dollars a month, five times a month, you can get a two-hundred-dollar-a-night hooker?" I think this is Gary's concept of the new math. Personally, I would love to be a fly on the wall when he teaches his son, Jackson, how to add and subtract.

Stuttering John wasn't interested in my Henry Kissinger mission of peace. In fact, he refused to put me through to Howard. It was only after I agreed to make the death threats the focus of my call that Stuttering John finally relented and put me through. My darker side was considering calming Melrose down on-air and then telling him that his mother wore Army boots, but the "segment" ended before I had the opportunity. Thank goodness!

Melrose Larry Green

Howard: "Here's a guy who hates you Melrose. Is this Dan?"

Dan: "Yes, hi."

Howard: "Quickly, what is it?"

Dan: "Well I just wanted to ask Melrose if he was still serious about the death threats he made to me. I'd like to apologize to him for upsetting him, I didn't realize that he would be so upset."

Melrose: "Oh, I was serious. I was serious, but I'll accept your apology."

Howard: "You made a death threat? Are you going around making death threats to people?"

Melrose: "Well, this guy..."

Gary: "Hold on. This is the guy that gave us the tape of him trashing you."

Howard: "Right."

Gary: "So then, after that day, he started calling the guy's house and leaving death threats!"

Howard: "Really?"

Melrose: "The guy was making fun of my mother."

Dan: "I had to have my home phone number changed to an unlisted number."

Howard: "You had to have your home phone number changed?"

Melrose: "That means you're famous, Dan!"

Howard: "What did Melrose say to you?"

Melrose: "They weren't death threats."

Dan: "He said 'that he was going to shoot me and blow my effing brains out!'"

Melrose: "Bobbeh meissehs! Bobbeh meissehs! That's not true!"

Howard: "He's going to shoot you and blow your effing brains out?"

Melrose: "I want to hear a tape of that Dan."

(Melrose: "Dan! Dan! Dan! I will fucking kill you! That's a threat! You hear me? You better watch your fucking back! I'm going to blow your fucking brains out! — And I'm not kidding, Dan!" — 6/26/96 3:30PM)

Dan: "But the thing is, I actually like Melrose. I just want to say that I think Melrose is an interesting person, and I hope that I didn't upset him too much because..." *(Click! Howard hung-up on me! My leader had wanted blood and I'd given him flowers. Once I was a vicious attack dog, and now I've become a tame house pet. Oh well. Perhaps if Howard had given me a little more air time I might have told Melrose that his mom wore Army boots!)*

Howard: *(To Melrose)* "All right. You know what? You gotta get out of here. I can't get caught up in your world. Come on. Stop it. Stop it! Stop it! Now you're being abusive. All right. Thank you Melrose Larry Green. Hey, your microphone's off. Take him outta here, Gary! The guy's a mental patient!"

The following day I gathered up my courage and decided to see Melrose in person at his New York book signing on West 33rd Street. Since Melrose was sooooo terribly offended by my comments about his mother, I decided not to arrive unarmed. As a precaution, I brought along a sympathy card to console him over his mother's death, and a four dollar bouquet of flowers from the local Korean grocer as a peace offering. Melrose took one look at me and laughed. What could he say? That's show biz!

To mend old wounds, Melrose even treated me to lunch at a Kin Yips, a nearby Chinese restaurant. Never able to resist being the purveyor of information about Howard Stern, Melrose shared this comment of Howard's which had been uttered to him during a commercial break the previous day: "Listening to Melrose talk about his relationships with women, is like listening to a person who plays wheelchair basketball talk about basketball."

THE MELROSE TRUTH TEST

1) He once ran for Mayor of Los Angeles and got over 1,000 votes.   T ❑ F ❑

2) He graduated from Brandeis and Cornell universities.   T ❑ F ❑

3) He's a virgin.   T ❑ F ❑

4) His father, Dr. Irving J. Greenblatt was a famous scientist.   T ❑ F ❑

5) His mother, Augusta Greenblatt co-authored numerous award winning books on medicine with his father.   T ❑ F ❑

6) He danced in one of Madonna's music videos.   T ❑ F ❑

7) He's a retard.   T ❑ F ❑

8) He thinks O.J. is not guilty.   T ❑ F ❑

9) He once got arrested for waving a Cajun fried fish in public.   T ❑ F ❑

10) He scalped two tickets at $100.00 each to the midnight premiere of *Private Parts*.   T ❑ F ❑

11) He once did Andrew Dice Clay's income taxes and screwed up so badly that the "Diceman" allegedly wound up having to pay an extra $68,000.   T ❑ F ❑

12) He appeared as the opening act for Jackie Mason at the Sahara Hotel in Las Vegas in November, 1997.   T ❑ F ❑

Answers:

1) T 2) T 3) Who cares? 4) T 5) T 6) T

7) F 8) F 9) T 10) T 11) T 12) T

CHAPTER 10

KING NORRIS

Being a Howard Stern fan can be a full-time job. From book signings and on-air contests, to Chat Parties and appearances on Howard's show, a devoted fan like myself can choose from a full menu of Stern-related activities.

Much of the feasting done at the Howard Stern trough is "officially sanctioned" — i.e. approved by Howard Stern himself. For an activity to merit Howard's approval it must be under his control, with all profits flowing directly to him. Although Howard loves to talk about his penis, he doesn't believe in over-exposing himself. Subjecting his public to too many for-profit endeavors, in too short a time span, can only sabotage and dilute said endeavors by boring the public. That's why Howard resists over-extending himself with too many projects. Like a master chess player, Howard employs a great deal of strategy before making any move.

In defiance of Howard's master plan, both his paid minions and non-paid Wack Packers refuse to show similar restraint. They will do anything to turn a buck. The zeal with which Howard's crew seek to capitalize on their leader's fame makes one believe that they need the money to buy food. Might Howard's rapacious hunger for keeping all the loot be the root of the problem?

Howard's producer, Gary Dell'Abate, has an appetite for earning extra dough that is exceeded only by the size of his legendary choppers. Perhaps the real reason Gary constantly licks his caps has less to do with his stated need to keep them moist, and more to do with his avaricious contemplation of reaping a windfall at Howard's expense. Gary constantly hosts events and appears at retail store openings and promotions. These appearances are announced *ad nauseum* during Howard's show. Howard has said that he wishes Gary wouldn't do them — a message that clearly hasn't penetrated Gary's thick, ape-like cranium. Howard once asked "What does Gary do at these events?". Jackie Martling answered him with this pithy reply: "He says here's so and so. Now where's my check."

Considering the fact that Jackie seems to spend more time hyping his own commercial empire than working for the betterment of Howard's show, he's one to talk! In fact, between souvenir tee shirts, mugs, hot dog relish, and what-not, there is hardly a crumb left at the Howard Stern smorgasbord that Jackie has not eagerly claimed as his own. I'm sure that in a dark, dank, fetid, flooded basement located somewhere in Bayville, Long Island (Jackie's home town), there lies a mattress stuffed and filled to the bursting point with Jackie's ill-gotten gain. One has to wonder — is there no limit to Jackie's appetite? Has he no shame?

When it comes to partaking in the feeding frenzy generated by Howard's fame, Stuttering John and Steve Grillo are also devoid of shame. The ever-increasing waistlines of all those seated at Howard's bountiful table is proof positive of their gluttony. I find it fitting that Howard ends each show by saying "And now, the most important part of the show — the plugs."

Despite the fact that Howard's Wack Packers are uninvited dinner guests, they show no hesitation whatsoever with regards to pulling up chairs and serving up the

Fred Norris

leftovers. Fred Schrieber, a.k.a. Fred The Elephant Boy, hosts wrestling events. Thomas Cipriano, a.k.a. Captain Janks, marketed a collection of his best Howard Stern related phoney phone calls. Laurence Greenblatt, a.k.a. Melrose Larry Green, has used his Brandeis and Cornell education to create a collection of his memoirs detailing his rise to fame as mental patient/irritant savant. Kenneth Keith Kallenbach, alleged girlfriend batterer and exhibitionist extraordinaire, parlayed his association with Howard Stern into a cameo role in a porno film (*Pussyman 9*). George Harvey, a.k.a. Crackhead Bob sells "Crackateer" memberships to his fan club for as much as $29.95. By the way, all of the above mentioned

Wack Packers with the exception of Elephant Boy have their own Web pages. Therefore, even fans with insomnia are not deprived of the opportunity to log-on and consume a midnight cyber-snack at the Howard Stern buffet.

Gold Membership in the Crackhead Bob fan club:

1) Official Crackhead Bob tee shirt
2) Original "Limited Edition" autographed photo (taken by Dan Wagner)
3) Membership w/password
4) Bumper strip
5) Auto window decal
6) Free bonus Crackhead Bob sunglasses and keychain!
"You get all this for just $29.95!"

Available now at http://www.crackheadbob.com

How fitting, then, that Fred Norris, who has so scrupulously avoided fattening himself at Howard's expense, should be one of the slimmest members of Howard's entourage. Fred has always come across as the most ethical individual seated at Howard's table. Perhaps Fred's amazing Kurt Waldhiem imitation in the on-air game *Guess Who's the Jew* is just an elaborate cover. That's what I considered when I heard Fred at long last plugging an appearance of his own. As it turned out, Fred's band King Norris was due to play at a nightclub near my home. In preparation of seeing Fred feast off the crumbs of Howard's celebrity, I polished my silverware, tied a napkin around my neck,

Crackhead Bob

and hungrily whiled away the hours prior to the sumptuous event.

Fred had announced that he would be playing at the Upper Dock Nightclub in Kings Park, Long Island on Friday, September 20, 1996. My wife had trouble understanding why I wanted to see him. I told her that I was curious. Would the affair turn out to be a traveling Howard Stern Show, or a serious concert? After all, Fred hardly seemed interested in capitalizing on Howard's fame. My wife then asked me if I was planning on including the experience in my already finished book. I told her that I wouldn't bother unless something truly spectacular happened.

I decided to bring my camera in case anything newsworthy occurred. Clubs usually forbid photography. I assumed that even if the club allowed me to take pictures, Fred wouldn't. I played out several scenarios in my mind. The most optimistic entailed my getting a few decent candid shots, and possibly, if I were extremely lucky, sharing a beer and a bit of chat with Fred during one of his band's breaks. This was as far as I dared imagine — I was well aware of how preposterous my thoughts were.

The Upper Dock, Kings Park, NY

The Upper Dock Nightclub is located on Old Dock Road. It is a small, well-tended club that reminds me of the stereotypical, rural, roadside biker hang-out. The place has an air of danger about it. I later learned from some of my more adventurous friends that the Upper Dock is considered to be a "rough joint". On the night of Fred's gig, the ratio of portly, red-shirted bouncers to patrons was about one to three.

While Fred's band was tuning-up, I ordered a long neck Bud and listened to the juke box. I was just starting to unwind when a huge fight broke out at the front of the club. It was unbelievable! Beer bottles crashed to the floor as innocent patrons fled in terror. From the juke box came the fitting strains of the Doors' song *Peace*

Fred Norris

Frog. Luckily, the bouncers managed to get the situation under control. I wondered why Fred and his band mates chose such an establishment to play in? What would come next — gigs behind a protective mesh of chicken wire?

After their tune-up, Fred and company left the stage. I snagged one of the numerous xeroxed promos for King Norris that the Upper Dock had taped to the walls outside the club. I figured that asking Fred to sign the promo would be a good way to start a conversation with him. Many people claim that Fred is very standoffish and unfriendly. I've even heard rumors that Fred refuses to sign autographs. Fortunately for me, Fred was very pleasant and gladly signed my souvenir. Perhaps Fred is only reluctant to sign things during Howard Stern events. To avoid being perceived as a groupie, I asked Fred to personalize the promo for a friend of mine who collects Stern related stuff. Fred wrote: "To John, thanks for listening. Fred Norris".

Just in case he remembered me from my Emmy scam, I fessed-up and told Fred that I was "The Emmy Guy". I asked Fred if Howard and the gang had really believed my far-out tale. Fred said, "You fooled them hook, line, and sinker." I told Fred that I thought they might have been playing along for the purpose of entertaining the listening audience. I then went on to say that of all the people in the studio at the time, I had been sure that he'd seen through me. Fred just looked at me and smiled in a way that confirmed my suspicions. By this time a few other fans had copied my lead and were eagerly waiting in the wings with copies of Fred's promo that they wanted autographed. I decided not to wear out my welcome and faded into the crowd.

While I talked to Fred, a voice in my head kept saying over and over: "I can't believe that I've written a book about Howard Stern, and yet here I am talking to his on-air cohort Fred Norris! This is so unbelievable! If Fred knew this, what would he say? I can't believe this is happening." Despite my state of disbelief I did my best to look normal and stay in control. I knew that if I came across as the obsessed fan I was, Fred would surely run for the hills.

Fred Norris rocks out

The Upper Dock has an outdoor fenced-in area behind the club with a wooden deck on one side. It was pretty stuffy inside, so I went out for some fresh air. A few minutes later, Fred and his bandmates came out, too. Fred seemed to be in a good mood, so I figured "what the hell" and struck up a conversation with him. I instinctively knew enough to avoid talking about Howard. Instead I talked about K-ROCK's recent change from a classic rock format to alternative rock. I lamented the fact that compared with the rest of the country, New York City has a terrible lack of decent music radio. Bingo! Fred and I were instantly on the same wave length. Fred said words to the effect of: "When I first left Washington, D.C. and came to New York's WNBC with Howard, I had expected to find great music stations. But when I got here (New York), there were hardly any." I asked Fred what kind of music his band played. To the best of my recollection, he told me that they play a sort of Texas-based blues-rock, psychedelic, Stevie Ray Vaughan, all-out rock and roll. He said that they try to lose themselves in their music. I could hardly wait to hear them!

Fred has a great sense of humor and quick wit. I mentioned a current newspaper article about a scandal regarding the warehoused psychiatric facility that's located next door to the Upper Dock Nightclub in Kings Park. Apparently, indigent patients and those without rela-

Fred Norris and fan

tives to claim them were buried in cemeteries located on the grounds. Some of the graves weren't even marked. At least one cemetery was covered over with dirt and planted with grass to disguise the fact that a cemetery lay underneath. In numerous instances, more than one person had been buried in the same grave. Without missing a beat, Fred commented: "Yes, but they only buried the schizophrenics in mass graves, Dan!"

I was surprised and flattered when Fred bothered to ask me what I did for a living. I told him that I was a professional photographer. He asked me if I

Fred Norris and fan

had a portfolio. This seemed like a strange question. I later learned that his band had agreed to meet with a photographer to consider getting some shots done, and she had showed up without samples of her work. How odd. I told Fred that I primarily shoot for magazines, designers, and advertisers.

Fred's response was to ask, "How do you go about getting work? Do you have to make cold-calls?" I replied, "Yes, I hate making cold-calls. Although some of my work comes from them, most of it comes from word of mouth, and existing accounts." Evidently, the same thing is true for radio. I know this doesn't sound too significant, but for anyone who has ever made cold calls it is a watershed of knowledge. Fred and I had found our common ground.

Fred told me that his band still needed some publicity photos. He asked me if I would mind taking some for them after the first set. He said that the band manager and drummer Frank Fallon could discuss what they needed with me. Although I was delighted and flabbergasted, I managed to squeak out with casual aplomb, "Sure, no problem. That would be cool." My fantasy was actually going to be realized.

Frank Fallon reminds me of Kramer from the television show *Seinfeld*. He wore a vintage Hawaiian shirt and a thickly ribbed retro brown corduroy jacket and sported a silly goatee and an ever-present beer. With his Irishman's gift for gab, Frank is the band's court jester — always ready with a joke or a quip.

Frank met Fred while working with him at K-ROCK as an advertising account supervisor. While at K-ROCK, Frank enjoyed working for Howard Stern's boss Mel Karmazin. According to Frank, Mel was pretty tolerant of his employees interests and lifestyles. All Mel really cared about was getting the job done. It didn't bother Mel that some of his employees drank too much, or burned the can-

Fred Norris

dle at both ends. Frank's description of the K-ROCK work environment sounded like the perfect place for "shock-jocks" and aspiring musicians.

The third member of Fred's trio is Robert Boyd the bass guitarist. He, too, has a goatee like an early 1960s beatnik. In his mid-twenties, Rob is about fifteen years younger than his chums.

Fred plays lead guitar and sings the main vocals. His ax of choice is a silver Fender Eric Clapton edition Stratocaster with active electronics. Fred is quite the guitar shaman. His soaring guitar riffs were heartfelt and tasteful. He even performed a little Van Halenesque finger-tapping. Much of the time Fred plays with his eyes closed and his face scrunched up in a mask of concentration and euphoria — an expression gleaned from MTV videos. I call it the classical musician-in-the-throes-of-orgasm look.

I got some great candid shots of Fred and his band. Some of the shots of Fred making faces are hilarious. In fact, I deliberately avoided showing some of these to Fred lest he try to confiscate or destroy the negatives. Celebrities are notoriously fussy when it comes to their public personae. Fred - ever the skeptic - even intimated that he thought there should be more pictures when I met with the band to review my shots. Naturally, I pretended not to hear his comment. Besides the photos of Fred making faces, I also had some shots of a groupie or two trying to get up-close and personal with him.

The Upper Dock has dreadful acoustics. It was difficult to fully appreciate the great show put on by Fred and his band. One of the best songs was *Silver Nickels and Golden Dimes* written by none other than the teen-aged Howard Stern. Seeing that Fred was playing within a short drive of Howard's home, and that the following day was a Saturday, I had hoped that Howard might even show up to hear his co-worker perform. But, I guess after being in a small studio with Fred for seventeen years, Howard has probably seen — and heard — more than enough of him. (At least this is what Howard is fond of saying on-air.) I'm positive Fred loves the opportunity music gives him to step out of Howard's shadow. I wondered what Fred

Fred Norris

would do if his music ever took off to the point where he had to chose between it and Howard.

Since the members of King Norris have day jobs, they rehearse and plan future gigs at night. On weekends they travel to as many gigs as possible. In light of these

Frank, Fred, Rob

facts, I'm not surprised that Fred — the only married man in the group — is reportedly having serious marital problems. I can't imagine that one would have any energy left after such a grueling schedule. Aside from the fact that Fred loves music, I wonder why he puts himself through this ordeal. Is Fred after a full-time music career in the rock and roll fast lane? Is it to escape from a bad marriage? Or perhaps to escape from a megalomaniacal boss?

The band played an eclectic mix of music. John Cougar Mellencamp's recent appearance on the Howard Stern Show doubtless had influenced Fred to include two of John's songs in his own line-up. He also did justice to some Hendrix and Clapton tunes as well. The trio played well together. Before the end of every number Fred would finally open his eyes, look in Frank's direction and count down the ending of the song with a flourish. I positioned myself on Frank's side of the stage

Frank, Fred, Rob

so I could capture Fred's expressions, which were invariably entertaining.

One part of the second set was revealing. Between songs Fred engaged in idle banter with his band mates, even doing some of his well-known impressions of Stern cast members Scott The Engineer, and Steve, the dimwit, Grillo. Unfortunately the audience at the Upper Dock appeared to have been recently lobotomized. They greeted Fred's snappy repartee with an eerie silence. Was I the only one getting the jokes? Anyway, during the idle banter

Fred happened to ask his buddies what song they would like to do next. Rob said he would like to play "visit the rest room". Fred said, "Oh, then you'd better go. Frank and I will play for awhile." At this point Frank piped in like a second grader with a full bladder "Ew, ew, ew, can I go too?". Fred said, "Okay, I'll just play with myself." — which he did. Frank and Rob left for the bathroom, and Fred just stayed, center stage, standing tall, eyes closed, and rocked out. There was clearly more than mere music being made on stage. This was pure psychodrama, as Fred played on, exorcising his private demons. In the dim light of the club, Fred cut a lonely figure indeed.

During a break between sets, I con-

Rob, Frank, Fred

ducted my impromptu photo session. First I had the band pose next to some trees behind the club. It was pretty dark, so I had to trust my judgement and wing it. The shots came out surprisingly well. However, I felt at a disadvantage by not having a hair and make-up person or a choice of wardrobe. The worst part of the shoot was trying to compose the shots in such subdued lighting. Of course the flash would provide enough light for the film, but it did little to help me see what I was doing.

This was all very strange. Their treating something as important as a photo session in such a catch-as-catch-can manner perplexed me. Why hadn't Fred asked Howard to recommend a photographer? Was Fred so determined to do his own thing that he would bypass Howard's helpful connections? I was surprised that the band hadn't asked me to shoot a studio shot on white seamless paper — the traditional backdrop for a publicity photo because it reproduces so well in the media.

Fred Norris

I think the glamour aspect of having flashes going off while they played, and the fact that people at the club could see the photo shoot in progress contributed to a sense of excitement that *the* Fred Norris and his band were actually gracing the club with their presence. It sure seemed to inspire some of the female attendees. Several of them threw their arms around Fred and demanded that he let them kiss him — which he did. Naturally, I preserved these moments for posterity. Luckily, Fred must have forgotten that I took these shots. For my part, I immediately put them in my ever-expanding Do Not Show To Fred Pile.

Next, I had the band pose beside the gray vinyl siding near the front of the club. We tried several different compositions. At one point I asked Fred to put his foot up on the siding at about waist level. Fred said he didn't think that was a good idea. However, I decided to have a little fun and told him to "just do it." We looked each other in the eye. Eventually he complied. Without the benefit of my professional mantle and a camera in my hand, I never would have had the nerve to insist that

Fred listen to me. It was a funny moment. I think Fred was as amused as I was. Of course the pose looked awkward, but after I had Fred put his leg down and his arm on the wall instead, everything fell into place.

From the way in which the shoot was progressing, I could tell that Fred and his bandmates appreciated my efforts not to settle for a humdrum shot. Finally, I had them pose by a three-foot-high metal pole capped with a halogen light. Even though the light was an incongruous element, it gave the photos a surreal look that appealed to my artistic sensibilities.

Fred Norris

Just before we finished the shoot a young woman whose name rhymed with chlamydia, I think it may have been Lydia, came over to schmooze with Fred. She barely looked old enough to drink. The situation was bizarre. Fred is about twice her age, or old enough to be her father. Lydia wore a black miniskirt and a red leopard print blouse. After informing us that she studied ballet, she asked if she could pose for some of the shots. Troublemaker that I am, I said only if she did an arabesque or a plié. She replied that she couldn't do those ballet moves in a miniskirt. Fred laughed. I just smiled. Eventually we let her off the hook with first position (standing straight with ankles together and feet pointing outwards). When I left later in the evening Lydia was still sitting at the same front row table she'd been occupying all night. She was watching Fred perform through eyes that were at half-mast. I bet she fell asleep before the set ended.

During the shoot, Fred mentioned Mel Blanc, one of his heroes. He told me that Mel Blanc's voice for Porky Pig was based on his disrespect and feelings of annoyance towards one of his bosses. I learned from Fred that this boss never even knew that he had supplied the inspiration for Porky. Why Fred chose to share this particular piece of information with me I'll never know. I wanted to ask him if it had anything to do with his feelings towards Howard, but I didn't have the guts.

All I could think of saying in reply was, "Yeah, that reminds me of the final scene in George Orwell's *Animal Farm*." I could tell that Fred enjoyed my analogy. Just then Lydia piped in with, "I always wanted to read *Animal Farm*." Once again Fred displayed his rapier wit with the comment: "Well there's still four more years until the next millennium, perhaps you'll make it!" The woman just looked at Fred. I couldn't stop laughing.

By 1AM I knew that I wouldn't be able to stay awake much longer. I had been up since six the previous morning. Although I wanted to stay until Fred finished playing, I decided to call it a night. I felt bad about being such a wuss. Frank Fallon promised to call me the following Monday to set up a time when the band could stop by my New York photo studio to review the shots. With the film still in the can, so to speak, I fervently hoped that I had captured something worthwhile to show them. That night I dragged my very tired body into bed and slept like a comatose patient. When I woke at noon the next day, it was tough convincing myself that I hadn't been dreaming.

Fred Norris

Frank called me on Monday as promised, and we made a date for the band to come by on Wednesday evening. Though I had already developed most of the shots and was happy with the selection, I offered to take some more shots on a white background. To put the matter to rest in a non-obligational way, I said I'd have a white background and lights set up on Wednesday so that the band could pose for more shots if they wanted to. Frank liked this idea.

Of course the subject of money came up. Previously Frank had offered to pay me about $150.00 for my work on Friday. I didn't have the heart to tell him what my fees really were. I knew that a high figure would scare them away forever. Even though it's Fred's band, they split the expenses three ways. I wound up charging the band only for the cost of the prints they received.

On Tuesday, Frank called me to let me know that Fred, "considering who he was, would want to keep/own all the negatives." I told Frank that I didn't work that way. Any shots that I take are my property, and the only thing I sell are prints of

my negatives and/or the rights to reproduce same in a very specific and defined manner. I was impressed with my own boldness. After all, my steadfastness could easily wreck my chances of doing another photo shoot. I wanted to learn more about Fred and his band. Without future opportunities to study them through my lenses, my adventure would come to an end. The issue was resolved by Frank saying he would relay my feelings to Fred and that Fred would discuss it with me himself if he wanted to. Poor Frank, I could tell that he didn't want to be stuck in the middle of this one!

On Wednesday, Frank told me that the band would get to my studio by six that evening. I was ready for

Fred Norris

them. I had loaded my cameras, and set up the lights and background. I had also stocked up on what proved to be the most important ingredient for a successful visit from The King Norris Band — beer!

Finally, I had sat myself down and given myself a "stern" talking to. I told myself to relax and not make a big fuss over Fred. I also vowed to avoid talking about the Stern Show too much as I knew that it would probably make Fred uncomfortable — or annoy him. Determined to keep a close check on my obsessive habits, I even composed a list to help me.

What Not To Do During A Fred Norris Photo Shoot

1) Don't fax the *Stern Show*.

2) Don't display the following: A) *Stern Show* memorabilia such as posters, tee shirts, videos, buttons, magazine articles, books, etc. B) Collections of original *Stern Show* photographs. C) The *Getting To Howard* manuscript.

3) Don't call Melrose, Kenneth Keith Kallenbach, Crackhead Bob, or Elephant Boy.

4) Don't log onto the Prodigy Howard Stern Fan Club Bulletin Board or surf Howard Stern related Internet sites.

5) Don't play the cassettes of your *Stern Show* appearances or Scores contest entries.

6) Don't ask Fred Norris to get you into Howard Stern related events.

7) Don't run out of beer.

Frank arrived as scheduled, shortly followed by Fred. They insisted that we wait for Rob to arrive before reviewing all the shots. Unfortunately, Rob had written down the wrong address. I suggested that Frank call his machine to see if Rob had left a message. This was a good idea as Rob had left a message that he was at a phone booth a block away from the studio. I accompanied Fred and Frank to the lobby of my building. From there Fred went one way and Frank another. I was starting to feel that my luck had run out when the guys returned after twenty minutes without Rob. After reluctantly returning to my studio, Frank called Rob's home phone. For some unknown reason Rob had decided to go home. Frank gave Rob the correct address and advised him to take a cab. A half an hour and one six pack later we were finally gathered together around the slide projector.

Frank Fallon

It was decision time. Fred and his band mates were happy with the shots. They asked me what I thought about them. I explained that while I thought the shots were very creative, I found them more appropriate for a magazine article or CD cover than for a publicity photo. To my way of thinking they needed studio shots. I told them that I would approach such a shoot by taking black and white group shots, individual head shots, and individual full body shots. This way a designer would have all the raw elements to satisfy any publicity need that might arise. I didn't press the issue. As usual, Frank kept the band moving by summarizing my thoughts and saying to Fred, "so you want to take some shots?"

Our little game of *Where's Rob?* had drawn us all closer together. Crisis can do that sometimes. So can beer. Fred said, "sure." I reviewed Fred's wardrobe. He had brought along two tee shirts, one black and one white, and an expensive designer tie-dyed shirt that was streaked with dark tones. After shooting a few polaroids, Fred chose the black tee shirt to be worn with his black motorcycle jacket. He looked like a Hell's Angel. Frank's outfits were the funniest of all. One ensemble consisted of dark jeans and a striped black and white shirt

Frank Fallon

that screamed prison uniform. Frank's clothing seemed to have been chosen with an eye to accentuating his sloping shoulders. Although I'm not a fashion consultant, I have two words of fashion advice for Frank — shoulder pads! Actually I loved Frank's eclectic look. He looked like a musician.

The biggest surprise of the shoot was Rob. The camera loves few individuals. Rob was one of the them. When I looked at Rob through the camera's view finder I had to remove the camera from my eyes to prove to myself that it was really him.

Robert Boyd

I was amazed at how photogenic he was. In fact, when it came time for doing the head shots, Rob required far less film than his friends.

The "boys" loved having their pictures taken. I must have shot close to three hundred photos in two-hours. Frank's consumption of cigarettes and beers was truly awesome.

Taking photos can be a real workout. Between setting up the lights, climbing up and down ladders, and trying to "work" the subjects I had really built up a sweat. Every few minutes I had to wipe the beads of perspiration from my forehead. I felt like Nixon during his famous 1960 presidential election debate. Frank noticed my efforts. In a gesture of friendship he said to his band mates, "Let's take Dan to a whore house after the shoot and get him laid!" The only response I could generate was a nervous laugh. I'm sure that my faced paled to the color of the white background. Of course Frank was being goofy, but... . In retrospect, what I should have done was say, "cool, where's the whorehouse?" In this way I could have seen if he was serious. What a call-in to Howard's show that would have made!

Robert Boyd

My last set-up was a bird's-eye view of the band. To do this I climbed to the top of a ladder. With one hand on the camera and one hand steadying myself by grasping the fire sprinkler pipes, I got my shot, which wound up being my favorite. By using a high vantage point and a wide angle lens, the faces of the band were enlarged, while their bodies seemed to recede beneath them. It's an amazing shot. I love the fact that their feet are hidden from view.

Robert Boyd

When the beer's gone, so is the band. That's Frank's motto. After I shut-off the lights on the set, Frank invited me to go for a few beers with the boys. How could I refuse? One day an anonymous Howard Stern fan, and the next day slamming down beers with Fred Norris. I didn't even bother to clean-up. Before I closed my studio door I took a last peek. The place was a mess. My white background was full of footprints, the kitchen counter was littered with empty beer bottles, and a cloud of smoke hovered over everything. It was a pleasure to leave it behind and head for the Molly Wee Pub on Eighth Avenue and Thirtieth Street. I left so fast that even my lens caps were spinning.

The Molly Wee Pub is a traditional Irish drinking bar. To witness a spectacle that rivals a Roman Orgy or a banquet with Henry VIII, just park yourself in front of The Molly Wee Pub on Saint Patrick's Day. Anyway, the Molly Wee is an establishment dedicated to serious drinking. The bar stools padded backs are covered in soft naugahyde. The cumulative wattage of the lights in the pub is probably less than fifty. Even though we had come in from the relative darkness of the outside, it took several minutes for our eyes to adjust. Next time I'll bring my spelunking gear. It's so smoky inside that I almost needed oxygen. The jukebox played a nice mix of classic blues.

Entering the pub reminded me of a scene from the television series *Kung-Fu*. As soon as we entered the bar all conversation ground to a halt. Fortunately we didn't have to showcase any flashy martial arts moves. The nocturnal denizens gave us the once over. After what felt like an eternity they slowly returned to their libations. I wondered if any of them recognized Fred. If they did, they certainly didn't show it. Frank wisely seated us near the front exit in case we had to make a run for it. As a newcomer to the group, I sat next to Frank and defended the outer perimeter from attack. Fred, the King, was flanked by Frank and Rob.

As it turned out, my apprehensions were totally baseless. After our baptism in beer we became nocturnal creatures, too. Fred ordered double shots of scotch and bottles of beer all around. For those of you shopping for Christmas gifts for Fred, he prefers single-malt scotch. I hardly ever drink, and I realized very quickly that I was in way over my head. I resolved to monitor what I said. The last thing I wanted to do was inadvertently mention that I was writing a book. Alcohol loosens lips. I wanted to make sure it would be Fred's lips that were loosened and not mine.

This was easier said than done. I could tell that Fred was extremely reluctant to discuss Howard Stern. Fred has said numerous times on-air that he is very loyal to the show. Take it from me, this is no mere exaggeration. Luckily, the topic of siblings provided the perfect chance to delve into Fred's psyche. Fred has one sibling — a brother who is four years older than he is. I asked Fred if they had a good relationship while he was growing up. Fred told me that his older brother used to beat him up all the time. It must have been quite a massacre, because Fred said that ever since they became adults his brother continues to apologize to him for his behavior.

It was obvious to me that Fred still harbors a bit of a grudge. I asked him if, other than the beatings, his brother had been nice to him. Fred said, "yes, but he could have been nicer." The look in Fred's eyes as he said this spoke volumes. It seemed natural to ask Fred how he got his brother to stop picking on him. Fred told me that when he turned fifteen he finally became taller than his brother. Fred is 6'2", and his brother is 6'. Fred said that one day his older brother was hassling him, and the cumulative effects of being beat upon year after year caused him to erupt. He grabbed his brother by the collar and slammed him against a wall. Then he looked him in the eye and said words to the effect of "if you ever touch me again I will kick the crap out of you!" I asked Fred what happened next. Fred said, "I told my brother that I would let him off for what happened in the past, which was more than he had ever done for me."

Fred Norris

At long last I was learning what made Fred tick. I asked him if he had ever played team sports. Apparently he hadn't. "I probably would have killed someone." he said. "I'm very ethical. I'm calm until someone crosses the line. Once during a game of touch football, I touch tackled my opponent, but he just kept running. So I ran after him and grabbed him in a bear hug. I was so mad!" Howard Stern has said that Fred knows how to kick ass, and I for one believe him.

We had two more rounds of drinks, with the bartender buying us the third round. Frank and Rob were getting a bad case of the munchies. Frank was the hungrier of the two. He kept getting up and reaching behind the bar so that he could grab small bags of potato chips. I think he must of eaten at least six bags. In my mind, I started to add up all the drinks that the boys had consumed since they got to my studio. It added up to quite a bit. By my guess they were each on their seventh or eighth bottle of beer and their third or fourth glass of hard liquor. Frank seemed partial to Bloody Marys made with extra vodka and no ice. Hey, wouldn't want to waste any space with mere frozen water. The funny thing about all the drinking was how well they handled it. Evidently this must be a regular part of the routine. I wondered how they ever got anything done.

I also wondered how Fred would be able to wake up in time for Howard's show the following morning. Frank, as the band's manager and person responsible for the general welfare of the crew seemed to also function as Fred's babysitter. It was getting late. Frank asked the bartender for the check. I think the bill was over seventy dollars. Pretty impressive for a corner pub. The band split the check three ways. I offered to chip in, but they wouldn't hear of it. After several attempts Frank finally managed to pour us out the door. Although Fred wanted to head home, he indulged his starving band mates in a trip to the pizzeria across the street. We each bought a greasy slice, which we then took outside and quickly wolfed down. The whole scenario reminded me of my teenage years. Frank and Fred live in the Upper East Eighties. Rob lives in the East Thirties. After agreeing to meet the following week and look over the shots, the boys stuffed themselves into a taxi and zoomed away. I watched the taxi until it disappeared in a sea of taillights. I couldn't believe the events of the previous five hours had really happened.

In the weeks that followed we met several more times to review the shots and make some selections. Fred was very pleased with the photos. Each time we met, the gang polished off large quantities of beer at my studio. I got the impression that any time the band accomplished anything, the occasion had to be celebrated with a trip to our favorite watering hole — The Molly Wee Pub. Of course I took advantage of these occasions to learn more about Fred and *The Howard Stern Show.*

Fred does a great imitation of Scott Salem, the engineer on Howard's show. I asked Fred why he thought it was so much fun for people to imitate Scott and goof on him. Fred said that it wasn't the imitation that was necessarily so much fun, it's the look that Scott gets on his face when you make fun

Frank, Fred, Rob

of him. Evidently Scott gets very irritated and his face scrunches up as though he were smelling something bad.

During our third trip to the Molly Wee Pub I struck gold. The mother lode. In the past, Frank had always sat between Fred and me, making it difficult to hold a conversation with Fred. This time I sat right next to Fred with Rob and Frank to his left. The evening started off with a bit of levity. The band had just returned from playing a gig in Los Angeles, opening for Ozzie Osborne on October 26th. They were in great spirits. Frank was joking with the bartender. It was the day before Halloween, and the bald bartender kept getting bumped in the head by a revolving rubber bat that was attached to an enormous replica of a beer can. The bartender asked Frank if he wanted a glass with his bottle of beer. Frank of course said, "do I want an ass with my beer?". I said, "you bet he does, and make that with a straw!" The gang started laughing. Once again it was Fred who supplied the punchline "ah, these hops are rather lumpy!"

KING NORRIS

Fred couldn't stop talking about the Los Angeles gig. He had never played in front of so many people. There were five thousand people in the audience when King Norris came on, and thirty-five thousand by the time Ozzie took the stage. This seemed like the perfect time to ask Fred what he hoped to achieve with the band. I commented that it must be very difficult trying to serve two masters. Working for Howard from before dawn and for his music until way past sunset had to be hard. What would he do if the band struck it big? What if they were the next Rolling Stones? Fred must have loved the comparison. He looked me right in the eye and said, "If that happened, I'd have to go with the music." Bingo. Not that I was really surprised. It must be very difficult playing second fiddle when you're born to play lead. (Guitar that is.) Besides which, Fred is over forty, an age when most bands have already made their mark.

Fred's musical clock was winding down. The time for tough decisions was at hand. No wonder Fred was so willing to threaten to quit when Howard was giving him a hard time several months earlier over Fred's beleaguered relationship with his wife.

Fred is very aware of others. A group of young men and woman who had been drinking at one of the nearby tables, most likely illegally, got up to leave. Before they left they returned their empty glasses to the bartender and thanked him. Fred looked at me and said, "What a nice, polite bunch of people." The incident reminded me of the fact that less than an hour earlier Fred had gathered the empty beer bottles in my studio and returned them to the beer carton they came in. Fred is no hypocrite. He practises what he preaches.

While we talked, a young couple sporting the grunge look came over and asked Fred if he was *the* Fred Norris of *Howard Stern Show* fame. They told Fred that he was their favorite person on the show. Fred was very cordial to them. I could tell Fred enjoyed being recognized. Fred had told me that he had trouble understanding why some fans behaved so strangely. One of the things that perplexed him the most was when suburban hausfraus wanted him to sign their breasts and other body parts at gigs. I agreed that this defied explanation. After all, I bet these same hausfraus are afraid to talk to strangers, and yet they let someone they've never met autograph their breasts.

Frank had given me a demo-tape of the band. On the tape, Fred does his great rendition of Howard's song *Silver Nickels and Golden Dimes*. I asked Fred what Howard and the gang thought of his version. Fred told me that his very professional and high caliber rendition of the song made his cohorts nervous. Evidently they felt threatened by it. They didn't know what to say. I imagine they weren't overly supportive. Fred seemed to think that they saw some underlying motive to his recording the song. I commented that Robin must have been supportive. After all, she is so nice on-air. Fred said that he "loved Robin, but that she carries a lot of baggage." Having read Robin's lengthy autobiography, I call this the understatement of all time.

Emboldened by the welcome direction the conversation was taking I asked Fred about Howard's legendary karate skills. Howard is a brown belt in Shotokan Karate. I laughed when Fred said, "Howard would fall down if you said, 'boo' to him." I said, "oh, come on — with Howard's height and weight advantage he could destroy me." Fred said, "no he couldn't. I've never seen your moves but you have something that Howard doesn't have — courage." Fred uttered this last statement prior to entering a cab with Frank and Rob. Once again I was left looking at red taillights and wondering if Fred had meant what he said, or if he was just testing me. I'm still not sure.

CHAPTER 11

HOORAY FOR HOLLYWOOD!

I love eating at Chinese restaurants. My favorite part of the meal is the fortune cookie. Recently I got a really great fortune. It said, "Fame and good fortune are coming your way. Lucky numbers: 07, 27, 96, 01, 12, and 54." What a great fortune. Usually I get silly Confucian proverbs such as, "He who understands everything, forgives everything." Not very useful. However, on Saturday, July 27th, 1996, my new fortune actually came true, and in ways that I could never have imagined.

In mid July, while surfing the Net, I came across a posting on a Howard Stern bulletin board announcing an open-call for extras in Howard's upcoming movie *Private Parts*. All I had to do was show up at one of two New York City locations and sign-up. This sounded too good to be true. What more could an obsessed Howard Stern fan hope for than to be on the big screen with his hero? To add profit to prophecy, I would even get paid for my cinematic debut! Over the past nine months I had participated in numerous Howard Stern related activities, but I was hard-pressed to imagine anything that could possibly compare with being in Howard's film.

The casting session for extras that I attended was held at the Palladium, a New York City club. When I arrived a long line stretched down the block. I learned that 3,500 extras were needed for a crowd scene that was to be filmed in Bryant Park behind the New York City Public Library. The scene was a re-creation of Howard's famous 1987 anti-F.C.C. rally.

While in line, I asked my fellow future extras if they were Stern fans. To my dismay, I was one of the only fans there. Evidently, the producers of *Private Parts* wanted to seed the cast with real actors. Perhaps they were afraid of Howard's fans'

◀ *Howard Stern fans*

Howard Stern

capacity for excess. Personally, I doubted if a mere thespian could muster the sustained frenzy necessary to portray a true Stern fan. Even the best Lee Strasburg method actors would be at a disadvantage in such a situation.

The casting session was far from organized. We were herded into the Palladium like cattle in groups of one hundred. To reach the staging area we had to climb up four flights of a very dark, damp, and smelly stairway. The experience reminded me of a documentary I once saw on meat slaughtering plants. I think this was done deliberately by casting agent Sylvia Fay to test our physical conditioning and desire. Outside there were rumors that we would be paid seventy dollars for the day. Supposedly, this was

the figure that extras had been paid in earlier *Private Parts* crowd scenes. Once our group (Group 5) was seated we were dismayed to learn that we would only be paid twenty-five dollars for a ten-hour day. That's less than the minimum wage! After taxes were deducted we would probably take home two dollars per hour. Shades of Kathie Lee Gifford. I told my fellow

Chauncé Hayden, Howard Stern

extras that I could make more money sewing in a sweat shop. They responded in chorus with "knit one, purl two".

If Howard is going to continue vilifying Kathie Lee vis-à-vis her sweat shop scandal, then he should put his *own* house in order first. After all, Howard employs

Howard Stern

interns for his radio show and pays people less than minimum wage for working on his movie. Both of these enterprises (radio show and movie) are highly profitable and lucrative. Why can't Howard share some of the wealth?

Even Sylvia Fay seemed embarrassed by the abysmally

low pay. She told us that we were to be available for filming between the hours of 10 AM and 8PM. She asked that anyone who was unwilling to work for this many hours, at this rate, to please leave. One woman got up and left. After the woman was out of ear-shot, Sylvia Fay conspiratorially whispered to those still remaining, "We didn't want her anyway!". Even though I am a die-hard Stern fan, I have to

Howard Stern

admit that I was half-tempted to leave myself. The time spent at the casting session, and travel time, and the actual working day added up to fifteen hours of indentured servitude.

A sign-in sheet was passed from person to person. Once this was done, Sylvia Fay asked us if we had any questions. I raised my hand and asked, "Can we shout out 'Fuck Imus', and stuff like that?". Every head turned to look at me. Sylvia Fay was too stunned to reply. My question was serious — this is exactly the sort of thing fans would really shout at a Stern rally. Evidently, my fellow actors were unenlightened, and unimpressed. They wanted to further their acting careers and started to network shamelessly. They asked Sylvia Fay how many head shots of them she would like for her files. They even wanted to know about hair and make-up. How ridiculous. It was a crowd scene, not Hamlet's soliloquy, for Christ's sake!

Sylvia Fay milked the cattle call for all it was worth. I guess being a casting agent for a crowd scene isn't terribly ego-gratifying. I would have chosen the actors for how loudly they could scream and how heavily their rabid mouths foamed. Parading us around and having us sit for inspection was totally preposterous. In truth, out of one hundred people, not one person was deemed undesirable. She took all of us who had stayed.

On Saturday, July 27th, 1996 I arrived on the set bright and early, full of anticipation, and ready for stardom. I was so excited that I had hardly slept the night before. The other extras and I gathered around under a massive tent, filled out paperwork, put on our identity tags with group numbers, and waited for our marching orders. Here's what we were handed:

Howard Stern

WELCOME TO
HOWARD STERN'S
PRIVATE PARTS

Prepare yourself for a truly memorable experience. Today, each one of you will be an integral part of this film's success and authenticity. We're going to ask you to listen closely to the directions given to you by the **Assistant Directors** (an Assistant Director is the person you will see on the set and in the holding areas wearing a **headset**, and screaming into a **bullhorn** until their veins are showing on their foreheads.)

Let's start with what is included here in your packet;

1. **VOUCHER** - IMPORTANT! This is your means of getting paid! Please take special care of it and take the time to fill it out correctly. Examples of the proper way to fill this out are posted in each holding area. Your voucher needs to be returned to an assigned CHECK OUT AREA at the end of the day.

(*Checking out at the end of the day proved to be a nightmare! It took about an hour, and a mixed group of Black and Asian gangster types threatened to beat up an acquaintance of mine who had hopes of cutting the line.*)

2. **MEAL TICKET** - This is very important; it is your pass to eat. Food will be distributed to you from a designated table at lunchtime. Don't forget, there's a whole lot of you here today, so please line up and be patient when the time comes.

(*Lunch was pretty good. It was packed in a brown paper bag, and reminded me of the kind of lunch dear old mom used to have me take to school. It consisted of a chicken sandwich, bag of chips, two chocolate chip cookies, an apple, can of soda, and a foil packet of mayo for the sandwich. Not too shabby, considering they were feeding a cast of thousands. We were also provided with an ample supply of coffee, doughnuts, drinks, and fruit. I guess they didn't want anyone to leave due to hunger.*)

3. **WRISTBAND** - Also very important! The colored wristband you are given designates your **group** (see the number) and proves that you are with the movie shoot, so please wear it at all times.

(*Everything is soooooo important! The wristbands were made out of a florescent green, orange, and yellow material. I wonder how they will remove all these bands in the final version of the film? — perhaps this will be accomplished by computer.*)

4. RAFFLE TICKET - Extremely important!!! This numbered ticket is your passage into mindless oblivion because we are giving away **TELEVISION SETS and OTHER COOL STUFF** to the lucky winners! Winners will be announced toward the end of the day so **stick around!**

(*The operative words here are **stick around.** The raffles were clearly designed to induce people to stay for the whole day. As it was, many people, with the exception of Howard's fans, succumbed to the heat and humidity and left early. The prizes were few in number, and many people never found out where to submit their raffle tickets — myself included.*)

THE SCENE

The scene we are shooting today celebrates Howard's galactic rise to #1 in the New York ratings in the mid-1980's. In it, Howard arrives with the rest of the cast of his show and his family to be greeted by his fans. This means that **YOU, YES, YOU**, are the biggest part of the scene's success. Without **YOU** Howard would be greeted by an empty field... now wouldn't that look stupid?

(*I just love it when people patronize me! My only question is: If we are so important, how come we are only being paid twenty-five bucks? One of the members of Howard Stern's Wack Pack, Fred The Elephant Boy, told me that the Wack Pack members were each getting one hundred and fifty dollars for the same work. Hey, I never accused Howard of running a democracy. He's the King of All Media and we extras are the lowliest of subjects.*)

MOVING TO AND FROM THE SET

Since there are so many of you we have sectioned people off into groups. Your group is designated by the wristbands you have been given. There are 2 Production Assistants (Assistant Directors in training) assigned to each group and you will be called to the set by groups. When your group is called, follow your assigned Production Asst. to the set, in an orderly fashion. Once on set you will be placed so that we can see you on camera. Please pay attention to the area in which you're placed. Each time you return to set, this will be where you should go, unless specifically instructed otherwise.

Once you're on the set, you'll take your directions from the people on stage using the public address system.

.....Just a couple of other things you need to know:

• **When you're in the park, stay on walkways and the lawn <u>only</u>!! Don't venture into any shrubs or plantings.**

• Please don't leave any cigarette butts on the lawn. (They're real hard to clean up.)

• Don't leave your valuables in the holding areas. We'll have security there, but we have no way of knowing which bag belongs to which person.

Thanks for being here with us today. We're looking forward to a terrific day, and an even better scene!!

Fortunately, it was a beautiful day. I was wearing shorts and a surfer style tee shirt. I had discussed wardrobe with several other Howard Stern fans. We were all in agreement that wearing something loud and easily identifiable would be a good way to spot ourselves in the film. Some fans arrived wearing loud hot pink, bright yellow, or vibrant lime green clothing. Not to be outdone, I was wearing what had to be, without a doubt, the most visible sign of demented fandom. I had boldly emblazoned the entire brim of my floppy, tan, porkpie hat with the word "HOWARD" in thick, black letters. Whenever the cameras started rolling, I made sure that my hat was prominently displayed. To complete my ensemble, I also wore my Revo aviator-style mirrored sunglasses. A friend of mine took a few crowd shots, and the effect completely blew me away — I was easily one of the most visible people in the entire audience!

My hat became a cherished souvenir. Over the course of the day I managed to have it signed by the following people: Howard, Robin, Fred, Jackie, Gary, Betty Thomas (director of *Private Parts*), Mary McCormack (she plays Howard's wife), The Interns — Stuttering John, Steve Grillo, Mike Gange, The Wack Pack — Fred The Elephant Boy, Melrose Larry Green,

Gary Dell'Abate, Betty Thomas

Fred Norris, Jackie Martling

Kenneth Keith Kallenbach, Captain Janks, The King of All Messengers, famous 60's pot smoker and Stern fan David Peel, and the rhythm guitarist for AC/DC — Malcolm Young. Betty Thomas had the nicest handwriting, and Robin had the worst. It took two tries to get Howard to sign the hat. At one point he had it in his hands and threw it back to me, saying "Maybe later". I persisted and succeeded in getting him to sign it. It would have made a silly souvenir to have everyone's signature but Howard's on it. Towards the end of the day I suffered a near catastrophe when my freshly autographed hat almost fell into one of the Port-O-San toilets.

Most of my fellow extras simply hung around waiting to be summoned to the set. However, I was born and bred in New York, and as I've said numerous times before, I'm a slightly compulsive, slightly rabid fan. As you may easily imagine I left skid marks on the sidewalk in my haste to reach my hero Howard Stern's altar — the stage set. I heard a primordial rock and roll jungle beat playing in the distance. Thump-tump-whump! The trees

around Bryant Park ringed the set like jungle foliage. Finally, I burst through the bush, and there, gleaming like a charcoal jewel, in the blazing sun was the enormous stage. Howard stood on the stage like a tribal shaman egging his followers on in a primitive dance of adulation and worship that transcended time. Nearby, sensitive to the

Robin Quivers autographing a fans bottom

shaman's every gesture and nuance was the rock group AC/DC. The drummer beat a rhythm on his tom-toms and high-hat that shook me to my very core. Slowly, cautiously, I advanced, closer and closer. The crowd recognized me as one of their own, and enveloped me in its embrace. Home sweet home. I assumed my rightful

Stuttering John

place.

Howard was clearly enjoying himself. He made comments such as "This is like Woodstock. Please don't eat the brown acid.", and "Fuck Imus", "I'm number one!", "The F.C.C. fucking sucks!", etc... Howard's hair was thick, curly, and lustrous. Personally, I am convinced it was a wig because the part where the hair meets the upper forehead looked very strange. Everyone was having a strange hair day. Gary had either re-grown his mustache for the filming, or perhaps it, too, was fake. Robin sported a medium length Afro wig that was darker than anything nature could possibly create. She wore a black outfit with beads that didn't do her ample physique any favors.

For his part, Howard was outfitted like an extra in a vampire flick. He wore a

Howard Stern

floor-length purple coat with black trim and a white pirate shirt with tufts of extra folded material that served the purpose of a tie, of sorts. I couldn't decide whether he looked more like the Little Prince in Antoine De Saint-Exupéry's book, or the rock star who was formerly known as Prince. When combined with Howard's 6'5" frame, the coat actually made him look at least a foot taller. Howard's next film should be *Gulliver's Travels*. They wouldn't even need any special effects.

During the original F.C.C. rally Howard and his crew wore fake prison stripes. At that time Howard was much heavier and Gary was much thinner. The passage of almost a decade saw Howard

Howard Stern

Stern looking slightly emaciated and Gary looking quite inflated. The Monday after the filming Gary made the following comments on-air: "The audience on Saturday was as cruel as they've ever been! They asked me when the baby was due, and then I was sweating, and a guy goes, 'Really hot when you're that fat, huh?'" Howard's reply to Gary's diatribe was, "Yeah, you are heavy. Your face is completely huge, and you're going to be in the movie. Some guy called you a 'Pumpkin face'. I heard that, that was funny!" I sympathized with Gary and the rest of the crew — the passage of ten years hadn't been very kind to me either.

Betty Thomas is the director of *Private Parts*. Her claims to fame are her acting performances in the successful television series *Hill Street Blues*, and her debut as a feature film director for *The Brady Bunch Movie*. Betty has a narrative style that's direct and unencumbered. As for Betty's wardrobe, all I can say is to reach Africa go Southeast at the next corner! She must have loaded up at Banana Republic's end-of-season sale. In fact, she looked like an extra for *Out Of Africa*. Her safari outfit was beyond belief. I think she may have even been carrying a canteen and a snake-bite kit.

Never a wallflower, Melrose Larry Green was on hand in full Howard Stern regalia complete with a heavy black leather motorcycle jacket with a cartoonish line drawing of Howard Stern's face. Over the course of the hot summer day, this jacket naturally became quite fragrant — undoubtedly enabling Melrose to secure extra elbow room for holding his signs. I have to give him credit. Due to the fact that the

Howard Stern

scene was a recreation of a 1980's event, I had hoped that he would come up with some sort of sign that could capitalize on the public's fascination with prophecy. Melly did not disappoint. He entertained the crowd with a sign that said, "O.J. Simpson will murder his wife in 1994".

Howard Stern

Howard and his listeners love to make fun of Melrose. At one point Gary led the crowd in a chant of "Melrose Sucks!". Never one to shy away from free publicity, Melly, marker and oaktag ever at the ready, quickly scribbled an aid for the hearing impaired which, despite bad spelling, echoed the crowd's sentiments exactly — "Melrose Sux!" Jackie pitched in with his own witty repartee by quipping, "Melrose if you were a foot closer, I could piss on you from this stage." The crowd heartily urged Jackie to at least give it a try.

Howard Stern

My duties as an extra were pretty easy and came quite naturally for me. All I had to do was pretend to be a rabid Howard Stern fan. I know some people might consider this is a stretch, but somehow, I managed to pull it off. Every time AC/DC hit a power chord, I raised my fists in syncopated rhythm. When Howard exhorted the crowd to chant, I was right there. Viewing the photos of myself in the crowd scenes was a frightening revelation. The only fans who out-performed me were some of the more adventurous female fans. After all they had secret weapons — bare breasts! Howard's producer Gary Dell'Abate encouraged them by

Howard Stern

saying, "Remember, this is a Howard Stern project, feel free to remove your tops! No, not now, later when the cameras are rolling!" The crowd could hardly be contained. We were out of control!

Jackie Martling, Howard Stern

Two fans rushed the stage. One was a woman with large, droopy breasts in need of Howard's signature. Howard was only too happy to comply and in the process cop a quick feel. He commented, "My, those are big ones." The other fan was a young, slender, tow-headed man who's only desire in life was to have Robin sign her name on his ass as he bent over and mooned the entire audience. I wondered if this scene will end up on the cutting room floor. (It did.) Either way, it seemed like quite a performance for twenty-five dollars before taxes. Once his ass had been "notarized", the young man returned to us mere mortals proclaiming in the most classic tradition, "I shall never wash my ass again." Judging from my front row vantage point, this was a vow that the young exhibitionist would have no trouble living up to!

As exciting as the onstage action was, it could barely compare with what was going

Howard Stern and Mary McCormack

Gary Dell'Abate, Robin Quivers, Jackie Martling, Mary McCormack, Howard Stern

Howard Stern

on underneath the stage, where some people were urinating. At one point, Stuttering John retreated to the lower level for a little nap, with the top half of his body hidden by the stage. I asked a fellow fan if he was okay, and was told, "Yeah, he's all right, just tired, that's all." "That's all", my aunt Minny! Personally, I think John was suffering the aftereffects of smoking a fat one.

But the real action under the stage was the impromptu love-making. As usual nothing beats reality. I was expecting a flurry of faxes and calls to Howard's show detailing love trysts during the day's filming. However, I was unprepared to witness the real thing. I saw one straight couple performing the "wild thang" under the stage while Howard was performing above the stage. Howard was correct, it really was just like Woodstock. Later in the day I spied a lesbian couple and a gay threesome doing their own versions of gymnastic floor exercises, and making some very creative uses of the aluminum tubing that was supporting the super-structure of the stage. (Just kidding — for a second or two I thought I was writing a fax for Howard's show.) Too bad

Howard's onscreen parents, Howard Stern

Howard Stern

Howard didn't have a camera on all the subterranean stage action, it could have been a highly marketable addition to his movie on video.

Even though I pride myself on being a roving reporter, I can't be everywhere at once. Evidently a gay coupling took place in one of the green and white Port-O-Sans. I found out about this particular sexcapade the following Monday morning during a listener phone-in to Howard's show. The listener told Howard that he had had sex with a male stranger in the Port-O-San. As the caller's name was John, he was immediately christened Port-O-Johnny. This aromatic union was facilitated through the communal abuse of powdered cat tranquilizers — prescribed by veterinarians for cats, but sometimes misused by druggies — a drug that's recently become catnip for Howard's imagination. Another listener, and obvious cat tranquilizer abuser, called into the show and gave this description of the effects of cat tranquilizers: "It's like if you sniff a Fellini film." Describing his experiences as an extra, Port-O-Johnny said, "There were a lot of weird people there." Howard offered this pithy reply, "You were one of them. You were in the Port-O-Johnny giving sex to somebody!" Jackie pitched in with his own remark, "It was so hot in there (Port-O-San), it must have been like a urine-filled oven!"

I was so glad that I had brought my camera. It proved to be a real bonus. I never expected to be so close to all the action. I had anticipated the event to be much more organized and restrictive, which was obviously hardly the case. I spotted dozens of people guzzling beers and smoking marijuana. It was a festival of Bacchanalian proportions. I photographed one adventurous couple. The women's name was Olana, and she had written

Stern Gang, AC/DC

"Howard #1" across her bare breasts with fire engine red lipstick. She was carried high above the crowd on her boyfriend's shoulders. (I had assumed at the time that they were boyfriend and girlfriend, but later learned that they had only just met.) The man's name was Henry. For obvious reasons, I nicknamed him O'Henry after the famous home-run hitter, Hank Aaron. Besides, Olana and O'Henry has a nice

Gary, Fred, Robin and Jackie

ring to it. The freshly minted duo asked me to send them one of the photos as a memento of their meeting.

O'Henry is a more committed fan than I could ever have imagined. He told me that he has a collection of over fifty tapes, with six hours of viewing each, of every Howard Stern *E!* Show episode. I asked him if he watched these tapes very often, and he told me "All the time! Someday, I will share these tapes with my children and grandchildren!" Wow, and I thought that I was a Howard Stern fan. O'Henry should work at the Smithsonian as a broadcast archivist.

The following week

Robin Quivers, Jackie Martling

during a conversation with O'Henry I learned that his name was even more fitting than I had earlier imagined. I asked him if he was still seeing Olana, and he told me that they had been in touch. He also regaled me with the things that happened to him later in the day after the filming was over. Evidently O'Henry and Olana had parted company early in the evening. Afterwards O'Henry "hooked-up" with a fellow Stern fan named Sheri, a West Indian who had given him the eye earlier in the day. O'Henry told me that he accompanied his new companion to the subway, to make sure she safely caught her train. Well, the train wasn't the only thing she caught. O'Henry told me that Sheri accompanied him behind a subway staircase and returned the favor with one of her own. There you have it, further evidence that when it comes to Howard Stern, fiction pales next to reality. The funny thing is that during my faxing days, I had always imagined all the sexual shenanigans to be a great big hoax. Maybe the joke's on me.

It had been an exciting, eventful, and surprising day. The prophecy in my fortune cookie, "Fame and good fortune are coming your way" had indeed come true. I had been blessed with the chance to be in Howard's film and would even be paid for the privilege. I also got a once-in-a-lifetime souvenir — an autographed hat with Howard and his crew's signatures. To top it off, I had been given one of the things I covet most — a great, true story that I could share with friends and readers.

But my day was not over yet. During the long, arduous check-out procedure that was necessary to receive one's measly twenty-five dollar check, I had yet another mini-adventure. (By the way, I never cashed the check. I figured that it would hold a greater value to me as a souvenir.) While waiting in line, I spotted a familiar looking man in the misty distance wearing a gray Animal Republic tee shirt with a mountain gorilla on it. This man was none other than Howard's cohort Jackie

Gary Dell'Abate, Robin Quivers

Martling. I couldn't believe it. He was in a parking garage waiting to collect his car. I just love a captive audience, and who's more captive than a man waiting for an

Robin Quivers, Jackie Martling

Robin Quivers

illegal alien to safely deliver his auto? I went over to Jackie and very politely asked him if it would be okay to have my picture taken with him. I knew that I was on shaky ground. It's one thing to ask for a favor at a public function, but it's really quite another situation to impose upon someone in a parking garage. I think the events of the day had contributed to my boldness. I needn't have worried. Jackie evidently saw my unease and put the whole matter to rest by saying, "Sure, it doesn't cost *me* anything!" Ha ha, Jackie always has his eye, if not his hands on the buck. Jackie further took control of the situation by putting his arm around my shoulder and drawing me close. I handed my camera to the parking attendant and he got off one quick frame. It was frame number 37 on a 36 exposure roll. Good fortune indeed.

Howard Stern fans

Stern fan

<u>Postscript</u>: On February 27, 1997, *Private Parts* opened with tremendous fanfare, receiving acclaim from fans and critics alike. In fact, it was the Number One Box-Office Hit in its opening week.

I was lucky enough to attend the much-touted Premiere at New York's Madison Square Garden thanks to the generosity of Crackhead Bob. For a fleeting instant, I caught a gratifying glimpse of myself looking like a psychotic refugee from *Gilligan's Island* in the corner of a shot. I have since been playing my own version of *Where's Waldo?* with the freeze-frame button of my VCR remote and my very own tape of *Private Parts*.

HOORAY FOR HOLLYWOOD 2.0 — THE FREE UPGRADE:

There have been several new revelations since my acting debut as an extra in *Private Parts* in July 1996. I

Stern fan

have since learned that the post-production for *Private Parts* included a day filming Gary Dell'Abate with Wack Pack members Elephant Boy, Crackhead Bob, Quentin The Stutterer, and Nicole Bass. They were filmed introducing various segments of the movie. These segment introductions served as a humorous way to separate the stages of Howard Stern's life.

Stern fan

Unfortunately, Gary was sequestered in a small trailer with the Wack Packers. Gary complained on-air that he was besieged by Wack Packers requests for future show appearances. Evidently, the Wack Packers were more annoying than life insurance salesmen. They all had agendas. Poor Gary.

Elephant Boy, as always, proved to be a fountain of knowledge. I asked him how much he and his fellow Wackers had been paid. He told me that they had received the Actor's Equity minimum of $540.00 for their labors. However, Elephant Boy, ever the Pollyanna, added that he was thankful for being given food and validated parking!

I was hardly surprised to learn from Elephant Boy that Gary was reportedly paid $2,250.00 for his day of babysitting and filming. Perhaps the extra compensation was really hazard pay for sharing a trailer with mental patients. Or maybe the money was payment for helping Stuttering John and Steve Grillo with the unpleasant task of grooming Elephant Boy's coif and facial hair.

Dan Wagner, Jackie Martling

CHAPTER 12

THE FEEDING FRENZY TOUR

O n December 6, 1996 I decided to make a one-day marathon tour of Howard Stern-related events. The idea of a tour appealed to me for a variety of reasons. I was curious to find out whether I had the fortitude to survive more than twenty-four hours of witnessing what can only be described as a barbaric feeding frenzy. The tour also interested me from an anthropological point of view. It presented a wonderful opportunity to see how Howard's critters feed in the wild untamed streets of New York City.

The first stop on the tour was HMV records at 46th Street and Fifth Avenue in Manhattan at 1:00PM, where Jackie Martling was to sign copies of his latest compact disc, *Sargent Pecker*. The second stop on my tour was one of Elephant Boy's wrestling matches, which took place at 9:00PM. After this, I would head to stop number three — Kenny's Castaways in Greenwich Village at midnight, where Stuttering John's band was making an appearance. My fourth and final stop was the New York Coliseum, for Gary Dell'Abate's Princeton Ski Shop Show the following day at noon. This was clearly a gruelling schedule.

Event #1: Jackie Martling

F irst stop HMV records. Even though Jackie Martling was appearing at HMV records to sign and promote his new comedy album, *Sargent Pecker*, he had announced on-air that he was willing to sign anything. Since I'm a troublemaker, I decided to see if Jackie was serious. On the way to HMV records I stopped off at a clothing store and purchased a three-pack of Fruit of the Loom underwear.

With my camera at the ready, I snagged the third spot in line. By the time Jackie arrived, at 1:30PM, approximately thirty-five people were waiting. I'm sure Jackie had hoped for a larger turn-out. After all, a year earlier Howard had amassed more than seven thousand people just two blocks away. Predictably, Gary put a listener on-air the following week who falsely claimed that Jackie only had four people waiting for him.

Since there were so few people in line, I knew that Jackie would try to spend more time with each person to prolong the signing. Howard signs his name at the rate of one signature every four seconds. If Jackie matched Howard's speed, then this signing would have been completed in less than

HMV Records

three minutes! I was glad that I had brought my undies. I had correctly reasoned that they would give Jackie something to have fun with.

Jackie breathed a sigh of relief when I told him that the underwear had not been worn. He even held them up for the amusement of the crowd. I asked him to write something humorous and nasty on them. Wondering what the head writer of Howard's show might come up with was exciting. Jackie drew a picture of a tiny penis over the crotch of one pair and wrote, "Your cock, Jackie". On the second pair, Jackie drew a small circle over the seat of the undies and wrote, "Your asshole, Jackie." Not exactly Shakespeare, but okay, I suppose. Perhaps writing for Howard Stern isn't as taxing as one would imagine.

Jackie was genuinely amused by my antics. As he signed my underwear, I start-

Jackie Martling

ed to photograph him. He heard the whir of my camera's motor drive and looked up. Jackie couldn't help but burst into laughter. He looked at the crowd and said, "I can't believe he's taking pictures of me signing his underwear." With that remark, Jackie jumped up and grabbed his crotch. Then he turned around, pointed his ass in my direction and grabbed it. Fortunately, I managed to squeeze off a few frames. Even though I didn't have time to focus, I was glad to have saved this bizarre moment for posterity.

After getting my stuff signed, I took up a

position near the end of the table Jackie was using to sign autographs and continued taking pictures. I figured that I might as well see what I could get away with. After a few moments Jackie looked at me, and in classic Howard Stern fashion asked, "Are you a homo? Are you a stalker?" Hmm, multiple choice questions. It was a tough decision. I looked at Jackie and replied: "I'm a gay stalker!" Hey, what did he want from my life? The fact of the matter was that Jackie had asked listeners to show-up for his signing. What did he expect — librarians wearing orthopedic shoes? Once again, my theories were verified — the Stern show treats

Jackie Martling

anyone that isn't a stripper or a celebrity as a mental patient, a homosexual, or a stalker.

My repartee with Jackie emboldened me to the point where I decided it was time to use my secret weapon. My fisheye lens! The closer one gets to one's subject with a fisheye lens, the more distorted and funny the results. I must have been within a foot of Jackie's nose when he turned to me and asked, "Hey, what are you shooting? — my boogers?" He looked so funny through my lens that all I could do to reply was laugh.

Eventually, Jackie decided to make productive use of my presence. He asked me to take a few pictures of him and his partners at Oglio Records. Jackie said that he wanted them for his Internet pages. Of course I was only too happy to oblige. I gave Jackie one of my business cards and in return he gave me his Internet address. Even the people at Oglio Records and their public relations company started inundating

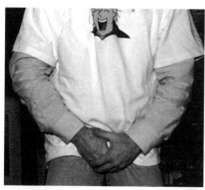

Jackie Martling

me with business cards. It was a wild situation, and much more than I could have hoped for.

A week or so later Jackie wound up using one of my photos on his Website. Jackie thanked me for the use of the photo by sending me a box of his Jokeland merchandise. The "care" package included shirts, CD's, videos, cassette tapes, and something called a Joke-In-A-Box that plays a prerecorded joke whenever you

Jackie Martling

tweak it's nose. I was overwhelmed by Jackie's generosity.

Unfortunately, Jackie's magnanimity was short lived. In early November 1997 Simon & Schuster published *Jackie Martling's Disgustingly Dirty Joke Book*. Imagine my surprise when I discovered that Jackie had reproduced one of my photos on thirteen different pages of his book without bothering to credit me or get my permission. This discovery prompted an immediate call to Howard's show to complain.

Howard and the gang, with the obvious exception of Jackie, couldn't stop laughing. Howard and Robin described Jackie's actions as being typical of his unprofessional, hippie-like behavior. In a reference to Jackie's having once allowed a listener to eat a marshmallow from his butt, I offered to settle the matter by having Jackie eat a Ring-Ding from my own butt. (Not that I would ever go through with such a disgusting thing — I don't think.)

Dan Wagner, Jackie Martling

Howard loved my suggestion. Even Fred piped in with, "Belly up to the butt-buffet!" Everyone was quite surprised when Jackie turned my offer down.

A day later Gary phoned me with the news that Howard wanted former New York City mayor, Ed Koch — who was currently serving as the judge in the television show *People's Court* — to take on the case. The suggestion thrilled me.

Unfortunately, it never

Jackie Martling merchandise

came to pass. According to Gary, Ed Koch didn't want to tarnish his judicial reputation by making light of *People's Court*. Gary and I thought that Ed Koch's attitude was pretty silly, given that *People's Court* is to law what *Hogan's Heroes* is to World War II. By the way, Jackie never offered to pay me for having used my photos. I guess I shouldn't be too surprised. After all, Howard and Robin never fail to remind their listeners that Jackie is cheap.

Event #2: Elephant Boy

What tour would be complete without a description and photographs of one of Howard's courtiers in action? It was with this sense of mission that I boarded an F train to my second tour destination — the Elks Lodge #878 in Jackson Heights, Queens. This was the site of one of Elephant Boy's numerous paid appear-

ances as a wrestling match bell-ringer and time-keeper.

The poet John Donne wrote: "Never send to know for whom the bell tolls". Fred, the Elephant Boy, would probably reply: "It tolls for he who rings the bell!" Yet this bell-

Elks Lodge #878

Wrestling match

ringer was only being paid $25.00! That's less than fifty cents per ring. After gas and mileage he probably was lucky to clear $20.00. If these are the spoils of celebrity, I'd rather be a fan.

My second reason for going to one of Elephant Boy's appearances was to deliver his completed headshots. Fred was in a rush to get them. No wonder. He was pathetically attempting to turn a 500 percent profit on the photos by charging $5.00 each for them. Many of the people at the wrestling matches

189

have become friendly with Fred. It was painful to see these "friends" induce Fred into giving them free photos. There wasn't much he could do about it. There's an old joke that goes: "What do you charge a three-hundred-pound professional wrestler for an autographed photograph?" Answer: "Whatever he wants to pay!" During the hour or so that I hung out

Elephant Boy

with Fred, he didn't make a single sale. He got lots of compliments on the photos, though.

The crowds at these wrestling matches are very scary. They are composed of "po, white, trailer trash". Many people brought their children, who were encouraged to yell insults at the wrestlers. I found the whole scene very depressing. The sight of Fred with the day's champion in the wrestlers' hot, stuffy dressing room was so Felliniesque that I was only too happy to oblige Fred by shooting some film.

Elephant Boy and the champ

Event #3: Stuttering John

The third stop of my tour was Kenny's Castaways, site of Stuttering John's band appearance. Even though Stuttering John was supposed to play at midnight, he didn't begin until around 1:30AM. Some may call this fashionably late. Personally, I felt like a marathon runner who has just encountered a huge hill with a strong head wind. To make matters worse, owing to John's late start, I had missed the last train home to Long Island and wound up having to sleep on the cold concrete floor of my New York City photo studio.

Stuttering John's behavior at Kenny's Castaways was pretty amusing. He acted as though he thought he was a major celebrity. It was obvious that he relished being in the spotlight. Before he began his set he went on stage and addressed the crowd. One or two yahoos in the audience shouted "Baba Booey". ("Baba Booey" is the Stern Fan's equivalent of the rebel yell.) Eventually my voice got hoarse and I stopped.

Steve Grillo and girlfriend

Quite a few members of the audience had absolutely no idea who Stuttering John was. In fact, I overheard one person exclaim, "Who's that pompous clown?"

John had his entourage with him, which consisted of his girlfriend, his underage-looking nephew, Steve Grillo, Steve's

Steve Grillo and girlfriend

girlfriend, and the rest of the band. I felt like a lucky anthropologist on the African plains witnessing a rare tribal ritual. Thanks to the alcohol and convivial club atmosphere, John and his entourage were really letting their hair down. There they were in their true element, displaying all the glory and splendor of their raw animalistic spirits. I circled upwind in a vain attempt to keep my scent from giving away my position.

Unfortunately, my camera's flash betrayed me. John came over and asked, "What magazine are you shooting for?" I replied: "I'm shooting for my book."

Kenny's Castaways

John gave me an amused look and chuckled. Emboldened by my own audacity I asked him, "John, would you mind posing with your wife? I mean girlfriend?" I had momentarily forgotten that John had weaseled out of marrying his girlfriend the previous summer as had been planned.

Stuttering John and Suzanne

Stuttering John gets paid

Even though they had recently had a baby girl, John, ever the perfectionist, felt the logistics of a beach wedding in the Hamptons required at least one more year to arrange.

What could be more fitting on a feeding frenzy tour than a chance to photograph cash changing hands? Luckily, I was in the perfect position to record such an event. In a nearby clearing, (read — momentary parting of the club's patrons) right before my eyes, were Stuttering John and what appeared to be a representative of the club paying John for the night's gig. (Perhaps John insists on getting paid *before*

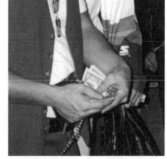
The Money!

he plays.) With trembling hands, I quickly raised my camera to eye level and shot. What a trophy. I could hardly wait to mount my trophy in my den and savor it whilst regaling friends with the tale of its origin and enjoying a fine cigar, a glass of twenty-year-old port, and a roaring fire.

My night at Kenny's Castaways was an unequivocal success. Not only was I able to capture the primitive rituals of Stuttering John on film, but I was also fortunate enough to bag the lesser sub-species of his genus — Steve Grillo. It was clear to me that both Stuttering John and Steve had temporarily landed far

Stuttering John

above their true stations in life as a direct result of being employed by Howard Stern. I enjoyed my field work as a Stern Show anthropologist.

Finally, after what seemed like an eternity, John and his band went on stage. I was curious to hear John perform live. His first album has one or two songs that are actually listenable. Gary gave him the best on-air put-down when he told John: "I heard your record shipped gold — <u>back</u> to the label!" The crowd looked bored. The only audience members that seemed to take any notice of the band were two women who looked as though they were more than just friends. This frisky-duo

Stuttering John

went in front of the stage area, faced each other, put their hands over their heads in a ballet-like position, and executed two wobbly out of sync pirouettes — and there I was thinking that my evening wouldn't be up-scale or cultural!

Stuttering John and his band

I'd seen and learned more than I had bargained for. It was time to make my exit. Before I left, I made a circuit around the club and shot a variety of photos of John, guitar virtuoso, in action.

Event #4: Gary Dell'Abate

After I stung Howard with my Emmy Award scam I kept vigil in front of my television set from 11 to 12 each night, waiting for Howard's *E! Show* to run my on-air appearance with Howard. Unfortunately my vigil was in vain. Scott Einzeger of the E! Entertainment Network informed me that my segment would never air for the spurious reason that The National Academy of Television Arts and Sciences refused to grant permission to show the Emmy on-air.

Scott told me that Howard keeps the Emmy in his office. This was later confirmed by Gary Dell'Abate during the final stop of my marathon tour at his promotional appearance for Princeton Ski Shops at the New York Coliseum Ski And Snowboard Show. Gary said that they have a running joke at the office, since reporters interviewing Howard about *Private Parts* assume he really won an Emmy. This is just what they predicted on-air during my appearance.

I took advantage of my providential meeting with Gary to ask him two questions. The first was: "Gary, whatever happened to my check for $522.00?" Gary answered by looking at me sheepishly and laughing. I said, "It was all bull, right?" Gary laughed and nodded his head in the affirmative. My second question was: "You guys weren't mad at me, were you?" Gary replied, "No, no, don't worry about it." I said, "Well, at least Howard got to keep the Emmy. I did it to meet Howard, not to be mean-spirited."

Personally, I believe that my segment never aired because Howard Stern didn't want to draw attention to the Emmy, lest he be forced to return it. Heck, I bet Howard wants to win an Emmy even more than Susan Lucci does. No wonder my scam worked.

Going to see Gary at the New York Coliseum was a great idea. After all, what could be better than having the opportunity to question a captive subject? Unfortunately, Gary wasn't in a very conversational mood.

Perhaps he felt uncomfortable in his low budget surroundings. Princeton Ski Shops had located the Gary/KRock booth in a dreary and remote section of the Coliseum. The walls of the booth were covered with cheesy black and yellow plastic rectangles bearing the KRock 92.3 call numbers. A large screen television and a VCR with a tape of music videos were placed catty-corner in the booth. On either side and perpendicular to the television were two wooden park benches. It would have been nice

Dan Wagner, Gary Dell'Abate

if these benches were for the show attendees, but such was not the case. The bench to the right of the television was occupied by two KRock promotions department interns. The left bench was used by Gary and a young man in charge of promotions.

Besides making money, Howard has said that he doesn't know what Gary does at these promotions. I have to agree, after seeing Gary in "action". Other than signing an autograph or two on ugly 8x10 glossies, all Gary did was park his butt on the reserved benches and gossip with his fellow KRock workers. It was quite obvious to me that Gary wanted to have as little as possible to do with the few fans who had bothered to shell out the eight dollar admission fee and show up.

I figured that as long as Gary was willing to sign autographs I might as well get one, too. I asked him to write something imaginative. Gary thought a while, grinned mischievously, and wrote: "To the lying Douche! w/ the Emmy, Baba Booey! Gary".

Trying to talk to Gary was like pulling teeth — and pretty enormous teeth at that. Gary mentioned that he needed to have a new headshot done. I was so excited at the prospect of getting another Sternite in my studio that I nearly wet myself. As casually as possible, I got on my knees and begged for the assignment. Gary said that he needed a conceptual photo. I guess when you're Gary, a beauty shot is out of the question. This explains the photo Gary was handing out. It depicted him from a distance wearing shades and holding a spray can with which he had just written *Baba Booey* on a brick wall. In an effort to secure the headshot assignment, I volunteered a concept of my own. I said, "If you want to stay with a teeth motif (as a joke I even pronounced the word motif, as mo-teeth!), then how about a close-up shot with a fisheye lens? It will make your teeth look enormous." Gary seemed to like the idea. In fact, he immediately proposed that his name could be written over his teeth on the finished photo. I gave Gary one of my business cards.

Whenever I deal with Gary, I never seem to be able to leave well enough alone. I doubted that Gary would hire me to do his headshot. Therefore, I played my only card. With a smile on my face I said, "By the way, I photographed someone you may be familiar with." Gary could tell by my expression that I was about to unload a zinger. Laughing, he said, "Oh yeah? Who's that?" I said, "Fred Norris. Ask him to show you the publicity shots I did for his band." Gary responded to my name-dropping with a quizzical look that was part smirk and part wide-eyed wonder. He couldn't decide whether to believe me or not.

One of the things that surprised me about Gary was his weight. He looked much thinner than I remembered when I had seen him during the filming of the crowd scene for *Private Parts*. I mentioned this to Gary and he told me that he had dropped sixteen pounds since Labor Day (over four pounds per month). I guess all the teasing and fat jokes directed at Gary had finally gotten his attention. I even asked him if he owed his weight loss to Metrex (the diet program hawked on the show). Gary laughed and said, "I throw up a lot. No, just kidding, I lost the weight by laying low." (Whatever that means.)

When Gary left to visit the men's room, I decided to question the interns. They told me that KRock doesn't even give them food or travel money. To add insult to injury, they even have to pay for the privilege of working. This payment is made to their respective schools for administering the intern program, evaluating their progress, and giving them four credits. What a sham! The interns even confirmed the fact that most of their time was spent being go-fers and cataloging tapes. KRock uses about twenty-five interns, most of whom never even get to see Howard Stern, much less participate in his on-air shenanigans. In fact, only five or so are needed during the morning time slot. Of these five positions, three are occupied by Stuttering John, Steve Grillo, and Mike Gange.

Gary always makes fun of the turn-out, or lack thereof, at promotional appearances by Jackie Martling and others connected with the show. All I can say is "people who live in glass houses shouldn't throw stones." During the hour or so that I hung-out with Gary only about ten people showed-up, many of whom were there just for the Ski Show and not to see Gary.

Compared to the interns, however, Gary is a big cheese. As such he must have felt compelled to entertain his troops. He did this by telling humorous anecdotes of his heroic exploits in the service of his general — Howard Stern. While listening sereptitiously, I was fortunate enough to hear Gary tell the following story about one of his experiences during an outdoor MTV awards show in Los Angeles during the late 1980s. The awards show took place in a huge circus tent. Surrounding the tent were dozens of trailers for the entertainers and their entourages. Even megastars like Dustin Hoffman were in attendance. Long picnic tables had been set-up for lunch and snacks. Gary was sitting at the same table as Stuttering John, Kurt Cobain, Courtney Love, Axl Rose of *Guns N' Roses*, and numerous unidentified people. All of a sudden there was a loud commotion at the end of the table. Courtney and Axl were screaming obscenities at each other. Courtney's husband Kurt just continued eating and tried to ignore the whole sordid scene. Meanwhile, Courtney was still screaming at the top of her lungs. Throughout the whole affair "Courtney was holding her new six-month-old baby under her arm like a loaf of bread." Gary: "John and I looked at each other and said, 'Isn't this the greatest!'"

Throughout the course of Gary's appearance I observed a constant stream of people employed by vendors at the Ski Show attempting to network with him. The method of networking with Gary never varied. The hopefuls would magically appear at Gary's right elbow with ski and hotel brochures at the ready. Once Gary noticed their presence they would ceremoniously open their printed matter and convey in hushed conspiratorial tones that the services depicted in said brochures were available, at no charge, for Gary's enjoyment. Gary would lick his teeth and gums, displaying obvious relish for the buffet of free items before him. Regardless of whether the free ski lodge or service was in Vermont, or New York, Gary would inevitably comment, "Oh great, I go there all the time!". With this salivating rejoinder Gary would take the brochure, printed matter, or card from the networking individual. Then the supplicants would thank Gary, nod their heads, bow, and take several steps backwards before making their exits. It was quite a sight.

Gary didn't seem very comfortable having me around. I was the only fan to stay for more than a minute or two. I even asked him if it was okay to hang-out. Gary said, "yeah, it's fine." However, I don't think he meant it. Maybe Gary was uncomfortable because he had tried to scam me about my payment for being on-air during the Emmy scam, or for not returning my calls when I had asked for advice about receiving death threats after my on-air appearance with Melrose Larry Green. Who knows? Perhaps Gary was uncomfortable with having someone witness the stream of people attempting to curry favor with him. Either way, due to the lack of fans in attendance I felt pretty conspicuous — and bored — just standing there. Besides, I didn't want to annoy Gary enough to jeopardize the remote chance of shooting his headshots. So, with a nod of my head, a handshake, and a mumbled goodbye, I, too, took the requisite backward steps and made my exit.

My first stop after leaving the New York Coliseum was the nearest one-hour photo lab. Looking at my photo of Gary was a shock. All I can say is, Howard really does surround himself with scary looking people. But hey, it's radio.

Gary is known by several nicknames, the most popular being Baba Booey. Howard used to refer to Gary as Boy Gary. He stopped calling Gary by this name after Gary complained that he was too old (about 35) to be called "Boy" anymore. Recently Howard asked Gary to wear an ape costume. Gary refused, saying that after he wore an ape outfit for the 1994 New Year's Eve Pageant, he promised himself that he would never stoop that low again. According to Gary, he is just a regular guy who is interested in sports and lives in Connecticut with his wife and kid. Howard, however, insists that Gary will have to wear an ape outfit again — if asked — and that he does in fact look like a monkey. (Gary is also often referred to as Mama Monkey.)

Decide for yourselves what Gary should be called. Perhaps this candid shot will help.

Gary Dell'Abate

<u>Postscript</u>: Due to the fact that Gary had been so uncooperative at his Princeton Ski Show appearance, I decided that a follow-up visit was in order. I didn't have long to wait. Several months later, during the "plugs" segment at the end of Howard's Show, I learned that Gary would be appearing at the grand opening for the Soupman at a store called the Bagel Boss, located a mere ten-minutes from my home on Long Island.

One of the problems with trying to obtain good photographs during an appearance is the time factor. The second problem getting a subject like Gary to cooperate. Therefore, I decided that the solution to these problems would be to get hired to take publicity photographs by the company sponsoring the promotion. That way I would have a reason for staying the entire length of the appearance, and would also have leverage with the person I was photographing (Gary).

With these goals in mind I gave the Soupman a call. I doubted that my plan would work. After all, why would they even want photographs? To improve my chances, I decided to make them an offer they couldn't refuse — an eighty percent reduction of my fee. After trying to reach the owner of the Soupman several times, I had no choice but to leave a message with one of the clerks at the Bagel Boss. My message was very simple: "Please give me a call, at 555-0U812, if you need publicity photographs taken during the Gary Dell'Abate appearance. My fee is one hundred dollars, and that includes 4x6 color prints." Talk about fire-sales. At that price I wouldn't even cover my film and processing costs.

Several days passed without a word from the Soupman. During this time period I began to regret my phone call. Maybe I had stepped over the line. Showing up at an appearance to take a few quick photos is one thing, but conniving to get hired could be construed as "stalking." Either way, I didn't have to debate the matter for long. Within another day or so, I received a call from Jack Freedman, the owner of the Soupman.

Gary Dell'Abate

Jack told me that my timing was perfect. It turned out that the Soupman was a franchise operation, and that Jack needed photos of crowds of people lining up to buy soup to show potential franchisees. Jack reasoned correctly that the best time to take such photos would be during an appearance by a member of the *Howard Stern Show*. I was amused when he told me that he would prefer it if the photos of the crowd scenes didn't include Baba Booey.

A week later I arrived at the Soupman. I could hardly wait to see Gary's expression when he learned that I had been hired to photograph his appearance. Within an hour or so, Gary made his grand entrance. He was very serious and businesslike. The first thing Gary did was shake hands and introduce himself to Jack Freedman, Jack's assistants, some people from the Bagel Boss, and last but not least — me. Jack introduced me by saying, "Gary, I'd like you to meet our photographer, Dan Wagner." As Gary and I locked eyes I could barely contain an ear-to-ear smirk. Gary's expression was priceless. He said, "You?" By way of reply, I smiled and gave him a sly wink.

It was fun to watch the wheels slowly turn in his monkey cerebellum. If I were to draw a cartoon of Gary, I'd have smoke pouring from his ears. I knew Gary would ask me how I had been hired. After ten minutes, Gary said, "So, how do you know Jack? Are you related, or something?" I replied, "No, I just called and asked them if they needed any publicity photos." Gary's face was a portrait of pure simian amazement. It's so satisfying to pull a fast one on him.

For the next two hours I was as photographically intrusive as a paparazzi on speed. No matter where Gary turned, there I was, zoom lens at the ready, and flashing away. I must have taken more than two-hundred photographs. I bet Gary saw spots for days.

I have to hand it to Gary. Despite being tricked, he was very professional and ultimately took my little prank in stride. In fact, he decided to make productive use of my presence, by asking me to send him some photos. Gary told me that he wanted the photos for his young boy, Jackson, because, "someday, I want him to see that people actually waited in line for my autograph." Gary's self-effacing comment touched me to the core. It made me feel somewhat guilty for acting like such a jerk. Gary, a class act — who knew?

Luckily, I quickly got over my false sentimentality and screwed on my wide-angle lens. I was going in for the "kill." For the final shots of the day I had Gary pose in front of the Soupman sign and pretend to eat from a large container of soup. Gary looked so silly that I could barely contain my laughter. Gary's a good sport — when he wants to be.

After the shots were done, Jack treated us to some of his fabulous soups. They tasted great. My favorite was the Lentil. In addition to the soup, Gary also had a lox sandwich, which Jack insisted on paying for. When the clerk asked Gary what he wanted to drink, he replied, "Anything but Snapple!" At the time Howard was still

angry about Snapple having withdrawn its advertising from his show. Talk about holding a grudge. Gary's behavior reinforced my belief that the Stern Show operates under a siege mentality.

By the way, I asked Jack how much Gary was being paid. He told me that Gary was getting close to two grand. Wow! Now who's the

Gary Dell'Abate

fool? There's a saying among salesman about taking all the customer's money that goes like this: "Never leave anything on the table." I guess Gary must subscribe to this philosophy, because he didn't leave empty-handed. Prior to his departure, Jack loaded Gary up with two enormous bags of bagels. My lasting impression of the day was Gary struggling with the heavy bags of bagels. All I could think about was the fable about the monkey with his hand stuck in the cookie jar.

Later in the week, Jack called me about using one of my photos for a full-page ad in *Newsday*. Since I had lost money on the photos, I was happy to make some extra bucks. Jack hired me to take photos at two more Soupman events where I was able to grab some shots of Steve Grillo, Crackhead Bob, and Elephant Boy.

Unfortunately, I was never able to substantially raise my fees. Whenever I tried (to raise my fees), Jack would ask me, "How come you charged so little the first time?" What could I say? — I'm an obsessed Howard Stern fan? Somehow, I doubted that he would understand.

CHAPTER 13

HAPPY BIRTHDAY, HOWARD!

Every year, on or about January 12th Howard's sidekick Robin Quivers throws an elaborate Birthday Party for him. Over the years the parties have become more and more grandiose. Gift-bearing celebrities and politicians drop by to wish Howard a Happy Birthday. Rock stars compete for the privilege of serenading Howard. The phone rings off the hook with calls from well-wishers.

Listening to Howard and his merry band of birthday revelers has always filled me with envy. In fact, the Birthday Show is usually my emotional low-point for the year. The event serves to remind me that despite my frequent interactions with Howard and his associates, I'm not a member of his inner circle. No matter how many Emmy Awards I give Howard, or how many photos I take of Fred Norris's band, or how many uncredited and unpaid photos I unwittingly supply for *Jackie Martling's Disgustingly Dirty Joke Book*, or how many free photos I give to his staff and Wack Pack, or how many times I set my pride aside and make a complete, on-air, fool of myself for Howard's amusement I will never, ever, be invited to Howard's Birthday Party.

The depth of my despair over being shunned yet again hit rock-bottom on January 13th, 1997, the day of Howard's 43rd Birthday Party and one of the coldest days of the winter. Each year Howard's party is held at a different location. That year it was held at Sony Music Studios, located near 50th Street and Ninth Avenue in New York City. An unrelenting wind whipped in from the West challenging only the hardiest — or craziest — to venture outside.

Clearly, only an insanely obsessed individual would chose to don headphones and listen to the festivities whilst freezing-to-death outside of Sony Music Studios on such a dreadful, ungodly day. But misery loves company, and at least I could comfort myself with the knowledge that I wouldn't be alone. A handful of similarly afflicted fans took turns sharing the scanty shelter afforded by a nearby doorway. I'm sure we were quite a sight. With our frost-bitten faces hidden behind woolen ski masks, and watery eyes peering through narrow slits, we resembled terrorists with advanced rigor mortis.

Despite the cold, one of the most painful aspects of my

Nicole Bass

birthday vigil was enduring the humiliating stares and laughs from arriving party-goers — several of whom had the audacity to stop and take snapshots. The experience reminded me of a mortifying memory from my youth. At the end of ninth grade, my Junior High School held a prom for the graduating class. Ever the loser, I spent the evening outside the barred gym windows peering in at the socially-functional members of my class. Towards the end of the evening I was spied by one of the class bullies, who wasted no time in mounting the stage, grabbing the microphone, and alerting the prom to my presence. Thanks to the efforts of a cruel yearbook

Stuttering John

editor my graduation photo was amended with the phrase: "Peeping-Dan!"

Before my Sony stake-out I had actually made a feeble attempt to crash the party. A block from Sony Music Studios I came across a limo driver who was busy eating his breakfast of coffee and blueberry muffins in his limo. The chauffeur had just

Fred and Mary

dropped two guests off and was listening to Howard's ongoing Birthday Show. My crisp twenty-dollar bill convinced the chauffeur to drive me the two-hundred yards to the studio's entrance. I waited for several awkward moments, in vain, for the chauffeur to open my door. With a silly grin, he turned to look at me and said, "Getting out takes another twenty." Unfortunately, I had just blown my wad, and so was forced to open my own door. Not exactly a dramatic entrance.

Amy Lynn

Upon exiting the limo I entered the studio and made a bee-line for the party. However, before I could walk more than a foot or two, an attractive woman asked me for my name. After double-checking the guest list, she informed me that my name wasn't on it. (Quelle surprise!) Since I had my camera bag with me I tried to convince her that I was with the press. Sensing an imposter, she asked me what magazine I was from. I hadn't expected such a tricky question. Maybe my brain was frozen. All I could do was mumble something about being a freelancer for *Broadcast Times*

Crackhead Bob

Magazine (I don't even know if such a publication exists.). From this point on things only got worse. She called one of the people in the promotion department to see if they'd heard of me. I was so nervous, that despite my frozen state I was actually sweating. Of course I was politely asked to leave. They wouldn't even let me hang out in the lobby.

The opportunity to photograph arriving and departing guests almost made my masochistic winter wait worthwhile. I managed to get several great shots. My favorites are: Fred and Allison Norris holding hands; Stuttering John wearing a goofy, brown, woolen cap; Dominic Barbara looking fatter than ever; sexy stripper Amy Lynn; Wack Packers Crackhead Bob, Nicole Bass, Elephant Boy, Uzo, Kenneth Keith Kallenbach and Captain Janks. Most of these photos were taken during a five-minute time

Dominic Barbara

span immediately following the party. The only reason the guests bothered to loiter in the freezing cold was to bask in the envious stares of those less privileged as they formed groups for further celebrating.

Before the group dispersed I managed to say hi to Uzo. She immediately remembered me from the previous summer's Chat Party. Imagine how I felt when she told me, "Dan, I could have gotten you into the party if you'd e-mailed me." Ahhhhh!!!!! Oh well, at least Uzo was nice enough to give me an official Howard Stern 1997 Birthday Party button. I almost

Uzo

felt guilty for having once considered Uzo a mere stray cat and Howard Stern profiteer.

Speaking of Howard Stern profiteers, let's not forget the famed bloated attorney — Dominic Barbara. It was rumored on-air that Dominic snuck three of his friends into Howard's Party. On top of this, Dominic reportedly bossed people around and complained that there weren't enough goody-bags for his friends. (Goody-bags contained a collectible Howard Stern Watch and other nicknacks.) After the party, Dominic went to the K-ROCK offices and allegedly tried to wrangle more watches. The following day, Howard and the gang publicly berated Dominic for his appallingly venal and obnoxious behavior, threatening to ban him from the show. Even Tom Chiusano, K-ROCK'S VP/General Manager, gave Dominic an on-air dressing-down. Tom told the listeners that over 600 people had been invited, and that the party was over-booked. One wise guy even opined that Dominic alone counted as more than one guest.

Over the course of the next few evenings, while watching the E! Entertainment Television shows of Howard's Birthday Party, I indulged in a festival of feeling sorry for myself, vowing that 1998 would be different. I would never again suffer the indignities of being a "poor little match-boy." For a whole year I toiled, plotted, and shamelessly sucked-up to Uzo. Finally, a year and several weeks later I was rewarded with the following e-mail:

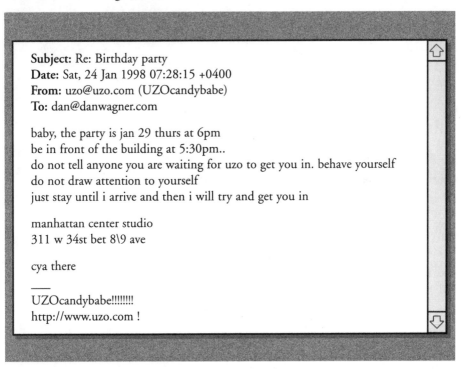

Subject: Re: Birthday party
Date: Sat, 24 Jan 1998 07:28:15 +0400
From: uzo@uzo.com (UZOcandybabe)
To: dan@danwagner.com

baby, the party is jan 29 thurs at 6pm
be in front of the building at 5:30pm..
do not tell anyone you are waiting for uzo to get you in. behave yourself
do not draw attention to yourself
just stay until i arrive and then i will try and get you in

manhattan center studio
311 w 34st bet 8\9 ave

cya there

___
UZOcandybabe!!!!!!!!
http://www.uzo.com !

God bless Uzo! God bless her home country, Nigeria! God bless her wonderful Website! God bless her silicon implants! God bless her e-mail punctuation, and God bless all her future lesbian conquests! Hey, wait a minute, she wrote, "i will try and get you in." That meant that even after a year of brown-nosing Uzo's burnt umber bum, I still might not get in. Time for some antacid medication.

P rior to receiving Uzo's e-mail I had desperately tried to win tickets to Howard's 44th Birthday Party. For the first time, the 92.3 K-ROCK promotion department offered listeners the chance to win two tickets to Howard's party. The contest was duplicated in all of Howard's major syndicated markets. This would be the first time that mere listeners would be allowed to mingle with the King of All Media, Howard Stern, at his Birthday Show. Normally, the party is filled with show sponsors, celebrities, show personnel and their families, and various insiders. To win tickets, *all* one had to do was be the ninety-second caller at various times throughout the day during a three-week period leading up to the party — no small feat! I tried calling so often that I wore off the writing on my "re-dial" button. It looked like Uzo was my last hope, provided the rumors that Howard might not even have a birthday party in 1998 were false. I, for one, doubted Robin's party-giving demurrals because:

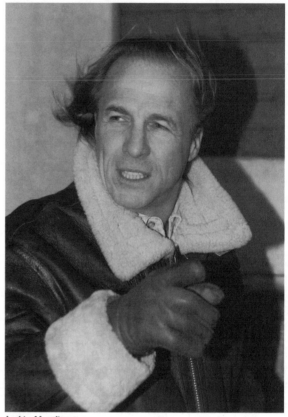

Jackie Martling

1) Howard Stern, being a self-confessed egomaniac and narcissist, would never tolerate a partyless birthday.

2) The Birthday Party is a huge ratings grabber for both the radio show and E! Entertainment Television. In fact, the E! show generates five half-hours shows from the event.

3) Robin and her fellow Stern staffers and crew would never risk the on-air wrath of their King by failing to honor his royal birth.

4) The show wives (Alison Stern, Allison Norris, Nancy Sirianni-Martling, Mary Dell'Abate, and Suzanna Melendez) would make their husbands lives miserable if they failed to give them a night on the town.

5) And last, and perhaps most important, the sponsors would miss their annual public stroking and schmooze-fest with Howard.

Actually, it was funny to listen to all the hollow protests that there wouldn't be a birthday party in 1998. Howard speculated that the party was postponed due to the recent birth of Gary Dell'Abate's son, Luke. This sounded like the best explanation by far. Although Robin is the "official" host of the party, most people believe that it's Howard's producer, Gary, who really does the work.

Some listeners thought that the party was delayed due to Jackie's absence from the show. Just before Christmas Jackie had gone on strike for more pay. A month later it seemed unlikely that Jackie would return in time for the Birthday Show, although many fans were betting that Jackie would make a grand re-entrance at Howard's party.

The majority of fans blamed Tom Chiusano for the impasse in resolving Jackie's situation and the status of the Birthday Show. Personally, I was half convinced that Tom was orchestrating the two events to flex his managerial muscles and save the station a truckload of money. Happily, I was mistaken. A week or so before the party became a reality, leaks were posted on the Internet that the birthday bash would be held at the Hammerstein Ballroom on 34th Street, just off Eighth Avenue — a mere five blocks from my photo studio. Yippee! Life couldn't get any sweeter when, on January 28th, 1998 (the day before the party) Jackie returned to the show. Now, with the stars in their proper alignment, the show would most definitely go on.

Unfortunately, the fans lucky enough to win tickets had to undergo a bizarre, macabre, hold-onto-the-edge-of-your-seat game of wait-and-see before they could find out whether or not they would be partying with Howard. In light of all the leaks, it was pretty silly to put the fans through so much abuse. After weeks of being left in the dark, the winners were finally notified the day before the party.

After the party a newfound friend of mine showed me the following copies of his winning ticket and a letter from Tom Chiusano:

<u>The Ticket:</u>

92.3 K-ROCK HOWARD STERN BIRTHDAY BASH '98

1998 HOWARD STERN BIRTHDAY BASH

HAMMERSTEIN BALLROOM
311 WEST 34TH STREET, NEW YORK CITY

THURSDAY, JANUARY 29, 1998
SHOWTIME: 7:00PM
DOORS: 6:00PM

NO CAMERAS, BOTTLES, RECORDING DEVICES
ALL ARE SUBJECT TO SEARCH AND CONFISCATION
ADMITTANCE IS NOT GUARANTEED

The Letter:

K-ROCK 92.3 FM RADIO

Congratulations on winning tickets to the 1998 Howard Stern Birthday Bash! We are extremely excited about bringing listeners into this special event, but we need your cooperation. This is the first time ever that we will have listeners at the Birthday Bash...it's an experiment! If all goes well this year, we'll make it a tradition. Since the event will be taped for radio broadcast, it is important that you act appropriately. Please be considerate — do not use profanities or partake in any dangerous behavior that may put you and others around you at risk.

(I wonder if the person who authored the behavioral manifestos for the extras in the Private Parts *crowd scenes also wrote this treatise?)*

Two other important things you should be aware of:

1. No bottles, cameras or recording devices will be allowed in the venue. All listeners will be subject to search and any necessary confiscation.

(Hmm, this letter is starting to remind me of the fascist flyers handed out during Howard's book signings.)

2. E! Entertainment Television will be taping this event for programming which will appear on E! Your presence and cooperation constitute your consent to being videotaped and your agreement that E! may use, without compensation, your name, voice or likeness in connection with its programming.

I hope you have a great time. Please help make this a night we will all want to remember.

Tom Chiusano
92.3 K-ROCK VP/General Manager

Despite the ample warnings to behave in a proper and decorous manner — a clear challenge for any fan — I later discovered that two fans had been ejected from the party for cursing and causing a scene because they couldn't hear the show very well. Evidently, while these two hellions were being thrown out, their fellow fans serenaded their departure with lyrics from a golden-oldie, "sha-na na na, hey hey, good-bye!"

Captain Janks

At long last my appointment with destiny was at hand. Even though Uzo had instructed me to meet her at 5:30PM, I decided to show up at 5:00. After plotting for a year I wasn't going to risk missing her. Besides, I correctly surmised that an early arrival would increase my picture-taking opportunities.

The Police Department had installed crowd control barricades in front of the Hammerstein Ballroom. To the left of the main entrance there was a line for ticket winners, and to the right a line for V.I.P.s, in this case show sponsors and guests. To my knowledge, the real celebrities were whisked through the ballroom's stage door on 35th Street.

Kenneth Keith Kallenbach

Although the line for ticket winners was approximately one fifth the size of the V.I.P. line, they were easily ten times as loud. I love to see other obsessed Stern fans let it all hang out. It's hard to calculate how many people are in a crowd, but I'd estimate the ticket winner line at around two-hundred and fifty. They were a hardcore bunch, which was no surprise. Anyone with the fortitude, perseverance, and stamina to phone K-ROCK thousands of times on the off chance of being the 92nd caller and winner of tickets to the social event of the year would have to be made of "stern" stuff.

Mike Gange

Tom Chiusano came out to address the fans and remind them to be good. It was a funny sight. Tom

Nicole Bass

is a tall, handsome, graying-at-the-temples, bespectacled man who reminds me of the Walt Disney cartoon character Jiminy Cricket. None of the fans took Tom very seriously. Since one of Howard's favorite sports is mocking Tom, I was impressed that Tom even dared to show his face. After a minute or two, Tom beat a hasty retreat to catcalls of "F-Penelope." (For those living on another planet, Penelope is the name of Tom's wife.)

Even Howard's fat intern, Mike Gange was heckled and called a "loser." Whenever I catch Howard Stern fans in action, I tend to regard them as the conscience of the nation, keeping the self-inflated posers of our great country honest. And at no time do they do this with more panache than when hurling derogatory comments at the infamous Melrose Larry Green. Melrose arrived with oaktag signs at-the-ready and an E! camera crew in tow, and began working the crowd. At one point he noticed me taking pictures of him, and singled me out for a hearty handshake whilst announcing to the fans, "Here's my good friend Dan Wagner!" I immediately turned pale with horror. What was Melrose trying to do? — get me killed? I shook my head "No," and jumped back as though he were a leper.

The V.I.P. crowd was pretty scary, too. Some of them resembled freak show denizens, which perhaps they were. I counted one dwarf, two midgets, one deformed giant, a tattooed lady, several cross-dressers, and a couple of dominatrixes. To complete the menage, there was a geriatric Wack Packer from yesteryear named 'Gina Man who looked like an escapee from a mental institution.

As for Wack Packer, Nicole Bass, he/she was the proverbial icing on the cake. Nicole was wearing a fetching shiny black minidress, stiletto high heels, and carried a teddy bear. With her long,

Ralph Cirella

Ratso Sloman

flowing red hair and larger-than-life muscles, Nicole looked like Conan the Barbarian on estrogen. I was so flabbergasted by Nicole's appearance that I almost forgot to take her picture. Luckily I snapped out of it, and snapped Nicole posing between two of New York's finest. Next to Nicole, the policeman almost look effeminate.

Speaking of looking girlish, I managed to photograph two of Howard's more elusive hangers-on. The first was Ralph Cirella, more commonly know as "Howard's girlfriend Ralph." Ralph is aptly nicknamed. His partially bleached blonde hair was teased, permed and highlighted. He looked more fay than RuPaul. Ralph could pass for someone's grandmother, but his head reminded me of a fruit salad. Howard insists that Ralph's straight, and I believe him, but nonetheless I wish Ralph would stop sending out such conflicting signals.

The second hanger-on to arrive was Ratso Sloman. Ratso's frugality is legendary. He reportedly gets his clothing from Goodwill, and recently purchased a waterfront house in a slum neighborhood for around $65,000. Ratso encouraged and somehow helped Howard with his

Ratso Sloman

first book *Private Parts*. Ratso's other claim to fame is his friendship with Bob Dylan and resulting book about Dylan's 1975 *Rolling Thunder Tour*. Ratso is also purportedly Melrose Larry Green's best friend. However, according to Ratso, he only tolerates Melrose because Melrose takes him to expensive restaurants. In an unparalleled act of friendship, Ratso once sent a tape of Melrose bad-mouthing Gary Dell'Abate to Howard for an on-air bit. Sound familiar?

Later in the evening, Ratso gave Howard Stern what was to become his favorite Birthday gift of the night — a videotaped copy of a porn flick called *Shane's Ultimate Fantasy*. Not surprisingly, Ratso was too cheap to give Howard a *new* copy

Fred, Jackie, Howard and Robin

of the videotape. The porno is about an old dominating man and his bevy of willing, gorgeous, young girls. Sounds like Howard's show — no wonder the tape was his favorite gift.

It was past 5:30PM, and still no sign of Uzo. In an attempt to calm my nerves, I sought the company of another would-be party crasher and friend of Uzo's named Marc. Uzo had successfully snuck Marc into Howard's party the year before. Marc was supremely confident that Uzo would get us in. According to Marc, "Uzo can do anything."

A few minutes later I learned what Marc's definition of "anything" encompassed. Marc told me that he had spent the previous night videotaping Uzo and a female friend of hers cavorting at a swank hotel until the wee hours of the morning. I bet Howard wouldn't mind getting a copy of that videotape for his birthday.

Finally Uzo showed up with a new, blonde, statuesque girlfriend on her arm and made her grand entrance. Marc and I greeted her as though she were the second coming of Christ. After all, she was our savior incarnate, and tour guide to the Promised Land of Howard's Party. In hushed conspiratorial tones Uzo told us that security was especially tight this year, but she would try her best to get us in. When we pressed her to divulge her plans, she informed us that she didn't have any plans — yet. Uh-oh! However, Marc wasn't the least bit worried because, "Uzo can do anything."

It was at this point that Marc and I discovered we were not alone. Uzo had three other friends whom she had promised to sneak into the party, too. Wow! For a self-

Fred Norris, Jackie Martling

proclaimed lesbian, Uzo has quite a set of balls. Who would show up next? — Cuban boat people? Actually, Uzo's friends were quite pleasant. They consisted of a bald, well-dressed investment banker; a tall, shy, thirty-something African-American man; and a young woman it seemed Uzo had just met. We were an eclectic bunch of people with the common denominator of being true-blue Howard Stern fans.

After a minute or two, Uzo had to go inside. However, before she left us, she promised to return and advised us to split up and try not to look too conspicuous.

Over the course of the next hour and a half Uzo returned several times to assure us that we had not been forgotten, and that she was still working on a plan to get us in. Uzo believed that our chances for success would be greatest after all the guests had been let in. I was a little doubtful, but what else could I do? At least it was a warm evening.

By 6:30PM most of the winners and V.I.P.s were inside the ballroom. Fifteen minutes later, Howard's security, headed by his loyal limo driver, Ronnie Mund, started gearing up for Howard's arrival. The squawks from their walkie-talkies pierced the night air. Some of the security personnel wore earphones. It was so 007. One would have thought that a head of state was arriving.

Howard Stern, Robin Quivers

E! Entertainment had sent a camera crew to tape Howard's arrival. I shamelessly attempted to suck up to the crew and to the security people as well. The last thing I wanted was to be pushed around and possibly have my camera smashed by a security guard, or crushed by an overzealous and overweight cameraman. Besides which, knowing where, when, and what the camera crew intended to do enabled me to make an educated guess about where I should stand in order to get a good photo of Howard Stern.

Suddenly the security guards went on full-alert and formed an impermeable human gauntlet just as Howard's limousine pulled up. The only gap in their shoulder to shoulder coverage was filled by the E! cameraman. Despite my educated guess, I had chosen one of the worst spots from which to get a candid shot of Howard.

Howard exited the limousine wearing a dark overcoat and his trademark dark sunglasses. One of the first people to greet Howard was his agent Don Buchwald. Ironically, Uzo's investment banker friend somehow managed to shake Howard's hand. Howard must have thought he was a newly hired security guard. Within seconds

Don Buchwald, Howard Stern

Howard made a dash for the ballroom entrance. I only got off one clear shot, but at least Howard is identifiable. Less than thirty seconds had transpired from the time Howard left the limo to the time he entered the ballroom. The camera crew and most of the security guards followed Howard inside and closed the doors behind them.

At this point the only people left outside were Uzo's five friends, myself included. We felt pretty miserable and stupid. Would we ever get in? Finally, around 7:00PM Uzo came out and gathered us together for a strategic huddle in a dark and out-of-the-way area a short distance from the ballroom entrance. Uzo looked as nervous and jumpy as an impala being stalked by a hungry lion. Fortunately, Uzo had devised a fantastic scheme for getting us inside.

Uzo's plan was as simple as it was brilliant. Upon signing-in, all the winners and guests were given a souvenir party button. The button served as proof of having gained admission and cleared security. Therefore, all Uzo needed to do was give her button and her girlfriend's button to us, and we could join the party two-at-a-time. As for Uzo, she's so immediately identifiable to everyone connected with the party that no one even noticed that she wasn't wearing a button — or else they were too distracted by the skimpy top that displayed her ample bosom.

With sweaty palms and a rapid heartbeat I boldly made my way towards the entrance. One of Howard's security guards asked me for my ticket. I was so nervous that I almost blew my lines. Thinking quickly, I told him that I had already been inside. He then asked to see my button. I looked down and realized that it had been partially obscured by the strap of

Elephant Boy and dance partner

my camera bag. My trembling hands moved the strap aside to reveal the button. I was shaking so badly that the security guard probably thought I had Parkinson's disease. Nonetheless, he allowed me to pass. Glory, glory hallelujah, I was in!

Once inside I did my best to blend in with the crowd. I was still paranoid. Suppose one of Uzo's friends got caught and spilled the beans? Or, suppose one of Howard's staff recognized me? I kept my eyes peeled for Uzo, so that I could return the party button that she needed to get the rest of her friends inside.

Howard really knows how to throw a party. Near the entrance to the lobby was an open bar staffed by jacketed waiters. Next to the bar was a lavish spread of gourmet foods. There were fresh fruits, crudités with dips, imported mozzarella in oil, a variety of breads and rolls, several hot pasta dishes, freshly carved roast beef and turkey, and more. My years of loyal listening had finally paid off. My share of this spread was long overdue payment for services rendered!

Speakers had been set up at regular intervals so that the audience could

Birthday party revelers

hear Howard's show, which was already in progress. Howard, Robin, Jackie, and Fred were seated behind two raised tables to the left of the main stage. The area in front of the stage which extended all the way to the rear of the ballroom was tightly packed with large round tables for ten. These tables were reserved for the most important guests. Dozens of servers raced through this obstacle course balancing trays of drinks and food.

Lonnie Hanover

The table for Howard's parents, wife, sister, and brother-in-law was closest to Howard himself. Seated at the next table were Fred's wife and some of the other show wives. Nearby, were the tables for the Wack Packers, with whom Howard frequently chatted on-air. However, according to Howard, the most important table was for Lonnie Hanover and his harem of Scores Girls. One of the funniest observations of the evening was Howard's comment that it was scary to see the two worlds of family and Scores Girls collide.

Although there were several balcony levels, only the first was open. The uppermost balconies were used for lighting and other production equipment. As far as I could tell, the balcony level was primarily for show sponsors and K-ROCK management. This is where Tom Chiusano and Howard's agent, Don Buchwald, held court. A second open bar and food area had been thoughtfully installed there, too. I found the balcony to be far more civilized and comfortable than the main floor.

The part of the balcony that extended above the main floor angled down in a procession of three or more "steps" that were about ten-feet wide. Each successive "step" was about two-feet lower than the one above it. On the uppermost steps were smaller, intimate, tables for the less important guests. The step closest to the stage was primarily used by the lighting technicians and E! crew.

The steps were fronted by a three-foot black metal railing that served double-duty as a place to steady my telephoto lens. It was a great picture-taking location. From this perch I was afforded an excellent view of the proceedings. Shooting down enabled me to get photos of Howard and the gang without their microphones blocking too much of their faces. The location reminded me of the tree-house blinds used by hunters. The best part of shooting from the balcony was that it kept me hidden from Gary and his flunkies. Gary is very suspicious and I knew that should he happen to see me, he would undoubtedly question my presence.

Howard's first guest was New York City Mayor, Rudy Giuliani. The mayor didn't arrive empty-handed. After wishing Howard a Happy Birthday, he gave him a "Rudy tie." Even Robin received a present of a "Rudy scarf." Howard loves to rub elbows with politicians. One reason for this is that it impresses his parents. The greatest moments Howard's father ever had was being on the stage during New York State Governor Pataki's inauguration and visiting the Governor's mansion. Howard mentioned that his mother always told him to dress as though he were going to meet the mayor, which sparked a spirited repartee between Howard, the Mayor, and Howard's mother who said words to the effect of, "yes, I always told him to dress like he was going to meet the Mayor — and just look how he turned out!" It's clear where Howard gets his rapier wit.

Ralph Cirella, Real Doll

Howard's next victim/guest, was the large-lipped, brassy, Yiddish-speaking, gal pal of Madonna, and self-confessed bisexual — the one and only Sandra Bernhard. Things usually get out-of-control when Howard and Sandra's mercurial personalities collide. Many fans are convinced that Howard and Sandra are sexually attracted to each other. It's too bad they haven't had the opportunity to procreate. Now that would be one scary-looking child!

Speaking of procreation, Sandra used Howard's party as a forum to announce that she was pregnant. Howard wasted no time in asking her if she had been turkey-basted, or if she had had sex with a man. Sandra claimed that she got pregnant the old-fashioned way. Unfortunately, Sandra wouldn't reveal who the father was, which of course led to some pretty wild speculation. Before leaving, Sandra presented Howard with a pair of edible male underpants. Knowing Howard, he'll probably make a listener eat them. I doubt his wife, Alison, would be interested.

During the course of the evening, Howard's sponsors showered him with gifts as they each received on-air acknowledgement. One gift that didn't receive any official notice or acknowledgment was a cute little multi-colored plastic, voice-altering megaphone costing fourteen-dollars that I had gift-wrapped, labeled, and dropped off at Howard's studio during the first week of January. At the time, I wondered if

217

Howard would ever get it, or if Gary Dell'Abate or an intern would wind up keeping it. I must confess that I was surprised and elated to see my present resting on Howard's table, a mere six inches from his elbow.

My little bubble of elation was deftly punctured by Howard himself on-air on February 20th, 1998, when I asked him how he had liked my birthday present, and he replied, "What was that?" After I explained what it was, and reminded him that the present had been clearly visible during his E! Birthday Show, he still claimed not to remember it, and even had the nerve to hang up on me.

Now back to the birthday show: Once Sandra's carcass had been picked-clean of juicy gossip, she was dismissed to go practice her Lamaze and Kegel exercises — or whatever. Sandra is a hard act to follow, and I wondered what sort of adventurous soul would rise to the challenge. Obviously, the job called for someone with a big ego and a great deal of ambition. In short, the job called for a politician such as George Pataki, the Governor of New York State and would-be future presidential candidate. Howard's face lit up like a Christmas tree when he saw the Governor. As for Howard's father, he probably soiled his undies. George Pataki sat on the guest couch next to Howard's table and unleashed a funny one-liner about not being the man who got Sandra Bernhard pregnant. Having Pataki go through the trouble of traveling all the way from Albany for Howard's party is proof-positive that Howard's star, if not his political clout, is on the ascendancy. What a coup!

Howard's Birthday Shows are frequently plagued with technical difficulties, and this show was no exception. The first major problem was with dysfunctional wireless microphones. Howard promptly called his engineer Scott Salem to task for this screw up which resulted in Scott Salem throwing a fit and leaving. Howard has labeled Scott a "loser's loser" — a name that Scott has never failed to live up to.

Another no doubt Scott-related fiasco was the inability of key fans to successfully call in to the show. Among those unable to wish Howard a Happy Birthday on-air were New York Senator Alfonse D'Amato and comedian Tim Allen.

Seeing Howard Stern perform a live broadcast from start to finish was fascinating. Over the past few years I had often wondered what it would be like to see Howard's crew in action. Howard's favorite on-air sport is berating Gary Dell'Abate and his helpers for being inefficient if not downright incompetent. Now I could see for myself whether or not Howard was being truthful. From my observations I have concluded that Howard was not only one-hundred percent truthful, but was in fact overly generous when he compared Gary, John, and Scott to the *Three Stooges*.

Gary and John ran around so much, and so aimlessly, that they reminded me of chickens with their heads cut off. Gary's primary job during a remote broadcast is to clear a path for the guests, adjust and/or hold microphones, and make occasional inane observations. Gary started out making $150.00 per week as Howard's producer back in the early 1980's with WNBC. As far as I'm concerned he was over-paid then, and he's overpaid now. Since going off of his diet drugs, Gary has plumped-up faster than Flip Wilson's penile implant. During the Birthday Show, Gary would reach down and hike up his tent-like pants at least ten times per minute. Hasn't he ever heard of suspenders? According to Gary he wears loose clothing to minimize his body fat. A week or two after the Birthday Show Gary related the following humorous anecdote about his weight gain which I've para-phrased: "I was having sex with my wife during her seventh month of pregnancy, and happened to comment that it was strange bumping into an enormous belly during lovemaking. My wife replied, 'Now you know how I feel.'" Perhaps Gary Dell'Abate should change his name to Gary Dell'Abelly.

Even Stuttering John and Jackie Martling looked terrible. John was fatter than ever, sported a full beard, and looked like a cross between Charles Manson and Burl Ives. As for Jackie Martling, one would have hoped that Jackie might have taken advantage of his one-month hiatus during the negotiation of his contract to work out at the gym or diet. Instead, Jackie, too, was fatter than ever and had gathered his thinning blonde hair into a ridiculous-looking pony tale. I imagine that Howard's intern, Mike Gange, must be very relieved that Gary, John, and Jackie have joined him in the fat boy arena. He is no longer Howard's sole target for fat-related humor.

The only members of Howard's team who have stabilized their physical appear-ances were Fred and Robin. Fred spent the evening working a small, grey, comput-erized box that triggered his legendary sound effects — a process that Howard refers to as "painting with sound." Robin seemed more relaxed than I've ever seen her. Throughout the evening Robin serenely gazed at the audience with a manner and deportment of an African Queen. Perhaps Robin's mood is a result of her new high-protein diet which consists of downing as many as four hamburgers per meal.

I think that Crackhead Bob is Howard's favorite Wack Packer because he was the only member of this auspicious group invited to sit on the guest couch and panel with a celebrity. After Howard, Crackhead Bob's second love is the Jets foot-ball team. He is never without his green Jets cap, and even has a Jets' logo tattooed on his arm. To see Crackhead Bob ensconced on Howard's guest couch with Baba Booey and Jets' quarterback Glen Foley was to see a truly euphoric man. From the expression on Crackhead Bob's face he clearly thought he'd died and gone to heav-en. That's why no one was prepared for what Crackhead Bob was about to confess to Howard. I know I wasn't.

Crackhead Bob announced on-air that his much awaited and heralded upcom-ing Valentine's Day wedding to his beloved Nina had been cancelled. Considering the fact that I'd spent months maneuvering myself into being Crackhead Bob's official wedding photographer, I was devastated. However, as bad as I felt at missing the wedding of the millennium, I was even sadder that Crackhead Bob was missing out on what might prove to be his only chance to get married. It's got to be a one-in-a-million shot for a half-

Glen Foley, Gary Dell'Abate, Crackhead Bob

paralyzed former Crack addict such as Bob to find a woman willing to marry him. Not to mention the fact that getting married would set Bob apart from the rest of the Wack Packers who seem incapable of forming stable relationships with members of the opposite sex.

Howard asked Crackhead Bob what had gone wrong. It's not always possible to understand what Bob is trying to say. Nonetheless, it seemed that Bob's wedding had been called off because his fianceé, Nina, didn't want an E! camera crew or the rest of the Wack Pack to come to her wedding. What she did want was for Crackhead Bob to spend some portion of their lives together as plain George Harvey, and not a Felliniesque caricature. Stuttering John interjected that Nina's alleged conversion to born again Christianity had something to do with her or Bob's change of heart. It was pretty confusing trying to figure out exactly what had gone wrong. Later, I even called up Bob's sister, Denise, to ask what was going on. Denise was too upset to discuss the matter in depth but did intimate that it might have had something to do with Nina having aspirations of becoming an actress, and that this might be for the best. When I asked Bob how he was doing he merely replied, "Now, I'm all alone."

Although I'll never get to take photographs of Crackhead Bob's wedding, at least I can count myself as being one of the select few to have received Crackhead Bob's official wedding invitation.

Howard Stern even allocated a portion of the on-air hijinks to the show wives. During this segment, Fred's wife Allison stole the show by simulating oral copulation with one of the wireless microphones, which inspired Howard to ask his mother if she'd ever given his Dad a "Monica Lewinsky." Howard's mother brought down the house by replying, "Who do you think taught her (Monica)?" Witnessing Howard's family in action was an added bonus to the night's festivities. His well-endowed sister Ellen said that she loved Howard and that he was the best brother in the world. Howard's father Ben spent most of the evening eating. Howard's wife Alison looked demure and aloof in a tailored suit more suitable for a business meeting than a Birthday free-for-all. Howard truly leads a double-life: by day a radio shock jock and Scores Topless Club aficionado, and by night a sedate, suburban family man who's afraid to leave his basement. Is it any wonder Howard recently announced that he's decided to start seeing a shrink.

Eventually, the open bar caught up with me and I high-tailed it to the men's

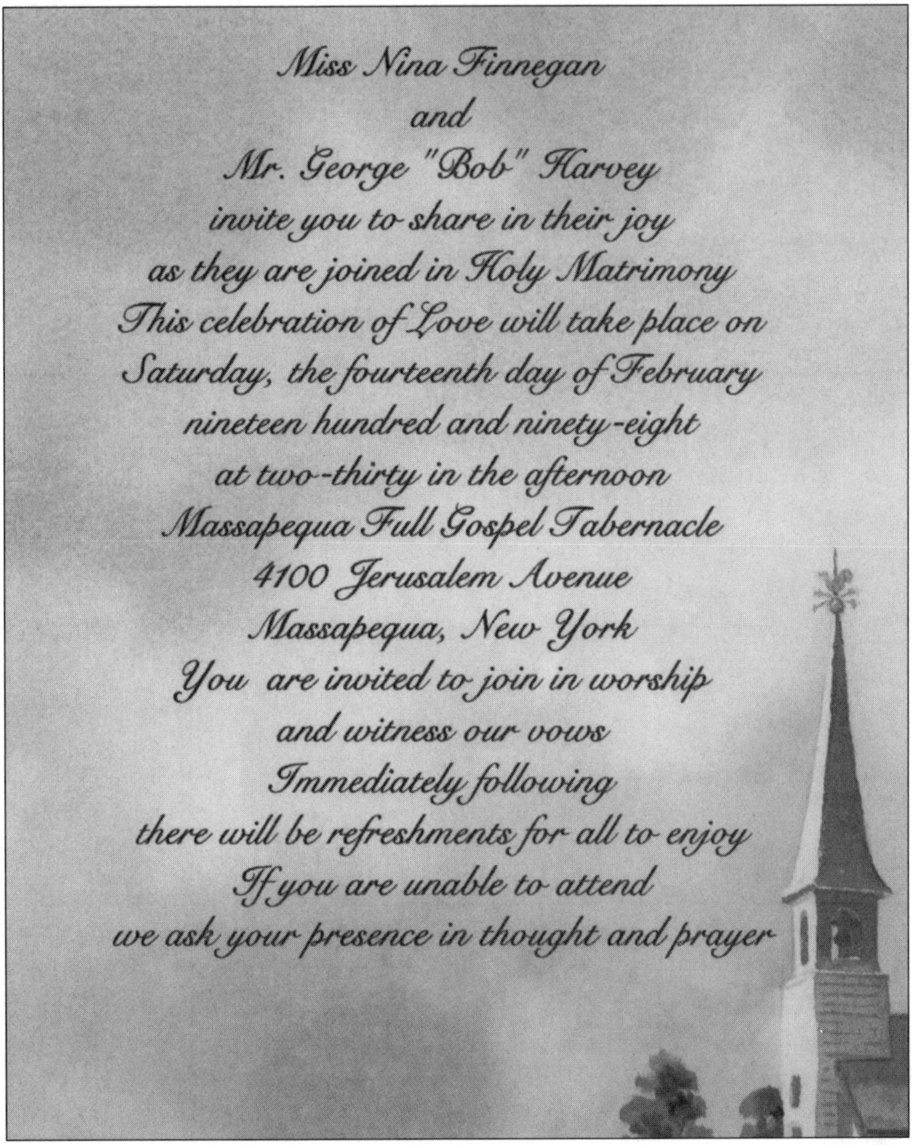

Miss Nina Finnegan
and
Mr. George "Bob" Harvey
invite you to share in their joy
as they are joined in Holy Matrimony
This celebration of Love will take place on
Saturday, the fourteenth day of February
nineteen hundred and ninety-eight
at two-thirty in the afternoon
Massapequa Full Gospel Tabernacle
4100 Jerusalem Avenue
Massapequa, New York
You are invited to join in worship
and witness our vows
Immediately following
there will be refreshments for all to enjoy
If you are unable to attend
we ask your presence in thought and prayer

room. After dropping a quart or two I looked to my left and was amused to find the comedian, and occasional Stern Show guest, Colt .40 Feinberg. Colt's "act" is based on sounding like an angry young black street hoodlum. Howard Stern has referred to Colt .40 Feinberg as, "the greatest black comedian who ever lived," although Colt is actually white. One of Colt's claims to fame is his enormous black afro. He even dedicated his e-mail address to his hair: digmyafro@aol.com. Colt is always "on" — a trip to the urinal being no exception. Colt sauntered up to the porcelain, reached down for his pants' zipper, and loudly proclaimed, "Okay, I don't want anyone to be intimidated when I whip out my penis." I laughed so hard that I nearly lost control and wet myself. Actually, it was considerate of Colt. 40 Feinberg to issue a stern warning because his penis really would frighten most men. It's so big that it spans three separate ghetto time zones: CPT — Compton Penis Time, MPT — Motown Penis Time, and HPT — Harlem Penis Time.

Upon leaving the bathroom I ran into Howard Stern's best friend Ralph Cirella. As a nearby E! crew filmed him, I asked Ralph to pose for a photo with me.

Colt .40 Feinberg

At Howard's 1997 Birthday Party he had been serenaded by Rolling Stone Performer-of-the-Year, Beck. I remember watching Beck's sensational performance on the *E! Show*. I doubted that Beck could be topped in 1998. I was wrong. For the next fifteen minutes or so, the entire audience was transfixed by the legendary David Bowie.

Bowie opened with his classic *Fame*, and closed with a new tune called *I'm Afraid of Americans*. The incredible sound system was augmented by a light show, smoke machines and dancing Scores Girls. After Bowie finished the crowd paid him the heartfelt tribute of falling silent for several seconds before bursting forth with sustained applause. Howard immediately rushed on stage and blurted out words to the effect of, "the first gift my wife ever gave me when we were in college was a David Bowie record." Later in the show, fellow Long Islander Billy Joel dedicated a song in honor of Howard's birthday via a satellite feed from the Nassau Colosseum. Unfortunately Billy chose to sing one of his trademark lethargic dirges. Howard's audience prefers loud, hard-driving rock and roll. I was surprised that he wasn't booed. Even Howard looked thoroughly bored. No wonder Billy's performance was cut from the show the following day. Of course Howard engaged in a little spin control, and the "official" reason given for cutting Billy Joel from the show was "technical problems."

Dan Wagner, Ralph Cirella

Also appearing by satellite, but not singing were Eddie Van Halen and his brother, Alex. Eddie was wearing spotted leopard fur culottes — one of the stupidest outfits I've ever seen. Howard and the Van Halens traded idle banter for a little while. The audience was disappointed that Eddie didn't play the guitar he was holding. Howard picked up on the audience's sentiment and told Eddie that they would have to appear live on his show and play for him at a future date.

The last performer of the evening was Megadeth with lead singer, David Mustaine. Megadeth was exactly what the crowd wanted — an ear-splitting heavy-metal band. Due to the fact that the party was almost over, everyone took the opportunity to let it all hang out. Wack Packer Kenneth Keith Kallenbach led a charge on to the stage and proceeded to throw his head up and down in classic heavy metal fashion. Ralph Cirella and Colt .40 Feinberg took turns abusing Howard's life-sized silicon Real Doll, whose wig fell off to reveal a large black velcro "X" on her scalp. The crowd became more uninhibited by the second. Elephant Boy and Alarmo (a red-suited performer hired by Slomins Alarm Company) mounted a smaller stage made of multi-colored plexiglass squares that were lit from below. The scene looked like a perverted version of *American Bandstand*. Joining Elephant Boy and Alarmo were a bevy of Scores Girls, and Hank "The Angry Drunken Dwarf" who was shit-faced drunk and promptly fell off the three-foot high stage and landed on his nose. Earlier in the evening Hank had failed a breathalyzer test with a result of .256 (twice the legal limit for a full-sized man in New York State). Poor Hank, the previous night he had fallen down a flight of stairs. His face was covered with bruises.

David Bowie

Surrounding the stage and urging the Scores Girls to show more flesh was a crowd of alcohol-driven men with high testosterone levels. Succumbing to the mood of my fellow revelers I decided to use my wide-angle lens, and proceeded to

Hank the Angry Drunken Dwarf

take some naughty photos looking straight up the Scores Girls' miniskirts. The Scores Girls got a big kick out of all the attention and really put on a show. Caligula would've been at home with this crowd.

Uzo and her special "friend" decided not to be upstaged by the Scores Girls and put on a floor show of their own that was positively bizarre. They rolled and jumped about in syncopated abandon. Earlier in the evening Uzo told Howard that she was out of the (massage) business, was in love with her new girlfriend, and had spent $10,000 over the last few days on a new wardrobe for her. Howard asked Uzo's girlfriend if she too, was in love. The woman received loud laughter when she answered that she was with Uzo for her money.

Shortly after Megadeth finished playing, Howard thanked everyone for coming and concluded the show.

Hank the Angry Drunken Dwarf

Most of the crowd, myself included, was reluctant to leave. It was weird and somehow unnatural for the evening to end so abruptly. I hung back trying to prolong the evening. Eventually, I had to join the crowd exiting the theater. As I made my way toward the lobby, I surveyed the scene for possible photo opportunities. A moment later Dominic Barbara approached me business card in hand, and asked me if I'd mind taking a quick photo of him and his wife, Irma. How could I refuse? I posed them together, asked them to smile, and quickly fired off the last three shots of the night.

As I boarded the nearby Long Island Railroad and headed home, I reflected upon the day's events. I still couldn't believe that I'd finally managed to attend a Howard Stern Birthday Party. Even though I was dead tired, I decided to put my exposed film in order so that it would be ready for the lab the next morning. I could hardly wait to see the shots. In my haste, I briefly opened my camera body and ruined the last three frames of the final roll of film from the party. I had never made such a stupid mistake before. Perhaps the night had been too exciting for my delicate psyche.

I knew Dominic Barbara would think I was a liar and a bum if I didn't send him the promised photo of him and his wife. But, the shots of him were ruined, so what could I do? Luckily, I remembered that I'd photographed Dominic and Irma during the premiere of *Private Parts*. After digging in my photo archives I uncovered the photo and

Howard Stern's 44th birthday cake

mailed it to the Barbaras in an expensive wooden frame. Some might consider my sending Dominic such a gift the epitome of shameless brown-nosing. It is! I am simply laying the groundwork for next year's birthday party. If Uzo can't come through again, Dominic is now indebted to me.

Who says getting to Howard is ever easy or straightforward?

About the Author

Dan Wagner had a wretched childhood. At an early age he promised himself that someday things would be better. He went to college, became a successful New York City photographer, married a beautiful Wellesley graduate, fathered two wonderful children, and settled into a suburban lifestyle on Long Island's North Shore, presumably set to live happily ever after.

Until a chilly fall morning in 1995 when Wagner awoke in horror, his blissful life shattered, as he realized he had become a truly monstrous creature—an obsessed Howard Stern Fan!